THE BRITISH LABOUR PARTY
AND
THE INDIAN INDEPENDENCE MOVEMENT
1917-1939

The British Labour Party
and
The Indian Independence Movement
1917-1939

MESBAHUDDIN AHMED

ENVOY PRESS, NEW YORK

The British Labour Party and
The Indian Independence Movement 1917-1939
©1987 Mesbahuddin Ahmed

Library of Congress Catalog Card Number LC 86-81908
ISBN O 938719 09 2
First Edition, 1987

PRINTED IN INDIA

Introduction

The policy of the British Labour Party toward the Indian independence movement was one of self-rule for the Indians. The party was, generally, sympathetic to Indian grievances. As the Labour Party played a significant part both inside and outside Parliament to advance the Indian cause, it is useful to analyse its attitude to the independence movement between 1917-1939.

This study starts from the year 1917 because in August of that year in historic announcement of the future policy of Great Britain in India was made. With the agreement of British parties and the approval of Parliament, this announcement laid down the principal of 'the gradual development of self-governing institutions with a view to the progressive realization of responsible government in India as an integral part of the British Empire'. The new policy came about partly because of the whole-hearted service rendered to the Allied cause by the people of India, and partly because of the rapid growth of the demand for self-government. It was a few months after the announcement that the Labour Party declared its policy of Home Rule for India, The study ends in 1939 because by that time the Labour Party had defined its policy for India as favouring either Dominion Status or independence under an Indian-drafted constitution. Since the Labour Party had not altered its basic position until the achievement of independence by India in 1947, the study ends in 1939.

This study is primarily concerned with the attitude of the British Labour Party to the Indian independence movement, although I have at times made references to the Conservative Party's attitude in order to clarify the difference between the two, since the Conservative Party was dominant in British politics throughout these years. I have considered at great length the Indian constitutional reforms and the stand taken by the Labour Party.

To my knowledge, no detailed work on the same subject at the same period and from the same angle as this study has been done.

Dr. G. Fischer published in 1966 a book entitled *Le parti travailliste et la decolonisation de 1' inde*, but he approached the subject from the point of view of analytical political scientist and not that of an historian. He did not scrutinise the historical events. I propose in this work to examine the stand taken by the British Labour Party, the second largest party in British politics at the time of the study and the one which championed the Indian cause, on the independence movement.

This study is based on both primary and secondary sources. With regard to primary sources, I have exploited, for example, the parliamentary debates of both the House of Commons and the House of Lords, the private papers of Labour members, and the Command Papers of the British Government relating to the Indian constitution. Annual reports of the Labour Party and its other publication were also used. Besides contemporary periodicals and newspapers, I consulted a number of books on the Indian independence movement and also the British Labour Party.

The study opens with the background of the early phases of the Indian freedom movement starting mainly from the year 1905. In that year Bengal was partitioned, resulting to unprecedented agitation in India. The partition of Bengal was the beginning of the end of the British Empire in India. Besides examining the Morley-Minto reforms of 1909 and the historic announcement of the British Government policy towards India, I have also dealt with the formation and development of the British Labour Party, as we are concerned in this study with the attitude and the reactions of the Party to the Indian independence movement.

The Montagu-Chelmsford Report of 1918, containing proposals for constitutional reforms for India is examined followed by the Government of India Bill of 1919 based on the Montagu-Chemsford Report. The Labour Party's attitude to the Bill is discussed at length. Also considered is the non-cooperation movement of the Congress Party and the stand taken by the Labour Party, and the Indian policy of the first Labour Government which remained in office for only nine months.

The Labour Party's stand on Indian constitutional progress comes next. The Commonwealth of India Bill put forward by the moderate Indian leaders in 1924 advocated the granting of Dominion Status to India. The Indian Statutory Commission, which was composed of representatives of the British political parties, was to survey the Indian situation and recommend changes on the existing constitution of India. The reaction of the Labour Party to the appointment of the Commission is examined. Indian political leaders at an 'all-party conference' attempted to reach an agreement on the framing of a constitution by the Indians themselves on the principle of full responsible government. A committee was formed to consider the principles of the constitution. The committee prepared their report in 1928. The main provisions of the report (known as the Nehru Report) have been discussed along with the recommendations of the Report of the Statutory Commission published in 1930. When the Statutory Commission was preparing its report, there occurred a change in the government of the United Kingdom. The Labour Party came back to office after the general election of 1929. The policy of the second Labour Government towards India is adumbrated.

While viewing the political situation in India and the first two Indian Round Table Conferences, the study first focuses on the Civil Disobedience movement which Gandhi started in 1930 in response to the handling of Indian affairs by the British Government when the Labour Party was in office. It then looks at the planning of the Round Table Conference, the first and second sessions of the Conference, as well as at the Gandhi-Irwin Pact reached in between the sessions.

The later part of the study states the criticism made in Parliament by the Parliamentary Labour Party of the National Government's India policy. This is followed with a discussion of the third session of the Round Table Conference. After the third session a Joint Committee of both houses of the British Parliament was formed to examine the White Paper proposals made at the end of the Round Table Conferences. The Joint Committee Report formed the basis of the Government of India Bill of 1934, which was then presented to Parliament. Parliamentary Labour Party took an active part in the debates on the Bill, which are discussed here at length. The Bill passed in 1935 came to be known as the Government of India Act, 1935. The study touches upon the working of the 1935 Act, the constitutional inpasse that followed the elections held in British India under the Act, and the Labour Party's views in this connection.

Acknowledgements

While acknowledging the contributions made to my work I would like, at the outset, to express profound gratitude to Dr. Els Witte whose kind help and valuable advice, during the years of my research, enabled me to complete it.

I should also like to record my indebtedness to my friends in the Department of History, Free University of Brussels—Mrs Machteld De Metsenaere, Mr Alain Meynen, Mr Guy Vanthemsche, Dr. Peter Scholliers and his wife Dr. Patricia Van den Eeckhout—for their constructive suggestions. I owe a great deal to the help of Mr Andrew Bryan and other members of the staff of the British Labour Party Archive in London. I am also grateful to Mr. Roger Brucher and the staff of the Brussels Royal Library for their constant help in supplying me with the materials for my research. Besides, I have received help from a large number of individuals both in Belgium and England to all of whom I offer my gratitude.

I wish further to express my thanks to Miss Rebeca McCormick, Research-Fellow of the Princeton University, USA, for her helpful suggestions. I owe a special debt of gratitude to my friend Dr. Marc Bergmans for his help in many ways in the final stage of my work, and to his wife, Dr. Joke Calcoen, I gratefully acknowledge the kind assistance. For any sort of errors in the text I alone am responsible.

I am much indebted to the Belgian Ministry of Dutch Culture for providing me with financial grant throughout the period of my research.

Finally, to my wife Jotsna and my daughter Tasmia, whose unmeasured sacrifices enabled me to see this work in complete form, my debt is beyond gratitude.

MESBAHUDDIN AHMED

Contents

CHAPTER 1

Background

Early phases of the freedom movement

The emergence of national consciousness among Indians during the nineteenth century was primarily the product of responses, both negative and positive, to the consolidation of British power. All Indians, whatever their religion, caste, or regional origin, immediately became aware of the foreign character of the Whites who ruled their land, as soon as they came in direct contact with the new rulers. The highly centralised character of British rule in India, especially after the Charter Act of 1833, promoted the growth of a pan-Indian nationalism. British rule had another peculiarity which served to unite the people of India in common opposition to it. Probably no foreign rule in India ever excluded the sons of the soil so completely from higher offices in the state—both civil and military—as did the British in the nineteenth century. Here was a common grievance which united Indians of all creeds and provinces against their alien rulers.[1] In its earliest phase Indian nationalism reflected only the big bourgeoisie—the progressive elements among the landowners, the new industrial bourgeoisie and the well-to-do intellectual elements. The first great wave of unrest which disturbed these placid waters, in the period preceding 1914, reflected the discontent of the urban petty bourgeoisie, but did not yet reach the masses. The role of the masses in the national movement, alike of the peasantry and of the new force of the industrial working class, emerged only after the war of 1914-1918. Great waves of mass struggle developed in the years immediately succeeding the War.[2]

The failure of the revolution of 1857 was followed by a period of reaction during which all anti-British movements in India were ruthlessly suppressed, while the people at large were completely disarmed. By the eighties of the last century the political depression was over and the public began to raise their head again. This time the policy and the tactics of the liberty-loving and progressive Indians were quite different from those of 1857. An armed revolution being out of the question, constitutional agitation was substituted in its place. In 1885, the Indian National Congress was established to organize Indian opinion and press for the removal of grievances.[3]

The Congress Party was founded by a group of Western-educated Indians, who also brought about the gradual revival of Indian national feeling. The birth of the Party marked an important stage in the growth of political consciousness and popular resistance in the country. In fact, it meant the beginning of a modest and constitutional, but at the same time, steady and continuous agitation. Initially its activities were mainly confined to bringing Indian grievances to the notice of the authorities in India and England.[4] The man who has been acclaimed as the father of the Congress Party was Allan Octavian Hume. Hume was one of the few members of the Indian Civil Service who sympathized with the people's aspirations to obtain self-government under British paramountcy. It was at his suggestion that the Congress was formed to enable all workers in the national cause to get personally acquainted with one another, to formulate a programme of activities from year to year and, incidentally, to form the nucleus of an Indian parliament which would in course of time prove that India was fit for any form of responsible government. Believing that the salvation of India could come only from Indians, Hume and his English colleagues, William Wedderburn, David Yule and Henry Cotton, took the initiative in giving shape and direction to Indian agitation. As a child of the British Raj, the inauguration of the Congress was cordially welcomed by Lord Dufferin, then Viceroy of India.[5] Having experienced the greatest difficulty in ascertaining the people's real wishes, he felt that it would be a benefit for the public to have some such responsible organization through which the rulers might be kept informed of Indian public opinion on matters of state.

The fundamental objectives of the Congress Party were three in number: first, to fuse all the different elements of the Indian population into a national whole; second, to regenerate gradually the nation along moral, social and political lines; and third, to form a strong union between Great Britain and India. A branch of the All-India National Congress Party was established in London in 1887. The office became the permanent centre of operation for the party's propaganda in England. This office was strengthened by the service of prominent members of parliament. Included in the list was James O'Grady, a Labour Party member of parliament. In 1890, the Governor-General recognized the Congress Party in a declaration stating that the Congress Party was 'perfectly legitimate' as a political organization. The party's status was confirmed by the Viceroy, Lord Hardinge, in December 1910, when he ceremonially received a deputation from the Congress Party.[6]

With the dawn of the present century came a national awakening in India and Bengal, which had suffered the longest under the British yoke, was the pioneer in the new movement. In 1905 the Viceroy, Lord Curzon, ordered the partition of Bengal. The announcement of the partition in the House of Commons led to widespread unrest in India. The general policy of Lord Curzon, particularly with regard to the political aspirations of the Indian people, and the high-handed and defiant manner in which he carried out the partition of Bengal, led to serious and far-reaching consequences of which he himself could not have dreamed.[7] His scheme ostensibly aiming at the improvement of an oversized and under administered province, was really a measure whose object was to break the growing solidarity of the political community which led India in opposition to government.

The constitutional methods for removal of grievances lost their appeal and new ways of bringing pressure upon government became popular. The year 1905 saw the beginning of a strenuous struggle between the self-assertion of the people on the one side and the attempt to suppress them on the other. The partition set the ball rolling and ultimately shook the imperial structure which the British had built with such care in India. As Gandhi truly prophesied, the partition of Bengal led to the partition of the British empire. The partition led to unprecedented agitation, which gained momentum around *swadeshi.** On an all-India platform, the agitation over partition identified itself with the *swadeshi* movement, directed towards the keeping up of anti-British and anti-government feeling. The speakers in agitation meetings dealt with the evils of British rule, the necessity for unity and patriotism, and

---

Swadeshi literally means 'of one's own country'. The word came to be used for articles manufactured and produced in India.

the boycott of English and other foreign goods.[8] The character of the agitation and its universality deeply impressed even Lord Morley, the Secretary of State for India, and he flatly contradicted Lord Curzon and his apologists when he admitted that the agitation against the partition was not the work of political wire-pullers and political agitators, but was the result of genuine feelings in the minds of the people that they were going to suffer a great wrong and inconvenience. Morley had also the candour to admit that the measure went solely and decisively against the wishes of most of the people concerned.[9]

A section of the English people and even the Conservative British journal like *The Times* as well as the *Manchester Guardian* made adverse comments and expressed sympathy with the feelings of the Bengalis and the anti-partition agitation. Against this partition the boycott of foreign goods was proclaimed as the national policy in a meeting at Calcutta. The original conception of boycott was mainly an economic one. It had two distinct, but allied, purposes in view. The first was to bring pressure upon the British public by the pecuniary loss they would suffer by the boycott of British goods, particularly the Manchester cotton goods for which Bengal provided the richest market in India. Secondly, it was regarded as essential for the revival of indigenous (*swadeshi*) industry which, being at its infant stage, could never grow in the face of free competition with foreign countries which had a highly developed industry. The two proposals, namely, refusal to buy foreign goods and the promotion of indigenous industry, were indissolubly bound up together. The first was known as boycott and the second as *swadeshi* movement—but these were merely two facets of the same stone. The boycott was the negative, and *Swadeshi*, the positive aspect of the same idea.[10]

The turning point in the history of the Congress is considered to be 1905. Whether constitutional or otherwise, the demands of the Congress were deemed aggressive in bureaucratic circles, and by the beginning of Curzon's rule the organisation had been identified with anti-British forces. The 1905 session of the Congress gave only conditional support to the boycott. But the Calcutta Congress in 1906, strongly under the influence of the extremists, adopted a new programme, sponsored by Dadabhai Naoroji, the old Father of the Congress himself. This programme proclaimed for the first time the aim of *swaraj* or self-government, defined as colonial self-government within the Empire, support of the boycott movement, support of *swadeshi*, and national education. *Swaraj*, Boycott, *Swadeshi* and National Education became now the four cardinal points of the Congress programme.[11]

As the movement spread, *swadeshi* and boycott began to be effective, and the government of the new province tried to suppress the anti-partition agitation with a heavy hand. The boycott movement was treated as seditious and anti-British, and was sought to be suppressed by the police. The meetings of protest and propaganda were disallowed, orders were in force to prohibit students from attending meetings or joining processions. The government also followed the policy of 'divide and rule'. It is true that many prominent Muslims joined the *swadeshi* movement, but the Muslims in general were encouraged to oppose the anti-partition agitation and arrange their own meetings in support of partition. They were told that one of the reasons for the partition of Bengal was to give the Muslims a province in which they were in a majority.[12]

The unrest had the fervour of a revolution and could not keep the entire Congress on the constitutional path. While the philosophy of revolution added considerable strength to the movement in general, the question of constitutional agitation or other methods divided the Congress leadership. In 1907, the Surat Congress saw a split between the moderates, led by Gokhale, and the extremists, led by Tilak.[13] The split became inevitable in view of the expectation of a liberal quota of constitutional reforms, hopes for which had been raised in Gokhale's mind by the talks he held with Morley, the Secretary of State for India. The moderates relied upon his liberalism and made every effort to prevent the nationalists from committing the 'Congress to an extremist programme'. The moderates viewed with apprehension any idea of the open struggle with the bureaucracy. and were not ready for taking the rough and narrow way to salvation, while the extremists wanted to capture the Congress and to make it an instrument for revolutionary action. In the process, the nationalists were isolated and suffered the onslaught of government repression in full measure.

The separation of the Muslims from the national mainstream and the formation of the Muslim League further strengthened the hands of Minto who, despite Morley's protests, took to severe measures of repression. Ordinances were issued to ban political activity and antiquated regulations were utilised to deport political leaders. It was not till the partition of Bengal had been annulled in 1911, that the movement subsided. An important repercussion of the repressive policy of the government was that the political agitation went underground and gave fillip to sedition, secret activities by the youth and resort to pistol and bomb as reprisals for severity of prosecution. The intensification of secret revolutionary activities was the most important development of the anti-partition agitation and the Morley-Minto policy of repression and reform.[14]

Morley-Minto reforms

Neither Morley nor Minto looked upon ruthless repression as the sole means of restoring peace and order. They also thought of bringing about some reforms in order to enlist the sympathy and support of the more moderate section of the people. The two principles of 'repression-cum-reforms' and 'rally with the moderates' became henceforth the watchwords of the British politicians.[15] The Morley-Minto scheme of reforms was first announced in December, 1906, and was finally passed into law as the Indian Councils Act of 1909. As a result of official inspiration, a few months before the announcement was made, a deputation of Muslim leaders led by the Aga Khan waited on the Viceroy on October 1, 1906. In connection with the impending reforms they demanded that the Muslim community should have a certain number of seats reserved for them and that these seats should be voted for, not by the general body of Indian voters, but only by Muslim voters. This demand by the Muslim leaders of what is known in India as 'separate electorate' was granted in the Indian Councils Act of 1909.[16]

The essential features of the Act may be described as follows:

1. The appointment of an Indian member on the Viceroy's Executive Council.

2. The appointment of Indian members in Provincial Executive Councils, and sanction for the creation of such councils where they did not exist.

3. The enlargement of legislative council, both at the centre and in the provinces, by an increase of both nominated and elected members.

The Act established the principle of representative government in the provinces and introduced a substantial measure of its practice.

Not only would provincial legislation now normally require the assent of non-official majorities in the councils, in all provincial matters they could now discuss administration, including the government's financial proposals. But there were serious limitations. Since the ultimate responsibility for the good government of India was still vested in the British Parliament, which meant, the maintenance by the central government of a wide measure of control over the provincial governments, the councils' field of action, both in administrative and legislative matters, was still severely circumscribed, and the constant necessity of having to refer to the centre and accept its decisions tended to give their proceedings an air of unreality. Moreover, though the politicians were now free to criticise the executive, they could not control it. Although the Indian members of the councils—not only the elected members but to some extent the nominated members also—began to assume the role of a regular opposition, yet it was a sterile opposition. To carry a resolution against the government might be hailed as 'a great moral victory', but it was not a real one; for the government was not obliged to bow to it.[18]

It should be pointed out that the Congress condemned the separate electorates created for the Muslims as designed to aggravate communal differences. It considered the franchise to be illiberal and rooted in the distrust of the educated classes. It regretted that the non-official majorities in the provincial legislative councils had been rendered illusory by the system of nomination, that provinces like Punjab and United Provinces had been denied executive councils, and that the Central Provinces had not been given even a legislative council. But, while disapproving of these illiberal regulations and urging modifications, the Congress gratefully accepted the reforms as a fairly liberal measure. The Indian nationalists interpreted them as an advance towards parliamentary government. The Muslims had every reason to feel satisfied with the regulations, for they provided them with separate electorates, a comparatively liberal franchise and weightage in representation. They had not been generally very enthusiastic about the reforms. The voice of extremism was not much heard. Most of the extremist leaders were in jails and their papers had been suppressed.[19]

Towards the end of 1910 India had a new Viceroy, Lord Hardinge, and a new Secretary of State, Lord Crewe, in place, respectively, of Lord Minto and Lord Morley. Both Hardinge and Crewe

felt that the unrest in India was chiefly due to the partition of
Bengal, and there would be no peace until this grievous wrong was
remedied. In a despatch of the Government of India of 1911 to the
Home Government, which was mostly inspired by the progressive
outlook of Hardinge, it was proposed that the partition of Bengal
should be annulled. It was also proposed that the capital of India
should be shifted from Calcutta to Delhi. That very year George V
and Queen Mary visited India and held a Darbar at Delhi. His
Majesty brought comfort to many a heart in India, by announcing
the annulment of the partition. Thus Bengal was restored its previous unity, and, the 'settled fact' was unsettled. The second
announcement that His Majesty made was regarding the shifting
of the capital to Delhi. The new capital was also welcomed as a
central place.[20]

The annulment of the partition of Bengal represented a partial
victory of the boycott movement. The wave of struggle which had
developed during the years 1906-1911 did not maintain its strength
during the immediately succeeding years; but the permanent advance
which had been achieved in the stature of the national movement
was never lost. Despite all the limitations of the extremist leaders of
those pre-1914 years, they had achieved a great and lasting victory.
The Indian claim to freedom had, for the first time during those
years, been brought to the forefront of world political questions;
and the seed of the aim of complete national liberation, and of determined struggle to achieve it, had been implanted in the political
movement, and was destined in the subsequent years to strike root
in the masses of the people.[21]

In 1914, the first Great War started. The initial reaction to this
tremendous event in India was a spontaneous rally to Great Britain's
cause. The men of the fighting races flocked to the colours, and all
sections of Indian opinion, except the most extreme, at any rate
in the earlier stages of the war, realized that the German threat of
world domination was as much a menace to India as to any other
country of the British Empire.[22] India's war effort surprised the
British people and the British statesmen. Prime Minister Asquith
acknowledged that "in all the moving exhibitions of national and
imperial patriotism which the war had evoked, there was none
which had more touched the feelings of the British people than the
magnificent response which the Princes and the peoples of India
had made to their need."[23] The war gave rise to a strange sort of

dual patriotism in India, somewhat similar to that in the White dominions. It evoked loyalty to Great Britain and heightened the sense of imperial unity, but it had an even more pronounced effect in developing a strong national consciousness. At first the twin sentiments of imperialism and nationalism went happily together, but as the war became prolonged the nationalist feeling asserted itself as the stronger, more confident and more articulate.[24]

The release of Bal Gangadhar Tilak (1914) and India's reaction to the war brought the nationalists into the forefront of Indian politics and set in the process of transfer of power from the moderates to the extremists, a process which was hastened by the terrible loss sustained by the moderates in the death of their two great leaders, Gokhale and Mehta, in 1915. But even before this the Congress, led by the old moderates, had already come to be looked upon as a backwater in politics—useless in the struggle for freedom. The thoughts of the nationalists had accordingly turned towards setting up a new organization for achieving it, and two great personalities, Annie Besant and Tilak, independently conceived the idea of starting Home Rule Movement on the Irish model.[25]

There was a general feeling among both the moderates and the extremists—except the die-hard section in both the camps—that the best interest of the country demanded that the extremists should be admitted to the Congress so that it might once again become what its name implies, namely the Indian National Congress, and not continue to be a mere party organization.[26] In December 1914 Annie Besant initiated negotiations with Tilak to persuade him to rejoin the Congress. Tilak was keen to return to the Congress fold, but he made it clear, that for the moderates' method of association with the government and mild criticism of its acts, he would "substitute the method of opposition to government, pure and simple, within constitutional limits." The deaths of Gokhale and Pherozeshah Mehta facilitated Tilak's entry into Congress.[27]

There were two Home Rule Leagues of Besant and Tilak and they acted in close cooperation. There was an informal understanding between them that Besant's field of work would cover the whole of India except Maharashtra and the Central Provinces, where Tilak's League would carry on the work. The Home Rulers assembled in large numbers at the Lucknow Congress in late December 1916 which marked the re-entry of extremists into the Congress.

At a joint meeting of the Committees of the Indian National

Congress and the Muslim Leaugue, at Calcutta, Annie Besant exercised her influence successfully to bring about accommodation between the two bodies on the question of communal representation. This common decision was the precursor of the Congress-League Pact which was signed at Lucknow and which was the basis of the resolution on self-government passed at the Congress in 1916 and which in its turn influenced the decision of Montagu on reforms.[28] The provisions of the pact were based on communal considerations. First, the right of separate electorate for the Muslims was admitted although the Congress had opposed separate electorates, all along, as anti-national and disruptive. Secondly, the right of the minorities to weightage was also conceded. This meant the Muslims would be given more seats than they were entitled to according to their numbers in provinces where they were in a minority as well as in the Centre. Thirdly, the minorities were given the right of vetoing a legislation, which concerned them and to which they were opposed. A provision was made that no bill or resolution affecting a community should be proceeded with, in any legislature, if three-fourths of the representatives of that community were opposed to it.[29] The communal demands once accepted, continued to figure in all later constitutional schemes.

The Home Rulers demanded self-government for India retaining the British connection. They wanted that the management of their country, its internal affairs, should be in their hands such as in the dominions. Though they demanded Home Rule as the birthright of the Indian people, the Home Rulers were emphatic in their assertion that they did not repudiate the sovereignty of the Emperor or the rule of the British people. The Home Rule Leagues created a significant impact on the national movement in India. For the first time, in 1916-17, agitation had been aroused on a nation-wide scale and a network of political committees covered much of India. The activities of the Home Rule Leagues bore fruit. A committee of members of Parliament was formed in London for the purpose of pressing forward the claims of India to self-government.

Anouncement of August, 1917

While in India such unforeseen changes were taking place in the opinions, attitudes and alignments of the political parties and leaders, public opinion in Britain concerning the Indian problem was also undergoing a radical transformation. In 1912, even the

Liberal Secretary of State for India, Lord Crewe, had disavowed the idea of dominion status as the goal in India; but within five years the British Government, due partly to the growth of Indian nationalism and partly, probably mainly, to the vicissitudes of the war, looked at the Indian problem from what was called a new angle of vision and committed itself to a policy intended to carry India over the first difficult period of transition from autocracy to democracy and to lead her to the goal of responsible government within the British Empire. In July 1917, Edwin Samuel Montagu succeeded Sir Austen Chamberlain, the Secretary of State for India, who had to resign as a result of the Report of the Mesopotamian Commission. Montagu was convinced of the necessity of a new approach to the Indain problem. Within a month of his taking office, he had persuaded his colleagues in the cabinet to agree to a policy which he announced in the House of Commons on 20 August 1917 in the following terms:

The policy of His Majesty's Government, with which the Government of India are in complete accord, is that of the increasing association of Indians in every branch of the administration, and the gradual development of self-governing institutions, with a view to the progressive realisation of responsible government in India as an integral part of the British Empire. They have decided that substantial steps in this direction should be taken as soon as possible, and that it is of the highest importance, as a preliminary to considering what these steps should be, that there should be a free and informal exchange of opinion between those in authority at home and in India . . . . Progress in this policy can only be achieved by successive stages. The British Government and the Government of India, on whom the responsibility lies for the welfare and advancement of the Indian peoples, must be the judges of the time and measure of each advance, and they must be guided by the cooperation received from those upon whom new opportunities of service will thus be conferred, and by the extent to which it is found that confidence can be reposed in their sense of responsibility.[30]

It was Lord Curzon of the Conservative Party who drafted the final version of the announcement, and not suprisingly Balfour and Montagu readily yielded to it because of the balance of influence and because, as a result of Curzon's masterly drafting, each found the formula not unsatisfactory. Curzon's major change was to insert the phrase 'responsible government' in place of 'self-government'. The announcement of August 20 was a powerful and revolutionary document, both in itself and in the effect it had on the course of the reforms.[10] Referring to Montagu's historic declaration, Josiah C. Wedgwood of the Labour Party said:

Edwin Montagu was good enough to consult me about the wording of those fateful three lines; (ref: The policy of His Majesty's Government. . . as an integral part of the British Empire.) but no one save Edwin Montagu could have obtained so liberal and far-reaching a declaration from that war-harassed Cabinet. Each member of the Cabinet had to be converted in turn, last of all Lord Curzon; and they never forgave him for what they came to regard as their moment of weakness.[32]

It will be observed that there was no novelty in the first part of the two-fold policy set out in this announcement. The appointment of Indians to official posts had been foreshadowed as long ago as 1833. The novelty of the announcement lay in the second part of it; for this was the first time that the goal of the British policy had been officially defined and moreover the proposed method of attaining it was precisely the method which had been so persistently rejected in the past. The longer phrase, 'the progressive realisation of responsible government in India as an integral part of the British Empire', defined the goal. For it implied that some day responsible government in India was to be completely realised without breaking its connection with the British Empire, and that could only mean an India fully governing itself on a parliamentary basis, yet still retaining its allegiance to the British Crown.[33] For *The Times* the real significance of Montagu's statement was that it was the clearest and most definite declaration of British aims in India which had been officially made since November, 1858. Such a declaration was overdue. The British Government's declaration was not only a forecast of permanent policy, but it was also a plain warning that the goal of self-government could only be very gradually attained.[34] The declaration, which became the preamble of the Reforms Act of 1919, was the response to the insistent demand of loyal and patriotic Indians for a goal and a policy.

We have so far discussed the early phases of the Indian freedom movement, 1909 reforms and the August Declaration of 1917. It is necessary at this stage to give an account of the formation and development of the British Labour Party.

Formation and development of the Labour Party

The Labour Party is unique in British history since it is the outgrowth of political agitation among the labouring population for parliamentary representation. The party came into being in February 1900, under the name of Labour Representation Committee. The name was officially changed to Labour Party at the 1906 annual conventions.[85]

Between the 1870s and the First World War a mass labour movement was formed in Britain. Trade union membership grew from about half a million in the mid-1870s to over four million by 1914. Underpinning the emergence of a mass labour movement in the last quarter of the nineteenth century was the growing predominance of regular industrial wage-earners, concentrated in substantial work units within the working-class population. By 1911 there were nearly one and a quarter million miners, providing a powerful and relatively prosperous bedrock for the labour movement. In transport, casual labour persisted on the water front and in road transport, but it was the steady work on the railways that grew fastest. The growth of mass labour movement from the 1870s was facilitated by the emergence of a more homogeneous industrial proletariat. The persistence of extreme differentiation of status within the working-class tended to restrict both the size and the political horizons of the labour movement.[86]

Out of the three general movements that helped form the Labour Party; namely the trade unions, the socialist societies—the most prominent one being the Social Democratic Federation (S.D.F.) the Fabian Society, and the Independent Labour Party (I.L.P)—the trade union movement was the most important from the point of view of membership and financial strength. The S.D.F. never developed into a very effective or influential organisation, but it did serve as a training ground for many of the labour leaders. Henry Mayers Hyndman organized the Democratic Federation in 1881, an advanced radical body whose original purpose was to campaign against government repression in Ireland, for land nationalisation and an increased working-class representation in parliament. Many of the original supporters left when it became clear that Hyndman intended to oppose the Liberals at elections. Subsequently the Federation adopted a socialist programme and, early in 1884, renamed itself the Social Democratic Federation.[87]

The Fabians were, from the very beginning, above all else collectivists. In 1889 they put forward their general point of view in *Fabian Essays*—the most important theoretical presentation of the peculiarly English brand of evolutionary development. By 1889, when the *Fabian Essays* appeared, the Society had made up its mind; and the group of exceptionally clever people at its head, including Bernard Shaw and Sidney and Beatrice Webb, proceeded to make a concerted effort to bring the growing independent labour movement over to their ideas. After that year they created numerous local Fabian societies in the provinces, leaving these bodies practically independent of the parent Society in London. Many of the local Fabian societies were subsequently merged in the Independent Labour Party, which they helped to leaven. Others survived to do active work, especially as promoters of Labour representation in the municipalities.

Politically, the Fabians combined two attitudes which seemed to many persons inconsistent, and caused a good deal of suspicion of them on that account. They favoured the creation of an Independent Labour Party, but were not willing completely to merge themselves in it if it was formed. This was because, in accordance with their 'gradualist' and evolutionary notions, they believed in a policy of 'permeation', that is, in trying to influence any and every party or group that could be considered to take up any of their ideas. They held that the workers ought to have a party of their own, but they did not believe that such a party would be fully Socialist, in their sense, or that work inside it could exhaust the possibilities of advancing the Socialist cause.

Nevertheless, the Fabian attitude was consistent, on the assumption that the Independent Labour Party would not be a fully Socialist party, but rather a political expression of the working-class point of view. The Independent Labour Party would doubtless be the most permeable of the political parties; but since the question was, in the opinion of the Fabians, one of evolution and not of revolution, it was important to permeate all parties.[38]

The Fabians neither secured nor sought large membership. They were a group of planners; and numbers would have destroyed the cohesion which was one element in their strength. First, the Independent Labour Party and then its successor the Labour Party accepted from them a large part of its programme. The Fabian Society was one of the bodies which joined in creating the Labour Representation Committee in 1900; but even thereafter it successfuly maintained its right to retain sympathetic members of other political parties within its ranks.

The Independent Labour Party, founded in 1893, established itself as a separate organisation, a new socialist group in competition, at least to a certain extent, with the S.D.F. and the Fabian Society.[30] The strategy of the party from its foundation was based on the conception of collaboration with trade unionists with the ultimate object of tapping trade union funds for the attainment of parliamentary power. It was primarily to defend this strategy that Keir Hardie fought tooth and nail against fusion with the S.D.F. His attitude was justified by the behaviour of the S.D.F. leaders at the critical moment of the formation of the new party—their intransigence at the foundation conference and their decision eighteen months later to secede. The objective of the I. L.P.'s founders was reflected in the programme adopted in 1893. The ultimate goal was socialism. The first priority was to secure the election of independent labour men to parliament. To this end the party adopted a programme of social reforms designed to avoid antagonising the unions and to appeal to a non-socialist electorate.[40]

Originating as a loosely coordinated federation of local labour clubs and parties, the I.L.P. long retained its decentralised character. The National Administrative Council, as its name suggests, had little executive or policy-making power. The branches often failed to pay their dues to the centre. The newspapers, Hardie's *Labour Leader* and Blatchford's *Clarion*, gave the party a national presence, but the centralising impulse of involvement in parliamentary politics was, for the time being, weak. Despite the numerical preponderance of the trade unions, the I.L.P. continued to be the effective element in the Labour Party right upto 1914. The period immediately before the war of 1914 was the great age of I.L.P. influence. MacDonald, as leader of the Labour Party in parliament and the most influential member of the I.L.P., occupied a key position, and made himself adept at the manipulation of the two machines, checkmating leftist tendencies in the I.L.P. by emphasizing the need for Labour unity, and combating excessive corporatism on the part of the trade unions by reminding them of their dependence on the devoted service of the I.L.P. propagandists.

The I.L.P. having acted virtually as a separate party during the war—though it had maintained its affiliation to the Labour Party throughout—did not at all like the change in its position involved in the appearance of the latter as a Socialist Party claiming the work and loyalty of all democratic socialists and thus threatening to push the relatively tiny I.L.P. into the background. The I.L.P. was halfhearted in its support of Henderson's effort to build up the Labour Party organisation in the constituencies on a basis of individual membership; but outside Scotland it did not positively oppose this, but sought rather to strengthen its own hold on the new local Labour parties that Henderson was busy setting up.[41]

It is important to realize that the move to form an alliance between socialist societies and the trade unions only came about after other socialist movements had failed. In fact, the founding of the Labour Representation Committee came at a time of intense political reaction. The socialist groups most involved in the flowering of socialist activity and propaganda in the 1880s and 1890s had spent themselves, and had seemingly failed to make any headway, especially among the working class. [42] Keir Hardie and his comrades of the Independent Labour Party realized that they would have to create an alliance with the trade unions. One of the reasons why I.L.P. wanted to make an alliance with the trade unions was that it would make possible the likelihood of an ever-expanding franchise which would give the right to vote to more working people. Besides, the inflexibility of the Liberals and the continued domination of political participation by the middle classes convinced Hardie and his I.L.P. comrades that a new political party was both necessary and possible. Henry Pelling in this context argued that their motivation was

to be discovered rather in the failure of existing political bodies to recognize, as the Socialists were prepared to do, the continually increasing importance of the labour interest in a country which, with a maturing capitalist economy and a well-established class system, was now verging on political democracy.[43]

There can be little doubt that the I.L.P. could have caused the Labour Representation Committee to declare itself Socialist had it wished to do so. The I.L.P. preferred to win the Liberal trade unions and keep them united on the policy of independent Labourism. It was wary of forcing the pace of the trade unionists along the path of socialism, which it nevertheless expected them ultimately to tread. From 1906 the process of winning over the Labour Party gradually to Socialism had been commenced;

particular resolutions of a Socialist character were put forward one by one for Labour Party approval.[44]

The Fabian Society's part, compared with that played by the I.L.P. in urging the Labour Party gradually towards Socialism was only a minor one, yet it was not without some importance. The Fabians, having a less responsible position in the Labour Party than the I.L.P. leaders, were in the fortunate situation where they could criticise the Labour Party for not being socialist enough; they were not necessarily obliged to incur the odium of restraining the enthusiasm of the socialist left-wing.[45]

The Labour Representation Committee had to contest its first general election within six months of being formed, and it is hardly surprising, when we consider the short time available and the lack of the resources, that the achievement was minimal. Out of their fifteen candidates only two were elected. [46] Hardie was one of the two candidates elected. In 1903 MacDonald, L.R.R.'s first secretary and the Liberal Chief Whip, Herbert Gladstone, concluded an agreement allowing the L.R.C. free runs in a number of constituencies. As a result twenty-nine candidates endorsed by the Committee were elected to parliament at the 1906 elections. When the 1906 parliament met, the L.R.C. took the name Labour Party, and elected a parliamentary chairman, Keir Hardie.

The parliamentary party was established in 1903,[47] but very little progress could be made until the election of 1906 placed a block of Labour members in the House of Commons. In that year a conference between the parliamentary party, the executive board of the Trade Union Congress and the executive committee of the Labour Party was held to coordinate the acitivities of the three groups. This conference brought the T.U.C. into closer agrement with the Labour Party, since the trade unions agreed to support all the candidates nominated by the Labour Party, and all labour men elected to parliament would adhere to the Parliamentary Labour Party. The parliamentary party was formed after each election or at the opening of each annual session of parliament.

Thus the Labour Party of Great Britain became an organized force in the nation. Its views were mainly those designed for the protection of the workers' interests. The early years were spent in consolidation and growth. In 1908, the Miners' Federation joined the Labour Party. By this time the party included many of the locally organized political federations espousing the workingman's cause, ninety-four trade councils, and some forty local labour bodies, besides an ever-increasing number of trade unions. Two years later the Scottish Labour Party with all its branches joined the Labour Party.[48] With this increased strength, the party was able to put up eighty-five candidates in the first election in 1910, and in the second, sixty-two, the decline being due to low finances. Out of these, forty members were elected in the first election and forty-two in the second. [49] This election saw the Labour Party emerge as a national organization, although its main strength still remained in the cities and in the heavy industrialized areas.

Between the first general election of 1910 and the outbreak of the war the Labour Party had not been transformed, but it had, nevertheless, changed significantly. In most of the great cities local Labour parties had taken over the duties of the trades councils. At the same time the councils were beginning to discharge their political functions more effectively. Since the trade unions remained the sheet anchor of organization this was as important as the establishment of local Labour parties. Likewise, in the mining constituencies Labour was unquestionably stronger in 1914 than it had been in 1910. Though the great industrial disturbances of 1911-14 do not appear to have done the Parliamentary Labour Party any obvious good at the time, it can be presumed that they did the older parties even less good. But it is impossible to say with certainty what the political consequences of the strikes were; it is likely that they made the local parties more militant. A probable consequence of this militancy was the attraction of many union members, who might not have been converted by the political activities of the party alone, to the Labour Party. At the same time there was an unprecedented rise in trade union membership.[50] It must be emphasized that Labour was operating on the basis of a highly restrictive franchise, and one which was probably peculiarly unfavourable to it. It is difficult for a mass working-class party to be politically successful when about half the working-class is voteless. Thus the constant extension of organization—particularly the attempts to make trade councils do serious political work—was designed to yield electoral dividends in the future. This the councils were able to do.

The Labour Party saw its function as the political mobilization of an already existing industrial class-consciousness: in practice it concentrated more upon the extension of organization, particularly in the constituencies, which was itself only the political side of an industrial organization that had grown rapidly in the late nineteenth and early twentieth centuries. The Labour Party was not based upon broadly articulated principles, but rather upon a highly developed class-consciousness and intense class loyalties, Accepting the Labour Party meant accepting not socialism but an intricate network of loyalties. In return, the Labour Party accepted its members as long as they understood its discipline and conventions. If it is objected that it has not served the cause of socialism or even the true interests of the working-classes the answer is that it was never designed to do so.[51]

The socialist objective of the Labour Party was not formally accepted until 1918 and it was in that year that the party approved a socialist formula drafted by Sidney Webb. British socialism, as propagated by the Labour Party, was to be founded on egalitarian democracy. The general objective of this democratic party was:

The gradual building up of a new social order. not on internecine conflict, inequality of riches, and dominion over subject classes, races, or a subject sex, but on the deliberately planned co-operation in production and distribution, the sympathetic approach to a healthy equality, the widest possible participation in power, both economic and political, and the general consciousness of consent which characterise a true democracy.[52]

Thus the Labour Party was committed to 'the inevitability of gradualism'. In 1918 there was no question of the dictatorship of the proletariat or even of working-class solidarity. But certainly in 1918 the Labour Party was competing against two strongly entrenched political parties, both of which had firm working-class support.

The organisational reforms of 1918 introduced a new element into the Labour Party, the hierarchy of local organizations of which the divisional Labour Party (called in other parties the constituency party) was the centre. This local organization has played an important role in the development of party tactics, and it has also provided the Labour Party with most of its brains. On the other hand the Labour Party was in 1918 and has since remained, fundamentally the trade union party. By thar year, however, the unions represented in the Trades Union Congress and the unions affiliated to the Labour Party were almost identical.[53]

The Labour Party accepted the right of the Indian people to govern themselves, but it recognized that the problem involved in developing self-governing institutions in a great continent inhabited by people who differ in language, race, and creed was not easy to solve. The party was sympathetic toward nationalism. But the leadership opposed the resort to violence, murder of officials, obstructive tactics in legislative councils, and boycotts.[54] The party sought to give to the Indian masses the potential power of bettering their economic conditions by political action. 'India for the Indians is a simple slogan,' said C.R. Attlee, 'but it is necessary to see what it means in terms of human life. There is no particular gain in handing over the peasants and workers of India to be exploited by their own capitalists and landlords.'[55]

The Labour Party formulated no Indian policy during the prewar years. The members in parliament criticised the stringent government policy. The party raised objections to the British policy in India in parliamentary debate on July 21, 1906, when the annual India budget was presented. After John Morley, the Secretary of State for India, introduced the budget with a laudatory speech on the conditions in India and the sound financial position of the country, James O'Grady of I.L.P. disputed Morley's contentions. O'Grady pointed out that chronic poverty of India was due largely to the high tax rate and the failure of the Indian Government to do anything to alleviate proverty. He deplored the gross neglect of public education and urged the establishment of agricultural colleges.[56] The attack was continued by Keir Hardie, another I.L.P.er, who proposed a resolution that would place the salary of the Secretary of State for India on the British estimates. He stated that this would provide parliament with greater control over Indian affairs. This resolution, however, was voted down as Morley advanced the opinion that if it was carried, party politics would enter into Indian affairs. Hardie's appeal for opening the higher offices in the Indian Government to the Indians was also ignored, and his accusation that it was British policy to reserve these positions for the exclusive domain of the British educated classes remained unanswered.[57]

Hardie undertook a trip to India in 1907 as a private citizen and not as a member of parliament or a representative of the Labour Party. On his return his views were recorded in a series of articles in the Labour press which he compiled into a book entitled *India* in 1909. In this book he says:

> It may be that all the provinces of India are not yet fit for the colonial form of self-government, but between that and the present soul-less bureaucracy there are many degrees of expansion in the direction of modifying bureaucratic power and enlarging the rights and liberties of the people. What I am trying to convey is that the people of India are fit to be trusted with such a large measure of self-government as would give them effective control over their own affairs and generally reduce British interference to the same limits as are exercised over the colonies in Australasia or South Africa.[58]

The Independent Labour Party was, both in domestic and foreign policies, more radical than the Labour Party. If O'Grady and Hardie should be excluded from the record, the other Labourites could be said to have continued passive anti-imperialism.[59] The Independent Labour Party's 1911 annual conference at Birmingham was significant with regard to India as Hardie moved an important resolution which was carried unanimously. The resolution reads:

> That this Conference declares that the immediate policy of the British Government in India should be guided by ideas of self-government and national responsibility. To that end it demands that the financial and economic policy of India should be put more under Indian control, and that the Councils recently established should be placed on a more popular basis and given wider powers of discussion and decision.[60]

Shortly after the passage of the Morley-Mintore forms of 1909, James Ramsay MacDonald undertook a private trip to India and, while he was there, he gathered enough information for his book, *The Awakening of India*, in which he censures the Indian Government for the heavy tax burden it imposed on the meagre income of the population. He believed that this burden was the principal cause for the poverty of the country.[61] MacDonald maintained that the Morley-Minto reforms were inadequate, even though they did provide a consultative authority. He wrote that the reforms did not produce a stable government, since the government while having to consult with the councils, was not obliged to follow the advice of the councils. He contended, nevertheless, that this, reform was the beginning of parliamentary government in India. He advocated the immediate alteration of the communal feature of the reform to give the Muslims only their proportional representation, and to grant them all the protections that they were entitled to.[62] At one point MacDonald mentions:

Coerced by her guardian, India will be an endless irritation and worry. Consulted by her guardian, and given wide liberty to govern herself in all her internal affairs, she may present many difficulties and create many fears, but that is the only way to abiding peace and to the fulfilment of our work in India.[63]

The Congress Party was so impressed with the book that it considered MacDonald for the presidency in 1911, but he declined because of his appointment to the royal commission, which investigated the Indian Civil Service, 1912-1914.

The Labour Party voiced its views over the Indian reforms bill in 1909 through Hardie, the party's considered expert on India. Hardie objected to the communal electorate. He claimed that he did not object as strongly to the special representation being given to the Muslims as he did to their being given special consideration out of proportion to their numbers. The Labourites insisted that the legislative councils should be controlled by elected Indian representatives. Hardie made a special plea by saying that when the reforms were adopted, an amnesty should be granted to all political prisoners.[64]

In the three years before the First World War, parliament reverted to routine matters so far as India was concerned. No important political debate on India took place till the war was over. After 1918 the Labourites became the principal champions of Indian nationalist aspirations in Commons.

NOTES

1. S.R. Mehrotra, *Towards India's Freedom and Partition*, New Delhi, 1979, pp. 10-11.

2. R. Palme Dutt, *India To-day*, Calcutta, 1947, p. 319.

3. Tara Chand, *History of the Freedom Movement in India*, vol. IV, New Delhi, 1972, p. 290; See also Subhas Chandra Bose, *The Indian Struggle (1920-1942)*, Bombay, 1964, p. 13.

4. R.S. Gautam, *Indian National Congress and Constitutional Changes in India (1885-1979)*, New Delhi, 1981, pp. 6-7; See also Lajpat Rai, *Young India*, New York, 1916, p. 123.

5, Pattabhi Sitaramayya, *The History of the Indian National Congress*, v l. 1, (1885-1935), Bombay, 1935, pp. 14-15. See also Sir William Wedderburn, *Allen Octavian Hume*, London, 1913 p. 63 et seq.

6. William Wedderburn, op. cit, pp. 87-90, For the early part of the history of the Congress see Sankar Ghose, *Indian National Congress : Its History and Heritage*, New Delhi, 1975, pp. 1-15.

7. R.C. Pradhan, *India's Struggle for Swaraj*, Madras, 1930, p. 78. See also Surendranath Banerjea, *A Nation in Making*, Oxford, University Press, 1925, p. 186.

8. M.N. Das, *India under Morley and Minto*, London, 1964, p. 43.

9. R.C. Majumdar, *History of the Freedom Movement in India*, vol. II, Calcutta, 1963, p. 11; See also Lovat Fraser, *India under Curzon and After*, London, 1911, pp. 388-9.

10. ibid., pp. 29-30; See also James Keir Hardie, *India (Impressions and Suggestions)*, London, 1909, p. 26; A. Hamid, *Muslim Separation in India*, Oxford University Press, 1967, p. 56.

11. R.P. Dutt, op. cit., p. 330; For general understanding on Swadeshi, see B.C. Pal, *Swadeshi and Swaraj: The Risk of New Patriotism*, Calcutta, 1954; See also S. Banerjea, op. cit., pp. 176-185.

12. V.D. Mahajan, *The Nationalist Movement in India*, New Delhi, 1976, p. 187.

13. M.N. Das, op. cit., p. 89; See also T.V. Pravate, *Gopal Krishna Gokhale: A Narrative and Interpretative Review of His Life, Career, and Contemporary Events*, Ahmedabad, 1959. pp. 228-231.

14. Bisheshwar Prasad, *Bondage and Freedom (A History of Modern India), 1858-1947*, vol. II, New Delhi, 1979, pp. 317-318.

15. R.C. Majumdar, op. cit., p. 258; See also Mary Minto, *India, Minto and Morley, 1905-1910*, London, 1934; Also B.R. Nanda, *Gokhale: The Indian Moderates and the British Raj*, New Delhi, 1977, pp. 296-313.

16. S.C. Bose, op. cit., p. 14; See also Stanley Wolpert, *Morley and India, 1906-1910*, Berkeley and Los Angeles, 1967; Also in B.R. Nanda, op. cit., an independent chapter deals with Separate Electorates, pp. 344-353.

17. R.C. Majumdar, op. cit , p. 259; See also O.P. Singh Bhatia, *History of India, 1857-1916*, New Delhi, 1968, pp. 116-118.

18. R. Coupland, *The Indian Problem (1833-1935)*, London, 1942, p. 44.

19. S.R. Mehrotra, op. cit., p. 122; See also R.P. Masani, *Britain in India*, O.U.P., 1962, pp. 86-7.

20. R.N. Aggarwala, *National Movement and Constitutional Development of India*, New Delhi, 1962, p. 69; See also Sir Courtenay Ilbert, *The Government of India*, Oxford, 1915, p. 131.

21. R.P. Dutt, op. cit., pp. 321-332; See also M.A. Buch, *Rise and Growth of Indian Militant Nationalism*, Baroda, 1941.

22. John Coatsman, *India: The Road to Self-government*, London, 1941, p. 40.

23. House of Commons Debates, vol. 66, col. 955. Hereafter cited as H.C. Deb.

24. S.R. Mehrotra, op. cit., p. 127.

25. R.C. Majumdar, op. cit., p. 354; See also M. Macdonagh, *The Home Rule Movement*. Dublin, 1920; Also Arthur H. Nethercot, *The Last Four lives of Annie Besant*, London, 1963, pp. 242-253.

26. ibid., p. 355.

27. T. Chand, op. cit., p. 449; See also Ram Gopal, *Lokamanya Tilak: A Biography*, Bombay, 1956, pp. 375-380.

28. ibid., p. 449.

29. R.N. Aggarwala, op. cit., p. 72; See also Ram Gopal, *Indian Muslims: A Political History, 1858-1947*, Bombay, 1959, pp. 129-132.

30. H.C. Deb. 1917, vol. 97, cc. 1695-6.

31. Richard Danzig, 'The Announcement of August 20th, 1917, *The Journal of Asian Studies*, vol. 28, Nov. 1968, pp. 25-36; See also Bipan Chandra, Amales Tripathi, Barun De, *Freedom Struggle*, New Delhi. 1972, pp. 119-120.

32. J.C. Wedgwood, *Memoirs of a Fighting Life*, London, 1940, p. 131.

33. R. Coupland, op. cit., pp. 53-4.

34. *The Times*, Aug. 21, 1917; See R.C. Pradhan, *India's Struggle for Swaraj*, Madras, 1930, pp; 131-133.

35. George Milton Ochs, *The Labour Party and the Constitutional Reform for India*, Illinois Univ. 1960, p. 5; See also A.W. Humphrey. *History of Labour Representation*, London, 1912.

36. James Hinton, *Labour and Socialism: A History of the British Labour Movement 1867-1974*, Sussex, pp. 24-38.

37. C.F. Brand, *The British Labour Party*, California, 1964. p. 4; See also James Hinton, op. cit., p. 40.

38. G.D.H. Cole, *British Working Class Politics*, pp. 121-4.

39. A.M. McBriar, *Fabian Socialism and English Politics, 1884-1918*. C.U.P, 1962, pp. 288-9.

40. James Hinton, op. cit., p. 58.

41. G.D.H. Cole, *History of Socialist Thought*, vol. IV, Part One, op. cit., pp. 421-2.

42. Tom Forestor, *The Labour Party and the Working Class*, London, 1976, p. 32.

43. ibid., p. 12.

44. A.M. McBriar, *Fabian Socialism and English Politics, 1884-1918*, London, 1962, p. 317.

45. ibid., p. 318.

46. Ivor Bulmer-Thomas, *The Growth of the British Party System*, vol. 1, 1640-1923, London, 1967, p. 176.

47. Annual Report of the Labour Representation Committee, 1903, p. 36.

48. G.D.H. Cole, op. cit, p. 230.

49. G.M. Ochs, op. cit., p. 15.

50. Ross McKibbin, *The Evolution of the Labour Party, 1910-1924*, O.U.P. 1974, p. 86.

51. ibid., p. 247.

52. G.D.H. Cole, *History of the Labour Party from 1914*, London, 1948,

p. 65.

53. Ivor Jennings, *Party Politics*, vol. III, C.U.P., 1962, pp. 459-462.
54. C.F. Brand, op. cit., p. 103.
55. C.R. Attlee, *The Labour Party in Perspective and Twelve Years Later*, London, 1949, p. 174.
56. H. C. Deb., vol. 161, 1906, c. 633 et seq.
57. ibid., c. 594.
58, J. Keir Hardie, *India*, London, 1909, pp. 78-84.
59. Tingfu F. Tsiang, *Labour and Empire*, New York, 1923, pp. 55-56.
60. Independent Labour Party Annual Report, 1911, pp. 103-4.
61. James Ramsay MacDonald, *The Awakening of India*, London, 1910, p. 92.
62. ibid., p. 178 et seq.
63. ibid., p. 302.
64. H.C. Deb., vol. III, c. 597.

CHAPTER 2

Indian Political and Constitutional Development and the Role of the Labour Party, 1918-1924

By 1918, the Labour Party had endorsed the policy of Home Rule for India and vowed to help the Indians in every way possible to bring about constitutional reforms. The party declared that it would endeavour to put pressure on the government in order to grant self-government to the Indian people. The party position until the general election of that year was moderate, that is, it would extend the right of self-determination to India within the framework of the Empire, stressing that self-government should be granted by stages.

When the Montagu-Chelmsford Report came up for debate in Parliament as the Government of India Bill, the Parliamentary Labour Party supported the bill, even though it was not satisfactory in its present form. The party, of course, criticised the autocratic powers of the central government, and also the communal and interest representation. It pointed out that, although the August Declaration of 1917 promised the beginning of responsible government in India, this promise was not visible in the bill. The Labourites advocated a directly-elected assembly and criticised the indirect form of election. Although the Government of India Bill was unsatisfactory, the Labour Party called upon the people of India to try it, and emphasized that they should agitate for Home Rule through constitutional methods.

The Labour Party in its 1920 annual conference reaffirmed its stand for the principle of self-determination for India and demanded adequate measures of autonomy for the Indians. The party condemned the repressive policy of the Government of India. The Labour members of parliament criticized the coercive legislation existing in India, such as the Rowlatt Bills. But in general, it was against the non-cooperation movement of Mahatma Gandhi. The Labour Party, which came to office for the first time in 1924 with Liberal support, and which stayed in office for a period of only nine months did little for the Indian cause. Of course, it was during that period that Gandhi, who was languishing in gaol, was freed by the Labour Government. But, it was also during their administration that the infamous Bengal Ordinance was sanctioned.

Soon after the announcement of August 1917, Montagu, the Secretary of State for India, visited India to study the political situation at first-hand, and to get what ideas he could on the subject of the actual wishes and demands of the Indian political leaders as well as of the Indian Government. Associated with his inquiries was the Viceroy, Lord Chelmsford. A joint report was signed by them in April 1918 and published in July of that year, shortly after Montagu's return to England.[1] It is known as Montagu-Chelmsford Report.

Montagu-Chelmsford Report

The following fundamental principles were laid down in the Report.[2]

(1) There should be, as far as possible, complete popular control in local bodies and the largest possible independence for them of outside control.

(2) The provinces are the domain in which the earlier steps towards the progressive realisation of responsible government should be taken. Some measure of responsibility should be given at once, and our aim is to give complete responsibility as soon as conditions permit. This involves at once giving the provinces the largest measure of independence, legislative, administrative and financial, of the Government of India which is compatible with the due discharge by the latter of its own responsibilities.

(3) The Government of India must remain wholly responsible to Parliament, and saving such responsibility its authority in essential matters must remain indisputable pending experience of the effect of the changes now to be introduced in the provinces. In the meantime, the Indian Legislative Council should be enlarged and made more representative, and its opportunities of influencing Government increased.

(4) In proportion as the foregoing changes take effect, the control of Parliament and the Secretary of State over the Government of India and the provincial government must be relaxed.

It was with a view to implementing these principles that the Report made detailed recommendations. The Report recommended that certain subjects of administration in each province should be 'transferred' to the control of 'ministers' chosen from and responsible to the majority in the Legislative Council, and on those subjects the Governor would normally act on their advice. The other subjects were to be 'reserved' to the control of the Governor and his Executive Council, whose members would still be officials and while discussing their policy with the Legislative Council, would be responsible not to it but, as before, to the Secretary of State.[3]

The reserved subjects were finance, land revenue, law and order, forests and commerce. The transferred subjects were agriculture, health, education, and local government. This system, known as dyarchy, was the brainchild of Lionel Curtis, a member of the Round Table group of Imperial Federationists, and a product of Lord Milner's 'Kindergarten'.[4] To safeguard the discharge of his duties in the 'reserved' field the Governor was to be empowered to enact any bill, including a money-bill, over the head of the Legislative Council if he should 'certify' that it was essential, but all such measures would be subject to prior approval by the British Government except in a 'state of emergency', when they would be subject only to subsequent disallowance.

It was recommended that at the end of ten years a commission should be appointed, with direct authority from Parliament, to examine the working of the system and to advise whether the time had come for complete responsible government in any province or provinces or whether some subjects now 'reserved' should be 'transferred' or, if matters had gone badly, the reverse should be done. Similar inquiries should be made thereafter at intervals of twelve years.

They proposed that the Central Legislative Council should be replaced by a legislature of two houses, the Council of State and the Indian Legislative Assembly, in both of which the great majority of members would be elected.

As a move towards breaking down the unnatural isolation of the States from one another and from British India, it was proposed that a Council of Princes should be established at the Centre, which, though purely consultative and concerned only with the common interests of the States, would by its mere propinquity to the new Indian Legislature encourage the recognition of the fact that the States had also common interests with British India.[5]

The Report disapproved of communal representation because it claimed that reserved seats for minorities would hinder the development of national feeling and of self-government. While conceding, however, that the Muslim representation had to be continued until some solution could be found, the Report did not recommend the granting of special representation to the Muslims in the provinces where they were in the majority. On the question of franchise, the Report was opposed to its any sudden extension that would include too many inexperienced voters.

Concerning financial arrangements, the Report recommended that the provinces should have separate resources. While conceding some degree of financial freedom, the plan recommended that the residual taxing powers should remain in the hands of the central government.

The official scheme did not provide for the plan to eliminate the Indian Civil Service from responsible control of Indian affairs because it felt that there were not sufficient trained Indians to assume the responsibility for the offices.[6]

In order to make the control of the British Parliament a reality, it was recommended that the salary of the Secretary of State for India should be defrayed from Home Revenues and voted annually by Parliament. This was to enable House of Commons in the Committee of Supply to discuss questions regarding Indian administration. The House of Commons was to appoint a Select Committee on Indian Affairs at the beginning of each session. That Committee was to gather information about Indian affairs and to report to the House before the annual debate on Indian estimates. The Secretary of State for India was to appear before it and answer questions.[7]

Three views were taken in India on the Montagu-Chelmsford Report. The 'Moderates', who had broken away from the Congress after the publication of the Report and who had formed a new organization of their own to be called the Liberal Federation, accepted it, but urged important amendments; the 'Home Rulers, declined to accept it, and urged amendments: the 'Extremists' declined it altogether.[8] After four days' discussion at the Conference held in 1918 the Congress declared that nothing less than self-government within the Empire would satisfy the legitimate aspirations of the Indian people. It further declared that the people of India were fit for responsible government. The Congress was of opinion that the Montagu-Chelmsford proposals were 'disappointing and unsatisfactory'[9].

The Montford scheme did not take India anywhere near her cherished goal since its only aim was to make a change in the pattern of government and nothing else. Annie Besant, the dynamic founder of the Home Rule League and an indefatigable fighter for Indian freedom, dismissed the Reforms as 'unworthy to be offered by England or to be accepted by India'[10]. It is interesting here to mention the following lines of Montagu himself which he put in his diary:

If we can get the details properly worked out and the Princes fitted in, I shall feel fairly satisfied but... always with the horror before me that the scheme will be acceptable to no one when it is published, and I am bound to say I am very apprehensive of this, because I do not think they like dyarchy.[11]

Legislation based on this Report was enacted in 1919.

The Labour Party and the Government of India Bill, 1919

In the years before the First World War began, the Labour Party continued its attack on the government's India policy. With the outbreak of the war there were radical changes, the Labour Party in England was split into the pacifist and nationalist groups, and unity was achieved only in 1918 at which time the party adopted a programme of socialism at home, and a policy of Home Rule for India. In the 1918 annual conference held at Nottingham, the Labour Party passed the following resolution on India:

That this Labour Conference endorses the policy of Home Rule for India, believing that the time has arrived when our brothers in all parts of India are capable of controlling their own affairs, equally along with South Africa, Australia and other British Dominions, and hereby pledges itself to assist in every way possible to bring about this much desired reform; further, we desire that all Labour Members in the British House of Commons shall do all in their power to bring pressure upon the present Government, without undue delay, in order that these people shall be given their just rights, which have been due to them throughout all time, including the right to self-government[12].

The resolution was hurriedly passed without discussion on the last day of the party conference. The conference demanded that the Parliamentary Labour Party should put pressure on the government so that the Indian people could have their just rights, including the right to govern themselves.[13] One will notice that the resolution did not demand any changes in the immediate future and that 'Dominion Status' for India was not mentioned in the resolution.

The Labour Party programme of 1918 maintained that India should have self-government by stages.[14] Party policy, as expounded later in the election campaign of December 1918, was more moderate than the resolution itself and even than the stand of the Home Rule League. It clearly followed the Montford Report. Lionel Curtis, the originator of dyarchy, was asked to write a pamphlet on India to be used by Labour candidates in the election. Curtis's draft, which was approved by the Committee on International Questions (that is, by Webb, Lowes Dickinson, the historian R.C.K. Ensor, and Leonard Woolf), was a restatement of the view that only provincial dyarchy was feasible at present: '...the number of people who could understand the meaning of a vote is small. To grant full responsible government outright, as in Canada and Australia, would place the government in the hands of a very few.' The leaflet, while stressing and exaggerating the diversities of languages and religions in the sub-continent, nevertheless visualised the task of Britain to encourage the development of national consciousness, and to transfer power completely in the long run.[15]

It was during this time that James Ramsay MacDonald wrote *The Government of India*, which while not being a statement of the official policy of the Labour Party, at least indicated the plan of one of its leaders. MacDonald objected to the system of dyarchy. He thought that a more workable approach would be to have the Governor appoint the executives with an understanding that some of the Indian legislative leaders be appointed.[16] Regarding communal representation, MacDonald said that special minorities should be granted only such representation as their strength would justify.[17] He recommended that the civil service should be opened to more Indians.[18] He expressed the view that the parliamentary controls should not be severed but should be lessened gradually. All control could only be eliminated when the Indians had their own responsible government.[19]

Montagu's reform scheme passed through the scrutiny of various commissions. One commission under the chairmanship of

Lord Southborough considered the problem of franchise, a second commission chaired by Feetham studied and reported on the division of functions between the centre and the provinces. The final reform proposals came to the House of Commons as the Government of India Bill and the second reading of the Bill was held on June 5, 1919.[20]

During the debates on the bill all attempts of the Labour Party to liberalize it failed. The principal reasons for the failure were the smallness of the group of Labourites in Commons and the lack of experience of parliamentary leaders. Even though Labour had improved its numerical position in Parliament in the 1918 election, it still could count only fifty-seven members, and the small numerical gain was more than offset by the defeat in the election of experienced Labour parliamentary leaders. One important factor that worked in favour of the Labour Party was the split of the Liberal Party which brought prominent radical Liberals into the Labour Party. One of the most prominent of this group was Colonel Josiah Wedgwood. Colonel Wedgwood added much luster to the Labour Party, and, while he was never completely accepted by all segments of the Labour Party, his power of debate greatly aided the party cause in the ensuing years.[21] He constantly championed the cause of India. Wedgwood knew India through his visit there and was always in touch with the nationalist leaders.

The Parliamentary Labour Party gave a qualified approval to the Government of India Bill, 1919. Speaking on the bill during the second reading in the Commons, B.C. Spoor, chief parliamentary spokesman for the party, who was in touch with moderates of the Indian National Congress, said that although unsatisfactory in itself, the bill seemed to contain immense possibilities, and it did point in the right direction. He criticised the autocratic character of the central government and the narrowness of the franchise. Spoor remarked:

The bill certainly does give, as has been claimed by the Secretary for India, a certain limited measure of responsible government in the provinces, but the central government there retains complete autocratic power. . . and if this bill becomes a Statute much strengthened and improved and in a much more democratic form, if we succeed in this we shall establish the beginnings of a partnership on terms of mutual confidence and goodwill between India and the rest of the Empire.[22]

Spoor in his attack on the bill said that it failed to meet the requirements of the Indian people because the Governors of provinces, that were to be granted partial responsible government, were given such sweeping veto powers that they would be able to overrule measures that they considered unsatisfactory. He protested that the bill was too narrow in scope, and that in the opinion of the Labour Party all powers, including control of finance, that affected the people in the provinces and that did not endanger the unity of the country, should be placed in the hands of the elected representatives of the people.[23]

J.C. Wedgwood went into details in his criticism of the bill. 'It would have been wiser,' he declared, 'to have been more courageous in constructing the bill.' It was defective in four respects: (1) lack of control of purse by the Indians; (2) the principle of indirect election and the small size of the Indian Central Legislative Assembly: (3) the smallness of the electorate; and (4) communal and interest representation. Colonel Wedgwood while criticising the bill said, 'In this bill the power of the purse is practically retained entirely in the hands of the bureaucracy.' Regarding the franchise suggested in the Government of India Bill and in the Report of Southborough, he thought it to be 'a very poor one'. He was surprised at the indirect election for the Indian Legislative Assembly because, he pointed out, 'in the Montagu-Chelmsford Report direct election was recommended.' 'Indirect election is unknown in English history,' he said. Although the constituencies would be too large in case of direct election compared to the elected members, he argued that the cure for it was to make the Indian Legislative Assembly a respectable size. The real complaint against this bill, as whittled down from the Montagu-Chelmsford Report, was the enormous increase in communal and interest representation.[24]

The bill, after having been read a second time in the House of Commons, was referred to a Joint Select Committee of the two houses. The committee was composed of fourteen members, seven from each of the houses of Parliament. Benjamin Spoor was appointed the Labour member on the Committee. The Joint Select Committee began by gathering information from leading members of the Indian political parties and from experts sent to London by the Government of India. Lord Sydenham, one of the

Conservative members of the Joint Committee, accused the Labour Party of accepting the views of the Congress Party. Although there is truth in the statement, the true significance of it is that it became the accepted Conservative Party view, especially of the reactionary Conservatives who insisted that British rule must be retained to ensure that the interests of the lower castes and the depressed classes would be protected.[25]. In all, sixty-eight witnesses were called, and upon the completion of this testimony the deliberation on the original bill took place. The amended bill was presented to the House of Commons on November 17, 1919. This was debated in the two houses of Parliament and on December 23, 1919, the bill was finally placed on the Statute Book under the title—Government of India Act, 1919.[26] The first election under the new constitution was held in India in 1920, and the new constitution came into effect the following year.

B.C. Spoor of the Labour Party moved a series of amendments during the proceedings of the Select Committee. In the first important amendment that he moved, Spoor demanded the transfer of more subjects to the jurisdiction of responsible ministers in contradistinction to executive councillors. He wished to reserve to the latter only the subjects of law, justice and police. The effect of the amendment would be to transfer to the elected representatives of the Indian people the control of municipal and district government, to be exercised through an organ similar to the Local Government Board in England, the control of irrigation, of the development of minerals, of land revenue, of famine relief, and of factory legislation, in addition to the control of education and public health which the bill intended. The second important amendment aimed at the extension of dyarchy to the central government; it demanded that not less than half of the Viceroy's Executive Council should be selected from the elected members of the Indian Legislative Assembly. In these and other amendments in the Committee, Spoor found himself in a minority of one.[27]

When the amended bill was submitted to the House of Commons on December 3, 1919 for the third reading, the Labour Party renewed its attack by proposing amendments that had been voted down in the Joint Select Committee. It was during the third reading that Josiah Wedgwood, aided by B.C. Spoor, managed to make the views of the Labour Party pointedly clear on the features of the bill that the Labour Party found repugnant. Wedgwood in his *Memoirs* says:

"Ben Spoor, on the Labour front bench, was my yoke-fellow on the India Bill. The rest of the party found the subject too difficult, but played up well in the lobby. The third reading we graciously accepted, and received unexpected compliments.[28]

In the debate that followed in the House of Commons at the third reading, Wedgwood reintroduced most of the amendments. He remarked that the promise of August 1917 was made not only of representative government but also of the beginning of responsible government and this was not visible in the bill. There was not even a pin's point of light, and the few subjects transferred to the Provincial Legislature were hardly a worthy gift from that great nation.[29] He was particularly vehement in his insistence that one-half of the Governor-General's Executive Council be chosen from the elected members in the Assembly, and he maintained that this was the only way that responsible government could be developed.[30] The amendment was defeated. Wedgwood criticized the portions of the bill which provided for the Council of State, the upper house of the central government. He said:

We do not see the necessity even for a double-chamber system in this country, still less in India, more especially when the Second Chamber and the Council of State is, according to the Report of the Joint Committee, going to be elected in the same way as the Indian Legislative Assembly itself. This will add to the trouble of legislation without the slightest improvement in the legislation that is passed.[31]

With regard to the election of members Wedgwood proposed direct elections. The Labourites wanted a directly elected Assembly capable of expansion and really representative of the electors of the country, instead of some form of indirect election drawn from foreign countries, which was not in accordance with British traditions.[32] These two amendments were negatived by the government votes. Wedgwood advocated that the central government of India be granted complete financial autonomy from the Secretary of State for India.[33] On the question of civil service Wedgwood wanted its control to be vested in the Government of India.[34]

With regard to the enfranchisement issue   Spoor said that while it was proposed by the Franchise Committee to enfranchise only 5,000,000 people out of the population of 315,000,000 of India, it was really difficult to believe that the English people were even taking a step in the direction of democratic self-government.[35] In a short speech after the entire bill had been read, and while acknowledging the defeat of the Labour Party amendments, he hoped that India would use the extension of political powers to the fullest advantage and that the people of India would continue their agitation for Home Rule on constitutional lines to secure a wider measure of self-government, for, the present measure was only one of the proposed steps towards the attainment of responsible self-government.[36]

On the third reading of the bill on December 5, 1919, William Adamson, Chairman of the Parliamentary Labour Party, summariz-ed the attitude of his Party towards the Government of India Bill in the following terms :

The Labour Party are prepared to admit that the bill is a definite move in the right direction, our principal criticism being that it does not go far enough, and that we are failing to take the fullest advantage of the help of the people of India themselves to assist us in the successful accomplishment of the great task we have in hand. The bill gives to the people of India a measure of control in the various provinces, but no real control in the central government. This is a mistake and will rob us of the sympathetic cooperation of some of the best elements of the population of India. We also regret the very limited franchise which this bill provides. On the face of it, is absurd that only five million out of a total population of three hundred fifteen million have been enfranchised by this bill.[37]

Even though the gallant stand was ineffectual, the action of the Labour members in the House of Commons demonstrated clearly that the Party wanted to advance the cause of self-government for India, and that the stout resistance offered by this group of stalwarts received the attention and the favourable comment of even their adversaries.[38]

The main provisions of the constitution established by the Act may be summarised as follows:

(1) The most important feature of the Act was that it made a part of the Provincial Executive responsible to the Provincial Legisla-ture. The Provincial Executive was divided into two parts—

councillors and ministers. The Provincial subjects were also marked into two categories—reserved and transferred. The councillors were placed in charge of the reserved subjects and the ministers were to run the transferred side. A fundamental departure from the old policy was that ministers were now made removable by and, therefore, responsible to the Provincial Legislative Council.

(2) Statutory rules were framed, for the first time, to separate the Provincial and Central subjects. In practice, a good deal of autonomy was conceded to the Princes in the administration of the transferred subjects. The control of the Government of India over the provinces in reserved subjects remained almost as before. The Government of India remained responsible to the British Parliament for the entire provincial sphere.

(3) The Government of India continued to be irremovable by the Central Legislature. The members of the Executive Council were responsible to the Secretary of State for India and to the British Parliament for the administration of India. This was the chief defect of the Act of 1919.

(4) The Central Legislature consisted, as the Report had recommended, of two chambers, but the Report's proposal that the upper chamber should be mainly nominated was set aside In the popular house at the Centre, out of about one hundred and forty-four one hundred and three were elected. There was a small majority of elected members even in the upper house. The franchise was extended, giving the right of vote to about ten per cent of the adult population of India. The method of election was direct in case of both the houses.[39]

(5) As regards finance, the allocation of Central and Provincial subjects included sources of revenue—customs and income tax being the major Central source, and land-revenue the major Provincial source. They were now empowered, within certain limits, to pass measures of taxation as well as other legislation without obtaining the prior sanction of the Government of India and the Secretary of State.[40]

(6) Although the Montford Report declared communal electorates as anti-national, the system was not only retained for Muslims, it was even extended to the Sikhs. In the rules that were made to implement the Act, the principle was further extended in the

case of the Europeans, Anglo-Indians and Christians in provinces where the influence of these communities could be weighty.

(7) Legally speaking, the powers of the Secretary of State for India remained as before. He was still responsible to the British Parliament for the 'superintendence, direction and control' of the entire Indian administration. But in practice, the Secretary of State and the British Parliament stopped interference in the administration of the transferred subjects in the provinces. In the administration of the reserved subjects in the provinces and the Central subjects, the legal control remained as before.[41]

The reaction of political parties to the 1919 Act was one of disappointment and dissatisfaction. But these were not yet prepared to break with the rulers. Motilal Nehru in his presidential address at the Amritsar Conference of the Indian National Congress remarked that the Act of 1919 was not based on the wishes of the people of India and its provisions fell short of the minimum demands made by the Congress. 'But let us not belittle the good that the Act does us. I would beg of you to work the new reforms, utilise them for the betterment of the country and continue to press and agitate for our full demands,' he said.[42] The Moderates welcomed the reforms, extended to them hearty support and pronounced them 'as constituting a real and substantial step towards the progressive realisation of responsible government.' But they suggested modifications and improvements not substantially different from those of the Congress.[43] In his presidential address of the All-India Muslim League Conference of 1919 held at Amritsar Hakim Ajmal Khan said, 'Looking at the reforms as a whole, we should welcome them as the first stone of the foundation of self-government.'[44]

Under Montagu, as under Lord Morley, political reforms in India were accompanied by coercion. During the First World War, political agitation came within the scope of the Defence of India Act. As the Act was to lapse with the end of the War, the government in India appointed a committee, headed by Justice Rowlatt, to devise new legislation. The recommendations of the committee were subsequently passed in two Acts, known as the Rowlatt Acts.* The repressive Rowlatt Acts were driven through India's Imperial Legislative Council at high speed, over the universal opposition of elected Indian members, who found their passage more humiliating and exasperating than the first partition of Bengal had been. The Viceroy in a speech delivered to the Imperial Legislative Council declared that his government was determined to carry the repressive legislations then on the anvil despite all opposition.[45] Jinnah and several of his colleagues resigned their council seats when the 'Black Acts' were passed in March 1919.[46] Gandhi condemned the Rowlatt Acts as symptoms of a deep-seated disease in the governing body. He called upon all Indians to pledge themselves to refuse civilly to obey such unjust, subversive laws, declaring a nationwide work suspension day during the first week of April 1919, as a prelude to the launching of a national 'passive resistance' campaign.[47]

On April 13 a protest meeting was held on an enclosed square, Jallianwala Bagh, at Amritsar. In spite of a ban on public gatherings of any sort, several thousands assembled there. To this place General Dyer marched a small company of soldiers. The soldiers barred the only exit and were ordered to fire on the crowd. Dyer's troops fired 1,600 rounds of ammunition killing (according to official figures) 379 and leaving 1,200 wounded without means of attention, the object being, according to his subsequent statement, to terrorise the population of the Punjab.[48] General Dyer made it clear in his defence that he went down to the Jallianwala Bagh intending not only to disperse an illegal assembly, but also to punish the crowd in a manner which would be an example to the whole province.[49]

When disciplinary action was taken against General Dyer and some other officers, his action and his attitude were supported by a

---

*One of them provided that any person who had in his possession any seditious document intended to be published could be punished by imprisonment not exceeding two years. In such a trial, it was relevant evidence to show that the accused had been previously convicted of an offence against the state or had habitually associated with a person so convicted. The other Act provided trial without jury and empowered the Executive to confine any suspect within a specified area and to arrest and search without warrant. (Tingfu F. Tsiang).

large section of the Press, by many members of the House of Commons, by an overwhelming majority of the Lords, and later in *obiter dictum.* The Labour Party condemned the Jallianwala Bagh incident with utmost indignation. We shall mention their views on the incident later.

Non-cooperation movement

The Jallianwala Bagh incident poisoned the political atmosphere in India. Gandhi took alarm at the situation which was then developing. In view of sporadic cases of violence of the masses against their rulers in Calcutta, Bombay, Ahmedabad and elsewhere, he declared that he had committed 'a blunder of Himalayan dimensions which had enabled ill-disposed persons, not true passive resisters at all, to perpetrate disorders.' Accordingly, he suspended passive resistance in the middle of April. In December 1919 the Congress decided for working the reforms, and Gandhi urged that the task of the national movement was to settle down quietly to work so as to make them a success. But the situation left no room for such dreams to be realised.[50] The tragedy of the Jallianwalla Bagh, the Rowlatt Acts and the Martial Law in the Punjab destroyed Gandhi's faith in the good sense of the Englishmen.

After the withdrawal of the Moderates, the Extremists took complete control of the Congress, which could adopt a revolutionary programme. The terms of the treaty of Sevres which was entered into between Turkey and the Allies were very severe and were resented by the Muslims of India. In this hour of agony of Muslims, Gandhi advised them to begin non cooperation movement against the Government. They accepted his proposal. The result was that Gandhi was sure of Muslim support if the Congress started the non cooperation movement. Some Hindu leaders were openly critical of what they called the folly of mixing up the Khilafat issue with that of national freedom.[51] In September 1920 a special session of the Indian National Congress was held at Calcutta, where the fateful resolution for non-violent non-cooperation was adopted by the Congress. The Calcutta decision was endorsed at the annual session of the Congress held in December 1920 at Nagpur. The Nagpur session will remain memorable for making two vital changes in the constitution of the Congress. Hitherto, the goal of the Congress was the attainment of self-government within the British Empire. The goal was now declared to be the attainment of swaraj, which according to Gandhi meant, 'swaraj within the British Empire, if possible and outside, if necessary.' Secondly, till then, according to the constitution, the Congress could employ only constitutional means to attain its objective.[52]

The non-cooperation movement turned the national movement into a truly mass movement on a giant all-India scale and gave further impetus to the political agitation and the British rule was shaken to its foundations.* The progress of the non-cooperation movement is summed up by Subhas Chandra Bose in his book *The Indian Struggle* as follows:

Throughout the country there was unparalleled enthusiasm. The 'triple boycott' had been fairly successful. Though the legislatures were not empty, no Congressmen had gone there. The lawyers had on the whole made a good response and the student community had come out of the ordeal with flying colours.[53]

Josiah Wedgwood of the Labour Party while commenting on the non-cooperation movement said:

It is right that those of us who have watched over and helped this new birth of freedom should now realize a factor that is growing clearer and dangerously clear. The Indian non-cooperation movement is not wholly inspired by desire for immediate Colonial Home Rule. There is also in the movement, hardly conscious it may be of itself, a fear of representative and responsible institutions.[54]

Throughout the year 1921, Gandhi's campaign proceeded remarkably. The Mahatma promised his followers swaraj in one year by 31 December 1921. To Gandhi swaraj probably stood for his own ideal of the subjection of the lower nature of man to the higher. But

---

*For the sake of clarity non-cooperation movement may be divided into two parts, one negative and the other constructive. Of the two, the negative is more significant; it consists of the triple boycott—the boycott of the legislative councils, the boycott of law courts, and the boycott of educational institutions. The positive or constructive part is stated in the last paragraph of the Congress resolution and consists of the adoption of *swadeshi*, encouragement of hand-spinning and hand-weaving, removal of untouchability, and the promotion of Hindu-Muslim unity. (J.P. Suda, *The Indian National Movement*, Meerut, 1969, p. 194.)

others read into it a political desideratum ranging from complete independence to Dominion Home Rule.[55] The non-cooperation campaign resulted in abstention from voting for the new Councils set up under Montagu-Chelmsford Reforms—of nearly two-thirds of the eligible electorate. The jails were crowded with 30,000 political prisoners.[56] The report of the Indian Statutory Commission maintained that Gandhi never found it easy to define what swaraj would mean in actual political practice; his accounts of it varried from time to time and were always nebulous. But the critical side of his doctrine was clear enough. Gandhi preached that British rule had impoverished India and destroyed its liberties. The existing government and all it stood for were satanic, and the only cure was to end it.[57]

Towards the end of 1921 Congress demonstrations became unruly and violent and Gandhi was no longer able to maintain the unity of his movement. The murmurings of discontent late in that year and early in 1922 portended an early return by some Congressmen to constitutionalism once the campaign was over.[58] The dissidents' opportunity soon came. The tragedy of Chauri-Chaura in February 1922 in the United Provinces, where twenty-two Indian policemen were burned to death by an infuriated mob of civil resisters, gave Gandhi a severe shock. He was surprised that non-cooperation could not remain non-violent. Being terrified by the prospect of finding India liberated overnight, without either the British army or police to assist Congress in maintaining order and preventing mass murder, Gandhi suspended the civil disobedience movement and in March 1922 its author and inspirer was arrested and sentenced to six years' imprisonment. After two years, he was released for appendicitis operation, but he did not resume active political agitation until 1929.[59] It is possible that this sudden bottling up of a great movement contributed to a tragic development in the country. The drift to sporadic and futile violence in the political struggle was arrested, but the suppressed violence had to find a way out, and in the following years this perhaps aggravated the communal trouble.[60]

The Labour Party continued to denounce the British policy for India after the Government of India Bill was passed in Parliament in 1919. The Party, at its 1920 conference in Scarborough, after reaffirming its stand for the principle of self-determination, demanded the 'full and frank application of this principle in the reorganisation of the Government of India in such a way as to satisfy all the legitimate aspirations of the Indian people.' One part of a resolution, moved by B.C. Spoor, M.P., on behalf of the Executive, reads:

The Conference denies the right of any Government to govern a country against the will of the majority; and while expressing the hope that all the people of the British Empire will prefer to maintain as parts of that Empire so soon as their aspirations have been dealt with in a thoroughly conciliatory manner by the granting of adequate measures of autonomy, it declares that the final decision must rest with those people themselves.[61]

He continued with a condemnation of the British action in the Amritsar massacre, and urged that the officials responsible for this atrocity be tried before a criminal court. Spoor called for 'the recall of the Viceroy as the only proof that can be given to India that this country is deeply moved by what has taken place and does not mean it to be repeated.'[62] He said that although the Government of India Act of 1919 was inadequate and in no real sense carried out the pledge given by the British Government in August 1917, and notwithstanding its very serious defects, the people of India should take the reforms as far as they had gone, to make the fullest possible use of them, and to continue the agitation along strictly constitutional lines. After pledging the support of the labour movement in Great Britain to India's cause of self-government, Spoor proceeded to condemn the Government of India for its vacillating policy. While on one hand the government solicited cooperation from the Indian people and desired the Indian adherence to the British Empire, on the other hand, it alienated Indian sympathy by acts of repression and violence.[63] The resolution was carried. John Scurr, a delegate from Buckingham Labour Party, who had contact with the Home Rule League leader Annie Besant, while speaking in that Conference appealed to the Labour members to insist in the House of Commons that the Press Acts and the Rowlatt Acts should come off the Statute Book, and that they must give the Indian people the liberty to say and do what they liked in the sphere of their political destinies.

B.P. Wadia, of the Indian National Congress, one of the delegation members attending the Conference, expressed his country's thanks and observed that in passing that resolution, and marking it in the way they had done the Labour Party had healed to a certain extent the wounds caused by some of the Britishers in India. He hoped the Labour members in the House of Commons would work for the repeal of the coercive legislation, which was Prussian in character and a disgrace to the fair name of Britain.[64]

On May 22, 1919, during the regular annual debate on India, two Labour M.P.s, Neil M'Lean and B.C. Spoor, moved for the suspension of the Rowlatt Bills. Speaking in the House of Commons Neil M'Lean appealed to the Secretary of State for India to express to the House his intention that the Rowlatt Bill, which outraged the sense of fairplay and justice that every Briton should hold, which laid upon the Indian people and around their necks a bond of servitude, and made them feel that they were a subject race, should not go through.[65] Spoor asked Montagu to remove the obnoxious and unjust Acts and to apply a more liberal policy and if he did that he would not only secure the gratitude of India and bring peace to that unhappy country, but he would go a very long way to securing also the stability of British Empire.[66]

Josiah Wedgwood, Labour M.P. said :

The fact that you are legislating against the unanimous wish of the people, whether it be good or bad legislation, is bound to damn that legislation and to give it no possible chance of operating with success. The Rowlatt Bills are not only against law, but they are against the people. It is these reasons which caused the explosion in India.[67]

With regard to the Punjab disturbances, Wedgood expressed that the Labour members were against the Jallianwala Bagh murder, against the way in which martial law was carried on in the Punjab, against Sir Michael O'Dwyer, who approved the act of Dyer later, and against the whole administration of the Punjab. He said, 'I agree with Mr Gandhi, the great Indian'. Gandhi said, 'We do not want to punish General Dyer; we have no desire for revenge; we want to change the system that produces General Dyers. That is what we must do.'[68] Spoor, while criticising the government, said that during the time of war promises were made to the Indian people and in a measure an attempt was made in the Act of 1919 to give effect to those promises. Yet at the same time they were promising the people of India that they would apply the principle of self-determination to the country and give them Home Rule, those activities were countered by repressive legislation throughout India and more particularly in the Punjab. 'They were countered not only by repressive legislation, but by acts that have been rightly described in the Commons as acts of unrestrained Prussianism,' he said.[69]

The Secretary of State himself denounced the Jallianwala Bagh massacre and said that there was one theory upon which General Dyer acted, the 'theory of terrorism', and the 'theory of subordination'.[70] Even die-hard Conservative like Churchill expressed his indignation over the massacre in the following terms:

That is an episode which appears to me to be without precedent or parallel in the modern history of the British Empire. It is an extraordinary event, a monstrous event, an event which stands in singular and sinister isolation.[71]

Earl Winterton, Conservative Member of the House of Commons, while commenting on the disturbances in the Punjab, said that though General Dyer stopped the rioting and the danger to the life of British and Indian officials, he believed less drastic methods might have succeeded equally well.[72] Spoor of the Labour Party appreciated the views of the Secretary of State for India concerning the question of the rule of force and added that if the spirit that infused his speech in the House of Commons directed the policy of the Government in Indian affairs in the months ahead, there was some chance of peaceful relations being re-established between India and Great Britain.[73]

When vote was taken on a motion, proposed by Viscount Finlay in the House of Lords, in which the conduct of the case of General Dyer was termed as unjust, one hundred and twenty-nine members supported it while eighty-six disapproved.[74]

The Labourites condemned Gandhi's non-cooperation movement. Thre were of course some exceptions. Ben Spoor and Fenner Brockway were among them. Fenner Brockway, who was a member of the Independent Labour Party, kept the Labour Party on the alert with regard to Indian question. Spoor and Brockway opined that 'Labour must not limit the right of an enchained nation in their struggle for salvation. Wedgwood considered that the agitation for liberty and justice was a sound phenomenon but it should confine itself strictly within the constitutional limits.[75] He always denounced the non-cooperation movement. In 1920 he was one of the fraternal delegates from the British Labour Party to the Nagpur conference of the Indian National Congress. In criticising the decision of the conference which confirmed the principle of non-cooperation to obtain self-rule by all legitimate and peaceful means, Wedgwood said that it would make more difficult the union between the Congress, Indian nationalism and the British Labour Party. He affirmed in one of his debates in the Commons that Indians should learn to exercise their responsibilities in organising an opposition in the Assembly on the model of the Labour Party in the House of Commons.[76] In reply to a remark made by the Prime Minister, Lloyd George, in Parliament ('Britain would in no circumstances relinquish her responsibility for India') Wedgwood said that their responsibility in India lay in assisting the formation of democratic self-government there. Continuing, he said, 'We want the non-cooperators to go on to the Councils and the Assembly, not to form part of the Government, but to form part of the Opposition to the Government, until they can become the Government themselves'.[77]

The prime minister in his speech threatened that if the non co-operators went to the Councils and conducted a campaign of opposition to the government in power, they would be regarded as bringing the reforms to nought, as a failure which was to justify them in withdrawing the whole of the dyarchy. Wedgwod replied to Lloyd George's threat by saying it as 'most unfortunate and a threat which as a matter of fact, it is quite impossible to carry out',[78] Spoor maintained that if the government wanted to destroy that non-cooperation movement, they could only do so insofar as they were prepared to do justice to the people of India in regard to the tragedies of 1919.[79]

A curtain of incomprehension came between Indian nationalists and British Labour in 1921. This is indicated in the absence of any questions on Indian matters from the Labour benches, except for a warning by Spoor in December 1921 against repressive measures. At the 1921 annual conference of the Labour Party, India was discussed; this time with a direct reference to the ineffectual Indian policy of the government. The Conference recommended that a more liberal policy be pursued for India, thereby reaffirming the position taken by the Parliamentary Labour Party in 1920 on the Government of India Act. In his address the Chairman of the conference sounded a note of warning and said:

The Indian people will for many years have cause to remember the murder of innocent unarmed civilians, the crawling and flogging orders of the British military authorities, and although they are not now retaliating by taking life or destroying property, they may be goaded into a war of defence similar to that obtaining in Ireland. India with its 300,000,000 population is answering British interference by quietly boycotting goods of British manufacture, and here again we find how the policy of coalition is affecting the economic life of the workers of this country.[80]

It is necessary to quote the illuminating resolution of the National Joint Council, the forerunner of the Trades Union Congress General Council, passed in February 1922, at the height of the crisis due to Gandhi's non-co-operation movement:

While realising the necessity of preserving order in India, the Council deplores the political arrests . . ., but also deplores no less the action of the non-cooperators in boycotting these parliamentary institutions recently conferred upon India by which grievances should be ventilated and wrongs redressed.

The resolution urged 'both Indian Democrats and His Majesty's Government to join in a conference, composed of all shades of political thought, to consider the possibilities of a peace based upon (a) an amnesty, (b) the dropping of the practices of non-co-operation, (c) a time-limit for the transition stages of partial self-government, (d) fresh elections, at least to the Legislative Assembly'.[81] The resolution was aimed at breaking the deadlock between the Viceroy and Gandhi. In December 1921 the Viceroy had braved Cabinet displeasure by making overtures for a round-table conference with Gandhi and other leaders but only if the non-cooperation movement was called off and the conference met without prior commitments. Gandhi was under pressure from the Liberals and some Congressmen not to push the civil disobedience to extremes if a conference could take place and he wavered.[82] The Labour Party resolution moved by Tom Shaw at the annual conference held in June 1922 urged the Parliamentary Labour Party 'to support any further legislation in the direction of securing for the people of India the same measure of self-government which is in operation in Canada, Australia and South Africa.[83]

During these post-war years the action of the Parliamentary Labour Party in the House of Commons was mainly condemnatory of the Indian policy of the British Government. The Labour members rose to the defence of the Indian nationalists and pushed for concessions to alleviate the repressive measures that were being enforced in India. Lieutenant-Commander J.M. Kenworthy, who was very active in Parliament about the Indian question, especially concerning the Indian Army, while speaking in the Commons in February 1922 said, 'Let us make it clear to the people of India if they only confine themselves to legitimate constitutional methods, even of agitation, that we will meet them half-way.' He reiterated that every help would be extended to the Indians towards developing self-governing institutions for themselves.[84]

Josiah Wedgwood stressed the need for giving the pledge of a time-limit for the granting of the next step in the reform scheme. By the next step in the reform scheme he meant complete autonomy for the provinces and control over finance in the Legislative Assembly. Further, he said, 'The next best thing that can be done now is to insist on fresh elections both for the Legislature and for the Council. If fresh elections could be held now it would not be a repetition of 1920.' Continuing, he said that their fight now would be to graft direct democracy upon India, and not to save for ever British administration in India. But, he maintained that it was no good either giving any pledge for the future, or having new elections now, unless at the same time the non-cooperators dropped their non-cooperation.[85]

B C. Spoor in his speech in the House of Commons on June 15, 1922 dealt with the Indian affairs and ventilated the views of the Labour Party. He deplored that over twenty thousand political prisoners were in gaol at present. The crime of these people was not that they were anti-British; it was simply that they were pro-Indian. Their aggressive assertion of independence, and their intense nationalism, have been stimulated by a long-continued 'series of bludering errors in British policy.' Referring to non-cooperation he said:

The policy of blood and iron can no more bring peace in India than it brought peace in Ireland. You cannot defeat non-cooperation by it. You can defeat non-cooperation by practising co-operation.

By this he meant 'the willing, ungrudging co-operation of British and Indian on absolutely equal terms in the maintenance of a commonwealth jointly enjoyed.' Spoor felt that there were certain specific things which should be done immediately. These were: (1) The political prisoners should be immediately released. (2) A conference which would include representatives of every school of Indian thought and representatives of the British Government should be immediately called to review the working of the system of diarchy besides reviewing the whole situation in India. The British and Indian Governments should give some indication that they were going to revise the whole Indian question long before the period of ten years indicated in the Act of 1919. (3) New elections should be held. (4) There should be a reduction in the vast military expenditure of India. Spoor said that Indians should be helped towards complete self-government at the earliest possible moment. 'As far as the Labour Party is concerned,' he said, 'we always have believed that India should be granted Dominion Home Rule within, at all events, a comparatively short time.' [86] Wedgwood emphasised that the Indian people should go on the councils and said when they realized that it meant governing India, 'the rest of non-cooperation would fall to the ground and be futile.'[87]

The views of the Labour leaders on Indian affairs were better expressed at the Bharat conference held on 30 December 1922 in London. Horniman, the chairman of the conference, expressed that the success of the British Labour movement would inevitably lead to the release of other people from the control of foreign imperialism and foreign capitalism. George Lansbury was a bit blunt in his speech when he said that at one time he believed that the British Labour Party could do great things for India. He did not so much believe it now. Addressing the Indians he said, 'Do not pin your faith to what English Labour or any external force could do for you. You should find your faith on your own strength and resolution.'[88]

Speaking on the non-cooperation of Indians Fenner Brockway of the Independent Labour Party said that in their opinion the Indian people had the absolute right to decide the extent and nature of their freedom, and the degreee of their allegiance to and connection with England.[89] Favouring non-cooperation as a means of protest against the British rule in India the conference adopted the following resolution:

The conference has the fullest confidence in the policy and programme of non-violent non-cooperation laid down by Mahatma Gandhi. It believes that the non-cooperation movement has reawakened the people of India to a true sense of their national responsibility in the way that no other means could have achieved and it is opposed to any proposal which would involve an infringement of that policy and programme.[90]

Labour's parliamentary strategy in 1923 was aimed at preventing the Viceroy's use of his special powers to pass bills rejected by the assembly so that the non-cooperators in India would not have additional grist to their mill. C.P. Trevelyan criticised the power of certification of the Viceroy as 'the old autocracy with a parliamentary cloak on'. The Indian assembly, he said, 'becomes a mere debating society, offering advice, but with no power or prospective power.'[91]

An important meeting, on behalf of India, was organised by the Labour Party and Indian residents in England at the Queen's Hall, London, on June 26, 1923 to discuss the question: 'Britain and India—apart or together', and inter alia, the Indian situation specially created by the high-handed certification of the salt tax. Ramsay MacDonald, the leader of His Majesty's Opposition in the House of Commons, presided. The object of the meeting was 'to support the constitutional movement in India towards Dominion status.' MacDonald delivered a long speech in which he referred to the Rowlatt Acts as 'that stupid piece of political blundering' which 'has been the cause of all the troubles. He denounced that section of the British people who had gone back on the war-time promise of self-government for India. He also declared that 'most of us who have liberal minds must accept Dominion status for India as the essential condition of imperial unity.' On the extra salt tax he said that he was not at all satisfied that it had been a financial necessity[92]. Trevelyan, while addressing the meeting, said;

What we in the House of Commons on behalf of the Labour Party have been complaining is that Lord Reading in his action in certifying first one bill and then another over the head of the Indian Assembly, has not been showing that understanding and discretion which we should have expected of him.

Continuing, he said that the Labour Party would help India on her way to self-government and self-realisation. He said:

The King's promise to us is a real promise, made by all that "is best in England. While others may deny it or may recede from it, Labour takes up the obligation.[93]

Before we pass on to discuss the attitude of the Labour Government, installed in office in 1924 for the first time in British history, it is necessary to give an account of the internal situation in India.

The first elections under the Reforms were held towards the end of 1920, and were boycotted by the Congress. The Liberals fought the elections and were returned in large numbers. Their policy towards the Reforms was that of 'responsive co-operation'. The elected members of the Central Legislative Assembly, which was formally convened on March 11, 1921, were forced to recognize the national feeling for independence. The first appeal requested the Government of India to introduce the principle of dyarchy on the central level and complete responsible government for the provinces. The failure of the government to give a satisfactory reply led to the introduction of a resolution for self-government for India. It was requested that the transference of all the subjects except the military and foreign relations to responsible Indian ministers of the central government be started, and that India be granted full Dominion status and self-government at the beginning of the fourth term of the Legislative Assembly in 1933. The general feeling among the Indians was that the British did not consider the Indians capable of governing their own country. When the resolution was voted, all the Indians favoured it and the officials voted against the measure. The resolution was forwarded to the Secretary of State for India. The following year another Indian resolution was passed. This one demanded that the British Prime Minister, David Lloyd George, clarify his stand on Dominion status for India.[94]

Under pressure from the Tory members, Lloyd George delivered in August 1922 his 'steel-frame' speech in which he described the Civil Service as the steel-frame of the Indian administration which must remain British. This speech caused widespread resentment in India, because the people were looking forward to the day when the power and the emoluments of the Civil Serivce would be curtailed and the people given thereby a due place in the administration of their country.[95] The Indians interpreted the speech as a repudiation of the August 1917 declaration of government policy. The aforesaid resolution also was forwarded to the Secretary of State for India. The following year. a third resolution was passed. This one urged the relaxation of control over the Indian government by the Secretary of State for India. However, the British Government took no action on any of the resolutions.[96]

Outside the Assembly, immediately after the suspension of the non-cooperation movement and the arrest of Mahatma Gandhi, the qeustion began to be mooted by the Indian National Congress, whether it would not be advisable to capture the councils. While Gandhi languished in jail, the leadership of Congress passed to C.R. Das, a great Bengali leader, and Motilal Nehru from the United Provinces, both of whom favoured taking advantage of the new Government of India Act. The Congress, then, was divided into two factions One group led by Das and Nehru, which came to be called the pro-changers, considered the circumstances unfavourable for civil disobedience and was attracted by the opportunities for political propaganda which the reformed councils offered. They came to the conclusion that the Congress should be induced to remove its ban on Council entry. The other group, known as no-changers, led by Chakravarti Rajagopalachari of Madras and Rajendra Prasad of Bihar, argued that civil disobedience was the sole means of paralysing government and winning *swaraj*. It was waste of energy, according to them, to undertake the council programme. The pro-changers had, before the release of Gandhi, already made up their mind. They were, however, unable to convince the Congress at Gaya in December 1922 to give permission for council entry. Undaunted by the rebuff, they launched on January 1, 1923, the Swaraj Party to fight the elections. The Swarajists won a majority of India's political activists to their policy of 'non-cooperation from within councils'. The no-changers were alarmed at the prospect of a split in the Congress, and a special session of the Congress was held at Delhi in September 1923, where the Swarajists were permitted to follow their programme. At the regular session held in December at Cocanada the Delhi resolution was confirmed.[97]

In the manifesto issued in 1923 by the Swarajist Party, it was stated to be the first duty of the party to demand that the right of the Indian people to control the machinery and system of government should at once be conceded and given effect to. 'In the event of the government refusing to entertain the demand, it shall be the duty of the members of the party elected to the Assembly and the provincial Councils, if they constitute the majority, to resort to a policy of a uniform, continuous and consistent obstruction to make government impossible.' It was also stated on their behalf that if their method failed to bring about the required change in the government, they would unhesitatingly join a civil disobedience movement.[98]

Just as the non-cooperation campaign formed the background for the work of the first legislatures, so Hindu-Muslim antagonism was by far the most significant movement during the lifetime of their successors. Individually, both Hindus and Muslims had been growing indifferent to all talks of unity, and some of them had seriously embarked on a programme of conversion, and consolidation of their respective communities.[99] Suspicion and bitterness were the inevitable result, and in the excitement of religious festivals occasions for dispute were only too easy to find. By the middle of 1923 communal riots were of almost monthly occurrence. In 1924 fierce outbursts occurred in many of the greater cities of the North. It is not surprising that against this background of bitterness the various attempts to find a constitutional formula on which Hindus and Muslims could agree failed completely.

Meanwhile, in England the government of Baldwin was turned out of office in January, 1924, and James Ramsay MacDonald, the leader of the Labour Party, formed the first minority Labour Government.

The First Labour Government

It is generally known that the British Labour Party came to office not by dint of its own parliamentary strength, but by the grace of the Liberals. In the general election held in Great Britain in December 1923 the Conservative Party won 258 seats, the Liberal party, 158, and the Labour Party, 191. The total Conservative vote dropped only slightly, and that of the Labour Party rose only fractionally. The Liberals improved their position slightly. But the Conservatives lost badly in terms of seats. Although they were still the largest party in the Commons, they were in a minority in the Commons and the country to a Labour-Liberal coalition.[100]

Stanley Baldwin resigned his office on January 22, 1924, and MacDonald became the first Labour Prime Minister. In fact, MacDonald did not take the responsibility of forming a Labour Government until he was assured that the Liberals would continue supporting him while in office. As the possibility of a Labour Government drew nearer, speculation as to the personality of the Labour Secretary of State for India was ripe. Josiah Wedgwood was generally looked upon as the candidate. His advent to the India Office was considered to be a foregone conclusion. The surprise of the Indian Press was great when Wedgwood was not sent to the India Office by MacDonald. The choice did not even fall upon Ben Spoor. The appointment of Sydney Olivier as Secretary of State for India was as unpopular in India as it was satisfactory to the British ruling class. On the average Indian, it did not make any impression that the new Indian Secretary was an old Fabian. What formed his judgment was the fact that Sydney Olivier was an old member of the Colonial Civil Service, an institution hated and suspected in India.[101]

Wedgwood fought hard to be Secretary of State for India or the Colonies. In the end he was driven to accept the Chancellorship of the Duchy, which made him a sullen and discontented colleague in the government. He was the cause of trouble, occasionally, in the Cabinet itself by his persistence in carping at Olivier's policy about India.[102] Indian problems were more fully and more frequently brought before the Cabinet, by telegrams, dispatches, and memoranda circulated by Olivier. But here the Cabinet was preoccupied with other subjects and too little familiar with the position to be able or willing to give these problems any effective discussion. In this department, however, there was a standing "Indian Committee" (Olivier, Richards, his Under-Secretary, Chelmsford, Wedgwood, Trevelyan, and S. Webb), which met frequently and, with one or two head officials, actually drafted the telegrams that Olivier freely sent.[183]

The Labour Government's policy for India was announced in a message MacDonald sent to India in January 1924. In this message he cautioned the Indians against their adoption of revolutionary or subversive means to attain their independence. He could foresee the ultimate independence of India only by constitutional means. In the course of his message to India, MacDonald said :

I can see no hope in India if it becomes the arena of a struggle between constitutionalism and revolution. No party in Great Britain will be cowed by threats of force or by policies designed to bring Government to a standstill; and if any sections in India are under the delusion that that is not so, events will very sadly disappoint them. I would urge upon all the best friends of India to come nearer to us rather then stand apart from us, to get at our reason and good will.[104]

The gravity of some of these words was immense. In one sentence he dispelled any doubt that might have been created somehow or other concerning the imperial policy of the Labour Party. Instead of giving any indication that, true to his profession of self determination and democracy, he would in any way modify the present unquestionably irresponsible and autocratic government of India, MacDonald pledged the Labour Party to the task of suppressing any attempt of the Indian People to free themselves by displeasing MacDonald and his task masters, the British bourgeoisie.[105]

George Lansbury, whose talents added greatly to the formulation of sound Labour Party policies and who was very sympathetic to the cause of India, in reply to a letter from Nehal Singh, an Indian nationalist, before the Labour Party came to office, said :

The Labour Party will soon be in office though not in power. . . . Labour men will be able to introduce a new spirit into the relationships which exist between the Indian people and the British people. Those of us who for years have been advocating a free partnership between the two people will continue to do our best to bring this about.

Nehal Singh, while commenting on the said statement, expressed that India under Labour would, in any event. be better off than under the Conservatives and even under the Liberals. But, on the other hand, he said, I see no signs of Labour rushing in to deliver India from the bureaucracy and make her self-sufficing in respect of her domestic affairs.[106]

The accepted maxim of British politics that the Indian question was not a party question but a matter of national policy guided the Labour Government. Lord Reading, the Gover␣ner-General, told the Indian Legislative Assembly on January 31, 1924, 'It is the policy of the British nation and not of any party.[107] He assured the members of the Assembly that the attainment of self-government for India was the ultimate policy of the British nation. Expressing the view he said, 'There is now a spirit in India, if I am to credit all I read, which is bent upon destruction of the Reforms unless it immediately attains that which it is impossible for any British Government to grant forthwith, that is, complete Dominion self-government.'[108] Lord Reading stressed that the advancement towards the goal of self-government was contingent upon the action taken by the Indian legislature and by the attitude of the Indian people.

The apprehension of the British Government centred around the emergence of the Swaraj Party. At the same time that the Labour Party formed the Government in England, the fortunes of election favoured the Swaraj Party and it was returned in the elections of 1923 as the strongest single group in the Legislative Assembly, as well as in most of the provinces, and in Bengal and the Central Provinces it commanded the majority.[109] The year 1924 opened with the Swarajists in the Councils and most of the Liberals outside. Both parties were in good heart; the Swarajists because they had triumphed at the poll; the Liberals because they regarded the new position of the Swarajists as demonstrating the validity of their own policy. But while in the matter of tactics, the two parties were radically divided, there was a substantial identity in their aim. In the first place, both Swarajists and Liberals were determined to press for early constitutional advance. They both agreed that the present constitution was unsatisfactory from the point of view of the national aspirations of India.[110] Because the avowed policy of the Swarajists was to disrupt the Government of India, the governmental authorities were fearful of the future, especially after Motilal Nehru, the leader of the Swarajists, was able to attract the independently elected members of the central legislature into forming a Nationalist Party with the Swarajist members. This new Party formed in February 1924 was pledged to ask the Government of India for full responsible government.[111] A motion was introduced in the Legislative Assembly by Rangachariar urging the revision of the Government of India Act of 1919. The steps recommended were: that a representative round table conference be summoned to prepare the scheme of a constitution for India, that the scheme should be placed before a newly elected

Indian legislature, and then submitted to the British Parliament for enactment.[112]

Sir Malcolm Hailey, who was then Home Member of the Indian Government, took an early opportunity of indicating the attitude of the government. He stated that many interests concerned had a right to know if any radical change in the system of administration was contemplated at an early date. He stated in emphatic terms that the answer was in the negative. The demand for immediate Dominion status was entirely new. It was inconsistent, he said, with the specific provision of the Government of India Act of 1919 that advance towards self-government was to take the form of successive stages. Sir Malcolm promised an immediate investigation of complaints against the working of the present scheme. In a subsequent speech he amplified the announcement by stating that if the enquiry revealed the possibility of advance within the Act, the Government of India were willing to make recommendations to that effect. On the other hand, if no advance was found possible without amending the constitution, the question of immediate progress must be regarded as an entirely open issue.[113]

The Labour Government was in a quandary as to the best policy for India. Perhaps the keynote of their policy was to achieve Indian co-operation with the British Government. Since the whole platform of the Swaraj Party demonstrated that the Indians had lost faith in the British policy, the Labour Government was determined to restore confidence between the Indians and the British. The Labour Government began making informal inquiries about the best procedure to bring the Indians and the British together. One plan under consideration was to send a royal commission composed of the former Secretaries of State for India and the ex-Viceroys, regardless of political party affiliations, to India to confer with the leaders of the Indian political parties. By holding joint sessions with the Indian political leaders the royal commission was to have worked out a new plan of constitutional reform for India. Neither this plan nor the suggestion that the Indians themselves should send a delegation to London were carried out, but Labour Government opinion was moving towards a plan that would use the parliaments of the two countries as bodies of inquiry. The joint commission did not materialize.[114]

Both the houses of the British Parliament severely criticized the

Labour Government for its indecision in formulating an Indian policy. The Conservatives were critical of the Labourites and they attacked the Government's action in releasing Gandhi from jail. The talk of releasing all political prisoners in India did much to incite the conservative element of the British society. The policy of the British Conservative Party to India was defined by the party leader, Stanley Baldwin. While laying down the lines of Conservative policy on broad national and imperial principles, Baldwin in his speech in May, 1924, in the Albert Hall, London said :

We regard the connection between India and ourselves as vital to both countries. While guiding our Indian fellow-subjects along the hard path that we have trodden, which leads to self-government within the Empire, we will firmly resist any attempt to bring about any form of separation. [115]

The Conservatives demanded to be informed of the validity of the rumours that the Labour Government was considering to revise the plans for the Indianization of both the Indian Civil Service and the Indian Army.

The Earl of Clarendon asked the Secretary of State for India in the House of Lords on February 26, 1924, whether His Majesty's Government had any statement to make with regard to affairs in India.[116] In reply Lord Olivier referred to the observations made by Sir Malcolm Hailey, who stated the views of His Majesty's Government in the Indian Legislative Assembly on February 18, 1924. Hailey said, 'I am anxious to emphasise that, in what I say, I speak with the full authority of His Majesty's Government.'[117] Lord Olivier said that His Majesty's Government were in sympathy with the purpose of the Home Rule Party in India. They were in sympathy, he declared, with the purposes of the Montagu-Chelmsford reforms; in other words, progress towards Home Rule. 'But their view is that.' Olivier emphasised, 'unless a parliamentary system is welded together by predominant common interests from its foundation in the electorate upwards no theoretical constitution that may be arrived at by a concordat among leaders of divergent interests, for the mere purpose of establishing an ostensibly democratic form, can prevent it from flying asunder'.[118] Referring to Lloyd George's 'steel frame speech' he said that it was impossible to associate the idea of perpetuating British service in India with the ultimate idea of Indian nationalism and responsible government.

He stressed that the proper line towards Home Rule in India depended on friendly co-operation.[119]

While speaking on an adjournment motion in the House of Commons on March 11, 1924, George Lansbury of the Labour Party dealt with the Indian question and said that the whole benefit of the Montagu-Chelmsford reforms was vitiated by the Jallianwala Bagh massacre, and because of the failure of the Home Government to take proper measures in dealing with those responsible. He wanted that the government should meet the Indians in a round table discussion to give them a little more self-government in order that peace might be preserved in India.[120] Though the members' questions and, the replis of Robert Richards, Under Secretary of State for India, on behalf of the Government were interesting, the debate in the Commons on April 15, 1924, raised by a member of the Conservative Party, was revealing, for it made clear the position of the British parties relating to India. All parties agreed that no immediate political advance could be contemplated. The differences between them were more or less verbal and hardly substantial. The Conservatives breathed fire and sword and advocated a policy of repression. According to them, the Indian National Congress was an organisation of the enemies of the British Empire, the Swarajists were obstreperous opponents of the government and Gandhi a rebel.

John Scurr, spokesman for the Labour Party, pointed out that the movement for self-government in India had been a continuous one since the founding of the National Congress Party, and that this evolving concept of responsible government was in keeping with British principles that the control of a national government should rest in the hands of its own nationals. He advocated the appointment of a commission to be sent to India to examine the grievances of the Indian people and suggest ways for a revision of reform at the earliest opportunity. Concluding, he remarked 'If provincial autonomy had been granted, and responsibility had been placed on Indian ministers for India's domestie affairs with regard to the provinces, we should not have had the trouble with which we are faced today.[121] The Liberal member, Hope Simpson, while defending the Labour Party deplored the failure of dyarchy and emphasized the need for change. He criticised the certification power of the executives. Referring to the provisions of the Act of 1919, which stated that a commission had to be sent to India in ten years, Simpson stated that there was nothing that would prohibit the sending of a mission to India before the decade had passed. 'We have got to encourage', he said 'the Indians to think that we are going to give them within a measurable time Dominion self-government.'[122]

Robert Richards, the Under-Secretary of State, said in the Commons that the Labour Government had authorized the Government of India to establish an Indian Government committee of inquiry to investigate the working of the entire Indian administration. Richards observed that the views of representative Indian politicians, who had come to the assembly in a perfectly constitutional way, and who advocated modifications of the Constitution about practical defects in the provisions of the 1919 Act, should be given full opportunity of constitutional expression and consideration before the recommendations of the government were nally formulated. Finally, he expressed the view that the Labour Government desired to establish contact with the Indians in the hope that a way might be found, by 'a full and frank interchange of views, to establish a lasting peace and enduring co-operation for the well-being both of India and of the Empire as a whole.'[123]

In April 1924, MacDonald, the Prime Minister, said to Indians:

We know of the serious condition of affairs in India and we want to improve it. Keep your faith in the British Government. An inquiry is being held by the British Government which means that inquiry to be a serious one. We mean that inquiry shall produce results which will be the basis for consideration of the Indian constitution . . . . which we hope will help Indians to co-operate on the way towards the creation of a system which will be self-government.[124]

This was followed by the appointment by the Labour Government in the following month of the Reforms Inquiry Committee presided over by Sir Alexander Muddiman. The Under-Secretary of State for India promised that as soon as the Muddiman report had been transmitted to the British Government, it would be placed before the British Parliament for consideration. But before the Committee could report, however, the Labour Government fell from power.

It is necessary to mention that while the inquiry was in progress in India, Lord Olivier stated in reply to a question in the Lords that His Majesty's Government were not in a position to form a

judgment whether Montagu-Chelmsford Reforms were really unworkable, as every progressive politician in India claimed, until the
Viceroy had had all his reports from his Provincial Governors and
that committee had gone thoroughly into the case and the evidence
had been heard and considered. With regard to the Swarajist proposal for drafting a new constitution by themselves and on the
question of sending a royal commission, Lord Olivier said that His
Majesty's Government recognised that it was just possible that the
result of the inquiry might impose upon them the duty of coming
to a conclusion whether some steps should or should not be taken
to re-examine the constitutional position. He asserted that it would
be so if it was proved to the satisfaction of the Government of
India that there were certain defects in the Montagu-Chelmsford
reforms, which could not be redressed 'within the four corners of
the Act' without some revision of its provisions.[125]

The remark of the Marquess Curzon of Kedleston, a Conservative, in the House of Lords debates, was blunt when he said that
the idea of the plan of a round table conference as proposed by the
Swarajists, to discuss the drafting of a new constitution for India,
had only 'to be stated to be covered with ridicule.' He said, 'I
cannot imagine a more unfortunate, or what would be likely in the
long run to be a more disastrous, method of endeavouring to cope
with the situation in India than resort to what is called a round
table conference.'[126] He warned the government that they only
represented a minority in Parliament and it must be perfectly obvious that 'it does not lie within their power, it is altogether outside
their capacity, to propose any sudden violent or drastic changes in
this matter.'[127]

The findings of the Mudddiman Committee were not made
public until 1925, and the recommendations were never acted
upon. The report contained two sections, the majority and the
minority reports. The assumption underlying the majority report
was that they were prevented from recommending any remedies
which were inconsistent with the Act, whether such remedies were
to be found by action within the scope of the Act or by the amendment of the Act itself. Their recommendations were therefore confined to a few minor adjustments. The minority report, however,
held that dyarchy had failed and 'the only cure to be had is in the
replacement of the dyarchical by a unitary and responsible provin-

cial government.'[128] The majority report revealed that in the opinion of the many witnesses who testified before the committee, the existing form of government was unacceptable. The majority of the witnesses were in favour of provincial autonomy and desired some measure of control in the central government. In general, the testimony indicated that the Indians desired at the centre the control of all subjects except defence, political affairs and foreign relations.

Specific defects in the constitution mentioned during the course of the investigation were: the failure on the part of the government to encourage joint deliberation between ministers responsible for the transferred subjects and officials in charge of the reserved subjects, the absence of collective responsibility among the responsible ministers; the conflict of interests between the reserved and transferred departments over administrative control; the failure of the civil servants to cooperate with Indian ministers responsible to the legislature; the restrictive financial control which prevented the Indian ministers from assuming any free course of action in their own departments; and the failure to grant true ministerial responsibility in the transferred departments. The executive certification power and the interference by the Secretary of State for India had deprived the Indian ministers of all but a vestige of responsibility. The majority report of the Muddiman Committee concluded that dyarchy really had never been attained because of the overlap of functions between the reserved and transferred subjects, and of the somewhat stringent supervision exercised by the executives over the action of the Indian ministers. The majority report granted that the dyarchy did offer valuable training to Indian ministers.

The minority report, which was written by the Indian members of the commission, was very critical of the lack of unity in the government at all levels, of the overlapping of responsibility and control, of the use of the certification powers of the executives, and of the stringent control exercised by the finance department. The system of dyarchy was roundly condemned, since, in the opinion of the committee, it had been worked the first three years by reasonable men and was found to be inadequate because of inherent defects, the principal ones being that the ministers lacked real responsibility, that there was no co-operation among various governmental departments, and that the financial settlement gave ministers inadequate funds for them to accomplish their assigned duties. In general, the consensus of the committee was that the dyarchy, at best, was working only with difficulty, and that a more liberal instrument of government was needed to develop an effective working administration.[129]

While the Labour Government was busy at home considering the course of action that it should take to improve conditions in India, the Swaraj Party was causing trouble in the Central Provinces and also in Bengal. In the Central Provinces the Swarajists being in absolute majority, there was no difficulty in putting dyarchy out of action. The Governor had no alternative but to take the administration of the transferred subjects in his own hands. In Bengal, although the Swarajists were not in an absolute majority, yet C.R. Das was able to enlist the support of some Muslims, and was able to render dyarchy unworkable. In other provinces the Party continued to make, now and then, demands for constitutional advancement.[130]

In July 1924, the Viceroy sent a message to the Secretary of State for India stating that under the existing laws the Governor of Bengal was unable to cope with the conspiracies and crimes of violence in the province. While Lord Reading emphasised that he could see no course of action other than resorting to extra-legal means to suppress disorders in Bengal, the Labour Government replied that it was in complete sympathy with the Viceroy's views and instructed him to assist the Governor of Bengal.[131] Thus the Labour Government sanctioned the Bengal Ordinance which was promulgated on October 25 of that year. It empowered police officers not only to arrest, but to imprison indefinitely, any person suspected of having the intention of committing certain crimes set out in the criminal code. It provided for trial by special commissioners, appointed by government, but it failed to provide any protection to the accused, inasmuch as the accused could not be present at the trial or be defended by a lawyer; further, this mock-trial could not be claimed as a matter of right; and finally the Ordinance dispensed with the necessity of even framing charges against people deprived of their liberty and allowed to rot in jail for an indefinite period of time. As the validity of an Ordinance only stood good for six months, the government introduced a Bill embodying the provisions of the Ordinance in the Beng Legislative Council when it was rejected, men of all parties—Moderates, Independents and Swarajists, Hindus and Muslims—uniting in its condemnation. But in spite of its rejection by the legislature, the government exercised its arbitrary powers and 'certified' it, and it became law.[132]

By this action the Labour Government resorted to the repressive policy that the Labour Party had criticized so severely under the previous administration. As the government sanctioned this epitome of inequity, it explained why it was charged with the betrayal of India. Instead of passing this ordinance, instead of bowing the knee to Lord Reading, who was once Lord Chief Justice of England, and upon whose advice it was passed, the Labour Government ought to have recalled him, and sent out as viceroy a member of the Labour Party who, with his strength and foresight, would have brought about a union of hearts between Britain and India by governing India in accordance with Indian opinion as expressed by the Indian legislatures.[133]

Lord Olivier, while speaking on the Bengal Ordinance in the Lords expressed that it gave unusual powers to the police and to the administration and which really took away from any one who was charged or proceeded against under it any protection for liberty. He said that any excuse whatever for saying that the Ordinance was aimed at any kind of political agitation in India should be without foundation. 'The Ordinance', he argued, 'was justified in the view of the Government of India on its merits, and justified in the view of the His Majesty's Government on the recommendation of the Viceroy and of his advisers, in whose judgment as to its necessity we had absolute and entire confidence'.[134] E. Thurtle, a Labourite, criticised the Ordinance in the House of Commons and remarked that the citizens of India were just as entitled to enjoy their constitutional liberty as were the citizens of England, and unless there were extraordinary conditions the Britishers, he said, were not entitled to put into force powers which were to take away from the ordinary citizen his most elementary rights.[135]

Whether this action was justifiable or not, in the eyes of the Indian nationalists the Labour Government's permitting the issuance of the Bengal Ordinance placed the Labour Party in the same category as the other British Political Parties. The one possible exception with regard to Labour's actions in India was Gandhi's release from jail, after a serious illness, and having served two years of a six-year sentence. But it was clear from the start that no major effort at conciliation was planned.[136] The pre-Labour Government speeches and writings of Labour leaders were full of good wishes for India. It was only when the time for giving at least an earnest of their good wishes came that they as a government failed. They failed India and they failed their own principles.[137] Lieutenant-Colonel Meyler said in the House of Commons that he was not in the least surprised that the people of India had been greatly disappointed by what had occurred since the Labour Government took office. Their promises had not been carried out.[138]

In its editorial entitled 'The Failure of India', the *New Leader* commented that the Prime Minister aimed at winning confidence in England, and to this end he postponed any attempt to apply Labour's own principles to India. To a certain extent this was unavoidable; Labour had no majority. There was much that labour might have done. It might have hastened the Indianisation of the civil service and the army. It might have contrived the inquiry into the next step towards constitutional reform in a way that would have impressed and reassured Indian opinion. The editorial further said that Labour governed India as Tories or Liberals might have governed it. Labour's failure to conciliate as it should have conciliated meant, in the end, that Labour must repress as Tories would repress.[139] MacDonald tried to justify later his inaction with regard to India in these terms :

I want to make it perfectly clear, especially to our Indian friends, that the action which the non-cooperators took, just when we were on the threshold of office, put innumerable obstacles in our way, gave us difficulties that made it quite impossible for us, for the time being, to do what we should like to have done, that, so far from assisting India in its progress towards self-government, it was most serious and, to my colleagues and myself, a most tragic disaster.[140]

The government of James Ramsay MacDonald remained in office for about nine months and on October 8, 1924, it lost a vote of confidence in Parliament. A general election took place on October 29. It was known as 'Red Letter' election. It was so called because of the use made by the Conservatives of a letter which they claimed had been sent to the Labour Party by Zinoviev offering the support of the Soviet Communist Party. The Zinoviev letter was a misfortune for Labour although it provided the Party with a magnificent excuse for its failure and defeat.

The election, of course, was far from being a disaster for Labour. It lost sixty-four seats and gained twenty-four, and was still ten seats better off (151) than in 1922; largely as a result of running more candidates, it put up its national vote by a million. The real losers were, again, the Liberals. They lost a hundred seats, and among the fallen was Asquith, whose long career thus came to a sad close. The Conservatives returned triumphantly with 419 members.[141] The nation then settled down to five placid years of solid Conservative rule.

Since 1918, the Indian Nationalist Movment had gone through an historic period full of exciting events. The attitude of the Labour Party during the period under discussion did not encourage optimism. Occasional pronouncements and stray resolutions put forward by individuals and passed in meetings created the vague notion that a Labour Government would somehow modify the relations between India and the Empire. When the Labour Government outraged Indian opinion by sanctioning the Bengal Ordinance, when Lord Olivier, the Secretary of State for India, rejected overtures for a round table conference, Indians were driven against their will to the conclusion that the Labour Party was tainted with Imperialism, and that India could not rely upon it for the realisation of its goal of self-government.

NOTES

1. V.P. Menon, *The Transfer of Power in India*, Calcutta, 1957, p. 18; See also by the same author, *Montagu-Chelmsford Reforms*, Bombay, 1965.
2. Cited in V.D. Mahajan, *The Nationalist Movement in India*, New Delhi, 1976, p. 289.
3. R. Coupland, op. cit., p. 58.
4. P.S. Gupta, *Imperialism and the British Labour Movement*, London, 1975, p, 40; See also Lionel Curtis, *Dyarchy*, London, 1920.
5. R. Coupland, op. cit., pp. 58-60.
6. G. Milton Ochs, op. cit., pp. 66-9.
7. V.D. Mahajan, op. cit., p. 290.
8. Annie Besant. *India: Bond or Free*, London, 1926, pp. 187-8,

9. Pattabhi Sitaramayya, *The History of the Indian National Congress,* vol. 1 (1885-1935), Bombay, 1935, pp. 153-4.
10. V.B. Kulkarni, *British Dominion in India and After,* Bombay, 1964, pp. 122-124.
11. E.S. Montagu, *An Indian Diary* (Edited by Venetia Montagu), London, 1930, p. 218.
12. Labour Party Annual Conference Report, 1918, p. 138. Hereafter cited as L.P. Report.
13. ibid.
14. Georges Fischer, *Le parti travailliste et la decolonisation de l' Inde,* Paris, 1966, pp, 130-1.
15. P.S. Gupta, op. cit., pp. 41-2.
16. J.R. MacDonald, *The Government of India,* London, 1919, p. 90.
17. ibid., p. 75.
18. ibid., p. 106.
19. ibid., p. 52.
20. H.C. Deb., 1919, vol. 116, c. 2341.
21. G. Milton Ochs, op. cit., p. 74.
22. H.C. Deb., 1919, vol. 116, c. 2363-69.
23. ibid., c. 2401.
24. ibid., cc. 2343-48.
25. G. Milton Ochs, op. cit., p. 82.
26. Tara Chand, op. cit., p. 465.
27. Tingfu F. Tsiang, op. cit., p. 51.
28. J.C. Wedgwood, op. cit., p. 156.
29. H.C. Deb., 1919, vol. 122, c. 468.
30. ibid., c. 689.
31. ibid., cc. 700-1.
32. H. C. Deb., 1919, vol. 122, c. 705.
33. ibid., c. 709.
34. ibid., c. 775.
35. H.C. Deb., 1919, vol. 122, c. 680.
36. ibid., c. 807.
37. H.C. Deb., 1919, vol. 122, c. 793-9.
38. G. Milton Ochs, op. cit., pp. 85.
39. R.N. Aggarwala, op. cit., pp. 84-5.
40. R. Coupland, op cit., p. 63.
41. R. N. Aggarwala, op. cit., pp. 85-6.
42. Indian Annual Register, 1920, pp. 350-351. Hereafter cited as I.A.R.
43. Tara Chand, op. cit., p. 468.
44. Ibid., p. 433.
45. ibid., pp. 32-3.
46. S. Wolpert, op. cit., p. 298.
47. ibid.
48. R. Palme Dutt, op. cit., p. 338.

49. Thompson and Garratte, *Rise and Fulfilment of British Rule in India,* New York, 1934, p. 610.
50. R. Palme Dutt, op. cit., p. 339.
51. A. Hamid, *Muslim Separatism in India,* (*1858-1947*), O.U.P., 1967, p. 144.
52. R. N. Aggarwala, op. cit., pp. 133-4.
53. S.C. Bose, op. cit., pp. 55-6.
54. J.C. Wedgwood, *Essays and Adventures of a Labour M.P.,* London, 1924, p. 141.
55. L.F. Rushbrook Williams, India in 1923-24 (A Statement prepared for presentation to Parliament in accordance with the requirements of the 26th Section of the Government of India Act), pp. 243-4.
56. M. Edwardes, *A History of India,* London, 1961, p. 327.
57. Report of the Indian Statutory Commission (also known as Simon Commission Report), vol. 1, Command Paper No 3568, p. 248.
58. R.J. Moore, *The Crisis of Indian Unity, 1917-1940,* Oxford, 1974, p.15.
59. S. Wolpert, op. cit., p. 307.
60. Jawaharlal Nehru, *An Autobiography,* London, 1958, p. 86.
61. L. P. Report, 1920, p. 156
62. ibid.
63. ibid., p. 157.
64. ibid., p. 159.
65. H.C. Deb, 1919, vol. 116, c. 688.
66. ibid., c. 693.
67. ibid., cc. 672-4.
68. H.C. Deb., 1920, vol. 131, cc. 1788-90.
69. ibid., c. 1738.
70. ibid., c. 1710.
71. ibid., c. 1725.
72. Earl Winterton, *Orders of the Day,* London, 1953, p. 100.
73. H.C. Deb., 1920, vol. 131, c. 1736.
74. House of Lords Debates, 1920, vol. 41, c. 376. Hereafter cited as H.L. Deb.
75. G. Fischer, op. cit., pp. 246-9.
76. ibid., p. 251.
77. H.C. Deb. 1922, vol. 157, cc. 1509-20.
78. ibid., c. 1520.
79. H.C. Deb., 1920, vol. 131, c. 1743.
80. L.P. Report, 1921, pp. 146-7.
81. L.P. Report, 1922. p. 37.
82. P.S. Gupta, op. cit., pp. 50-1.
83. L.P. Report, 1922, p. 204.
84. H.C. Deb., 1922, vol. 150. c. 937.
85. H.C. Deb., 1922, vol. 152, cc. 1060-1,
86. H.C. Deb., 1922, vol. 155, cc. 599-606.
87. ibid., cc. 654-5,

88. I.A.R., 1923, pp. 548-9.
89. ibid., p. 550.
90. ibid., p. 551.
91. H.C. Deb., 1923, vol. 165, c 737.
92. I.A.R., 1923, pp. 540-1.
93. ibid., pp. 543-5.
94. G. Milton Ochs, op. cit,, pp. 103-4.
95. S.C. Bose, op. cit., p. 75.
96. G. Milton Ochs, op. cit., p. 105.
97. Tara Chand, op. cit., vol. IV, pp. 3-4.
98. R.N. Aggarwala, op. cit., p. 143.
99. Ram Gopal, *Indian Muslims: A Political History*, *(1858-1947)*, Bombay, 1959, p. 161.
100. Robert Rhodes James, *The British Revolution*, *(British Politics, 1880-1939)*, London, 1977, p. 465.
101. 'India and the British Labour Government' by M.N. Roy, *The Labour Monthly*, vol. 6, April, 1924, p. 204.
102. 'The First Labour Government' by Sidney Webb, *The Political Quarterly*, vol. 32, January-March, 1961, p. 15.
103. ibid., pp. 20-1.
104. *The Labour Monthly*, vol. 6, 1924, op. cit., p. 207.
105. ibid.
106. *Indian Quarterly Register*, vol. 1, 1924, pp. 266-7. Hereafter cited as I.Q.R.
107. Tara Chand, op. cit., p. 52.
108. I Q.R., vol. 1 (January-June), 1924, p. 119.
109. Tara Chand, vol. IV, op. cit., p. 53.
110. Rushbrook Williams, op. cit , p. 270.
111. G. Milton Ochs., op. cit., p. 108.
112. Tara Chand, vol. IV, op. cit., p. 54.
113. R. Williams, op. cit., p. 276.
114. G. Milton Ochs, op. cit., pp. 109-110.
115. *The Times*, May 3, 1924.
116. H.L. Deb., vol. 56, 1924, c. 320.
117. Quoted by Lord Olivier while speaking in the House of Lords, H.L, Deb., vol. 56, 1924, c. 333.
118. H.L. Deb., vol. 56, 1924, c. 334.
119. ibid., c. 342.
120. H.C. Deb., vol. 170, 1924, cc. 2291-4.
121. H.C. Deb., vol. 172, 1924, cc. 1279-81.
122. ibid., cc. 1275-8.
123. ibid., cc. 1285-9.
124. Cited in an article entitled 'The present position in India' by David Graham Pole, *Labour Magazine*, vol. 9, April, 1931, p. 560.
125. H.L. Deb., vol. 58, 1924, c. 775-6.
126. H.L. Deb., vol. 56, 1924, c. 358.

127. ibid., c. 361.
128. R.C. Majumdar (General Editor), *The History and Culture of the Indian People*, vol. XI, Bombay, 1969, p. 396.
129. G. Milton Ochs, op. cit., p. 117.
130. R.N. Aggarwala, op. cit., p. 145.
131. H.L. Deb., vol. 58, 1924, c. 833.
132. V.H. Rutherford, *India and the Labour Party*, London, 1928, pp. 6-7.
133. ibid., p. 9.
134. H.L. Deb., vol. 60, 1925, cc. 835-9.
135. H.C. Deb., vol. 179, 1924, c. 1450.
136. Richard W. Lyman, *The First Labour Government*, 1924, London, 1957, p. 214.
137. 'The trust of Empire and Mr. MacDonald a trustee' by M. Abdullah, *The Labour Magazine*, vol. 7, April 1925, pp. 225-6.
138. H.C. Deb., vol. 174, 1924, ec. 1665-6.
139. *New Leader* (I.L.P. Journal), October 31, 1924.
140. H.C. Deb., vol. 186, 1925, c. 746.
141. R.R. James, op. cit., pp. 473-5.

CHAPTER 3

The Labour Party and the Indian Constitutional Progress, 1924-1930

From 1924 till the formation of the Second Labour Government in 1929, the British Labour Party was not much concerned with the Indian problems because of the internal economic conditions in England. Still, some Labourites did not lag behind in attacking the Indian policy of the Conservative Government.

While the first Labour Government was still in office, an Indian delegation, which included Annie Besant of Home Rule League, arrived in the United Kingdom and presented to the India Office a memorandum containing a general draft of their constitution prepared by the National Convention. The draft advocated for granting Dominion Status to India. Later, the National Convention drafted the Commonwealth of India Bill which was not accepted even for the second Reading in the House of Commons, although the Labour Party made an appeal for it.

An important event of the aforesaid period was the appointment of the Indian Statutory Commission (also known as Simon Commission). Although the Commission was due in 1929 as per the Act of 1919, the Conservative Government appointed it in 1927. This Commission was to make recommendations for the development of responsible government in India. The Conservatives advanced the date because they thought that the Indian question should be disposed of by themselves, so that if the Labour Party came to power next they would not be in a position to make any further concessions to the Indians. The Commission was composed of the British members only, which was vehemently resented by the Indian People because of their exclusion from that body. Some Labour members in Parliament, of course, advocated for a mixed Commission of both Indians and British. But it bore no result. Finally, the

Labour Party also nominated two of their members on that Commission.

In India, the political parties decided to draft a constitution for themselves during this time and a committee, headed by Motilal Nehru, was formed in this respect. The committee was to consider the principles of the constitution for India. Their report (known as Nehru Report), prepared in 1928, could have no effect because the British Government had already announced the appointment of the Simon Commission. The recommendations of the Simon Commission Report, published in 1930, included autonomy in the provinces but responsibility at the centre was no where in sight. The Indians condemned the report of the Simon Commission as there was no mention of Dominion Status in it. The report also did not satisfy the Labour Party, although the party appreciated the tremendous work undertaken by the Commission.

In 1929 the Labour Party came into office for the second time with Liberal support. Although, after taking office, it declared that it intended to fulfil the British policy statement of August 1917, with regard to India, the government would not consider questions of policy that would involve constitutional changes until after the Statutory Commission Report was published. Later, in June 1930, the Labour Government announced that a round table conference of both the British and Indians would be held to discuss the Indian constitution.

Commonwealth of India Bill

The Conservatives made it clear beyond all possible doubt after coming into power in 1924 that they would not move an inch beyond the framework of the Act of 1919, and held out an open and undisguised threat that there might be a setback in the reforms after ten years if the Indians did not behave properly in the meantime. The fears of the Conservatives, caused by the temporary assumption of power by the Labour, passed away like an evil dream, and the British Government could now pursue its traditional policy towards India.[1]

In India the Moderates, who advocated independence by constitutional means, attempted to advance a positive programme for constitutional reform. Annie Besant formulated a plan to gather all the elected representatives from all Legislative Councils of the country into a convention to write a constitution for India. Early in 1924, this group was formed into a conference which adopted the name of the National Convention of India. The extreme nationalists were not represented at the Conference. The Conference laid down the essentials of a constitution which would confer Dominion Status on India. The first session of the National Convention met in April 1924, and appointed seven committees to consider and report on various problems in connection with the drafting of the constitution.[2] Once the draft of the constitution had been approved by the entire convention, it was to be submitted to the Indian and British governments.

While the Labour Government was still in office, deputations of Indians on behalf of the Indian National Convention and consisting of such eminent persons as Srinivasa Sastri and Annie Besant visited England, interviewed the Secretary of State, talked to the members of Parliament and held meetings to explain India's demand for Swaraj. One such meeting was held at Queen's Hall in London in June 1924, and at this meeting a British Auxiliary to the National Conference was organized. Robert Smillie, a Labour member of Parliament presided over the meeting where George Lansbury, another prominent Labourite, was in attendance with Annie Besant. The meeting emphasised the need for granting provincial autonomy to the people of India.[3]

The National Convention drafted the Commonwealth of India Bill after the Indian delegation came back home. The Indian National Congress and the Swarajists had never accepted and endorsed that particular bill: but all sections of Indian progressives, practically all intelligent Indians interested in politics, emphatically concurred in the position on which that bill was founded, namely, that if there was to be any hope of an acceptable new constitution, it must be one framed by consent among Indians, and in accordance, primarily, with Indian ideas. And, conversely, that no acceptable scheme could be expected to be devised by any commission imbued with any presumption in favour of the ideas of a Conservative Parliament or of the India Office or of the Government of India and its bureaucracy as then constituted.[4] The delegation returned to London again with the bill and it was introduced in the House of Commons as a private member's bill late in 1925. In Commons' debates of July 1925, MacDonald stressed the Labour Party's view about the bill, stating that the British Government had a great obligation to the liberal Indian politicians who had drafted the bill. He acknowledged that it was not in its final form, but the people who drafted the bill had the interests of India at heart. He said :

There is no doubt that with the goodwill of both sides of the House, and the determination of both sides of the House to make people of India comfortable and contented within the British Commonwealth, this matter may be pursued.[5]

Lansbury, Wedgwood and Lee-Smith supported the bill.

The Commonwealth of India Bill would have granted India responsible self-government with some limitations. The Governor-General, who was to be the chief of state, was to retain control over defence and foreign affairs. All control by the India Office was to be terminated. India would be a federated state with the residual powers remaining in the hands of the provinces. The central legislature was to be composed of two houses. The upper house was to have 150 appointed members. Provincial representation in the upper house was to be proportional to the total population of the country. The lower house was to be double the size of the upper house. Members were to be elected by popular vote from a restricted electorate. The Government of India was to be conducted by a prime minister and his cabinet, who would be responsible to the elected lower house of parliament. A committee composed of members of the cabinet would assist the Governor-General with the problems of national defence and foreign affairs. The provinces would be autonomous regions in the federal state. All communal and special representation aspects of the 1919 Act were to be abolished, but in the transitional stage, provision was made so that both the Muslims and the Europeans would be allowed to retain special representation for a period of five years. Civil service was to be divided between the federal government and the provincial governments, and each would have complete authority in its own sphere.[6]

The Commonwealth of India Bill received a cool reception in the House of Commons. The Labour Party made a direct appeal to the House to make a friendly gesture to India by supporting a second reading, but this appeal fell upon deaf ears, since the Conservative Party was in power with a comfortable majority.

Meanwhile, the official Labour Party programme was reviewed at its annual conference in 1925. On behalf of the Executive Committee George Lansbury introduced a resolution that recognised the right of the Indian people to full self-government and self-determination. The resolution declared its agreement with the conclusions of the minority report of the Muddiman Committee. It stressed that immediate steps should be taken to place the Indian constitution on a permanent basis and that all coercive measures and repressive legislation should be withdrawn. The resolution further demanded that a statutory commission, as expressly stated in the 1919 constitution, should be established at the earliest possible moment and urged the Secretary of State to examine the Commonwealth of India Bill, and to call a conference of representatives of the various Indian parties, with a view to the immediate application of a constitution in accordance with the wishes of the Indian people.[7] Fenner Brockway of the Independent Labour Party seconded the resolution and remarked that so far as India was concerned the resolution was very important, because representatives of the government were telling the nation that the policy of the Labour Party was the policy of the government. The resolution was approved by the conference.[8]

However, when the Labour Party's policy for India as adopted by the conference of 1925 was under consideration by the Parliamentary Labour Party, there was a sharp divergence of opinion on the parliament tactics to be used. The majority of the Labour MPs. supported MacDonald who thought that since the Labour Party was the chief opposition party, its tactics should be constructive. The minority, led by Lansbury, thought that the party should adopt an obstructive policy.[9] In the House of Commons debates in July 1925, the Labourites discussed the Indian problems. Referring to the reports of the Muddiman Committee, J.C. Wedgwood regretted that although the diarchical system was mentioned as unworkable, it had to be continued till 1929. He advocated that provincial autonomy should be given to the Indians because security of the Empire would be maintained by that and at the same time education in self-government could most safely be attempted. On the question of franchise he said, 'If we want to get an educated

Indian electorate, an extension of the franchise is the best means of starting that education on right lines.[10]

Ernest Thurtle, another Labour M.P., also criticised dyarchy and said that it was neither government by the bureaucracy nor government by the democracy, and it had entirely failed to satisfy the desires of the Indian people. He told the House that the most moderate Indian politicians were dissatisfied with the diarchical system. Thurtle wanted the government to accept the recommendation of the minority report of the Muddiman Committee and suggested that a committee be immediately formed to go into the whole matter so that long before 1929 the government would be able to put forward, as a result of the work of that committee, a scheme which would be acceptable to the Indian people. [11]

MacDonald in his speech expressed the hope that the government would lose no time 'in getting an amendment of the Montagu-Chelmsford reforms by allowing and providing for the special representation of Indian labour'.[12]

A few months later, in 1925, the Government of India (Civil Services) Bill was placed in the Commons by Earl Winterton, the Under-Secretary of State for India for second reading. It was a bill 'to amend the provisions of the Government of India Act by exempting proposals for expenditure upon certain salaries, pensions and other payments, from submission to Indian legislatures.'[13] Speaking on the Bill, John Scurr, a Labourite, told the House that when the question of Indian self-government, examination of the grievances of Indians came up, it was always said that the 1919 Act could not be altered and that the Indians must wait until the Royal Commission was appointed in 1929. That is said when the question affects the Indian people, but when it affects our people, a measure of this kind is brought in, attempts are made to rush it through, and it is found that we can alter the Act of 1919 quite easily, he said. Scurr wanted the bill to be withdrawn stressing that India should be placed exactly upon the same terms and conditions as the Dominions in the British Empire. [14] Wedgwood regretted that at a time when the Swarajist Party seemed to be adopting the sensible course of cooperating in the development of democratic institutions, the government was altering the Act of 1919, in an undemocratic direction, in the interests of the civil service.[15]

Mention may be made here of the first British Commonwealth

Labour Conference held in London from July 27 to August 1, 1925, where the Indian delegation attacked the Labour Party for its policy in regard to India. Chaman Lall, Member of the Legislative Assembly of India, in his speech bitterly criticised the first Labour Government. He mentioned that MacDonald himself said that India must have freedom, and that the two essentials of that freedom were first, that the Cabinet must be made responsible to the people of India, and that the finances must be handed over to the representatives of the people. But he said that when the Labour Party came into power nothing was done in that regard. Chaman Lall further pointed out that the Indians asked the Labour Government for a round-table conference to discuss their position but that too was denied.[16]

Wedgwood, who was present at the conference, got indignant at Chaman Lall's accusations at the British Labour Party and said that as far as the freeing of India was concerned that depended very largely on the way the Indian legislators made use of the powers they already had. He said 'It is all very well to say self-determination : we want to know what sort of self-determination you want.'[17]

N.M. Joshi, another member of the Indian Legislative Assembly, said that he did not ask whether they were better off under the Labour Government. That government was in office only a short time, but it was for them to reply why they did not do more. He hoped the next Labour Government would give them self-government. He referred to the problems of Indian labour and said that they found it most difficult to fight the battles of labour because, in the first instance, the forces against them were not Indian capitalists alone, but British capitalists and the British Government which supported them. He told the conference that he was not under any delusion that responsible government would do very much for the masses at once, but if they were given self-government their fight would be easier because then they would have to fight only the Indian capitalists and the Indian Government.[18]

Litile notice was taken of the Indian problem in the 1926 annual Labour Party conference because of the general strike of that year. The Independent Labour Party published a report in 1926, on conditions in India and an outline of policy in which they stressed that the best course would be for the British Government to declare frankly that it was prepared to reconsider the whole question of its relationship with India on the basis of self-determination and self-government. The report suggested that the government should announce its readiness to end the external British control and should prove its new spirit by withdrawing immediately all repressive measures in India and declaring an amnesty for all political offenders. The report said that if the confidence of India was to be regained British sincerity must be evidenced by a recognition of the urgency of the problem and by an unmistakable gesture of goodwill. [19]

It is to be noted that Hindu-Muslim strife flared up in different parts of India in 1926. There was a recrudescence of communal riots. The causes which generally led to inter-communal rioting were the slaughter of cows which outraged Hindu feeling and the playing of music before Mosques at prayer time, which gave offence to Muslim feelings. There was considerable tension all over the country because of rioting. The general election of November 1926 was held under the shadows of Hindu-Muslim riots. It was contested by nationalists in the name of the Congress and there was a great improvement in their strength in many of the provincial legislatures, for example in Madras, and Bihar. The whole-hearted cooperation of all sections of Congressmen, which was not forthcoming in 1923 when the Swaraj Party ran the elections, was responsible for the improvement. The final tally of the election showed that the Swaraj Party had lost heavily but still remained the largest party in the Central Legislature. In the provincial elections the Swaraj Party lost heavily in the provinces of Bombay and in the Central and the United Provinces. [20]

This decline in the political fortunes of the Swaraj Party was viewed by the Conservative Government in Great Britain as an Indian approval of British constitutional policies for India. The Conservatives' policy for India was the maintenance of the *status quo*, that is, the maintenance of the constitution of 1919. The guiding figure of the government's Indian policy was the Secretary of State for India, Lord Birkenhead, who privately acknowledged that he was not in sympathy with the constitution of 1919. He insisted that he was at least willing to give the system of dyarchy in the provinces a chance, even though he was convinced that any responsible government for India was a mistake. Birkenhead did not believe that the Indians were capable of sustaining responsible self-government for several centuries to come. He was convinced that the strength of the British in India was because they alone were capable of governing the country. With these convictions, Lord Birkenhead was determined to suppress all violence and other activities that in his mind were subversive.[21]

The first discussion of the Conservatives' policy for India was held in Commons while the 1926-27 budget was presented. Earl Winterton, the Under-Secretary of State for India, in his speech said that the temporary alliance that had been formed between the Congress Party and the Muslims had broken down, and that there had been a noticeable increase in tensions between the Muslims and the Hindus. He remarked that the natural result of gradually increasing the power in the hands of Indians themselves, and thus augmenting their interest in practical politics, was a tendency at least fifty years old and brought out more clearly the real depth of the cleavage existing between Hindus and Muslims, and it therefore followed that that result could not have been avoided by any system of extension of self-government. Winterton said that it was for Indians themselves to show how far they could overcome in the future that 'great obstacle' to their progress and unification.[22]

The Parliamentary Labour Party members did not offer any strong objections to the government's policy of *status quo*. Wedgwood made the major speech from the Labour bench. He reiterated the Labour Party's stand on communal representation and said that he did not consider communal representation as a permanent feature of the Indian constitution. He said that as soon as the two major religious groups were politically educated, that form of representation could be eliminated. Wedgwood, while speaking on the representation of labour and depressed classes pointed out that the Reforms Inquiry Committee made certain recommendations which had not yet been carried out. He said that one of the most important recommendations was that there should be at once additional representation of labour and of the depressed classes on the Legislative Councils and in the Assembly. He told the House that the Noble Lord (Earl Winterton) while answering a question the other day, seemed to indicate that there was to be additional representation of labour on the Legislative Council, but he said nothing about the Assembly. Wedgwood emphasised that it was in the Assembly that the most important labour legislation was to be carried out. He suggested that the only way to get labour or the depressed classes safely represented on the Legislative Council or in the Assembly was by reduction in the franchise qualification so that they might have votes like any other citizen of the Commonwealth.[23]

H. Snell, another Labourite, in his speech stressed that if the Indian people were to have any extension of self-government in a couple of years' time, the enquiry into the faults of the constitution should be started shortly. Commenting on the religious strife he said that the difficulties which those unfortunate differences had created should not be exaggerated. Snell maintained that the religious differences were temporary, and that out of them great good might come.[24]

Other Indian questions that were mentioned in the course of debates in the House of Commons concerned the Indian Army, and the detention of political prisoners by the Government of India. F.W Pethick-Lawrence, a left wing Labourite, while speaking on the Indianisation of the Army pointed out that one of the difficulties in granting Home Rule to India was that Home Rule without control of defence, without a truly Indian Army officered by Indians, could only be an imaginary and illusory form of self-government, and that complete self-government could not come about for India until she had an army which was really composed not only of Indians but manned by Indian officers.[25] The same view was expressed by J. Scurr when he said that Indians themselves should have the control of the army if real Dominion Status was to be conferred upon India.[26]

Lieutenant-Commander J.M. Kenworthy of the Labour Party regretted the fact that the Indian Army could be used outside the confines of India at the will of the Governor-General in Council, after a declaration of a state of emergency. He demanded an amendment of the Government of India Act providing that Indian troops were not to be used outside India, without the consent of the Indian Legislature.[27]

Deploring the policy of coercion pursued by the Government of India, Lansbury said that imprisoning people without trial was the worst kind of policy to bring about any settlement of the disagreements which existed between England and the people of India. 'We want the Government of India and the Secretary of

State for India to treat the Indians as equals and as people whom we want to be free partners with us in rebuilding the world,' he declared.[28]

E. Thurtle, another Labourite, pointed out that the imprisonment of Indians, some of whom had been languishing in gaol for more than two years without trial, was not only a mistake, it was a crime, and the longer that crime continued the deeper the shame on the government which countenanced it. He said that British justice demanded either that these men should be brought to public trial, or that they should be released forthwith. Referring to Bengal Ordinance he said, 'In our view there was never any necessity for this most extraordinary measure, and we think that if Lord Oliver made a mistake it was because he was misled by his advisers.[29]

H. Snell, Labour M.P., criticised the existing system of government in India and expressed the view that the present system reduced the efficiency of government without developing any sense of direct responsibility in policy. He asserted that responsibility could only be increased by granting the Indian people a further measure of self-government. He warned that if it was delayed too long the non-cooperative attitude might have an unfortunate re-birth. He said that the Indians were looking forward to the day when the provincial governments would be autonomous, when the Government of India would become responsible to the Indian people. Snell remarked that the Labour Party believed both in the will and in the ability of the Indian people to direct and control the machinery which belonged to their social life, and it would support the Indian people in every peaceful endeavour that they made to get the blessings of self government in their own time.[30]

In keeping with the policy of the Labour Party, the left wing Labourites again reintroduced the Commonwealth of India Bill as a private member's bill and this time also it could not have a second reading, as the government by this time had proposed to send a royal commission to India with a view to investigating the constitution. The 1927 Blackpool Conference of the Labour Party moved a resolution which declared that the royal commission, to be appointed under the Government of India Act, should be so constituted and its method of doing its work so arranged, that it would enjoy the confidence and cooperation of the Indian people.[31]

In another resolution put forward at the same conference by Fenner Brockway of the Independent Labour Party advocated for the withdrawal of all coercive measures and repressive legislation prevalent in India. In his speech Brockway said that if a royal commission were to inquire into a new constitution, 'the best first step that could possibly be taken was to win the trust of the Indian people by releasing the Indian political prisoners'.[32]

Appointment of the Statutory Commission

It was an auspicious moment for the Indian nationalists when in November 1927 the Viceroy, Lord Irwin, made an announcement, regarding the appointment of the Indian Statutory Commission (also known as the Simon Commission). The intention of the British Government in passing the 1919 Act was to take a decisive and distinctive step towards the gradual development of self-governing institutions in India. The Act provided for the setting up at the end of ten years of a Statutory Commission for inquiring into the working of the system of government and to make recommendations for the development of responsible government. Since the Statutory Commission was due in 1929, it was rather surprising to find a Tory Government advancing the date of the Commission. The Indian National Congress had been pressing since 1920 for a round table conference for revising the constitution for an early introduction of Dominion Home Rule, but this demand had been consistently turned down by the British Government. The Conservatives wanted to dispose of the Indian question while in power, so that the Labour Party, if they happened to succeed them, would not be able to make any further concessions to the Indian demand for Home Rule.

Since the next general election in England was due in 1929, the Conservatives considered that it would be it prudent to create the Statutory Commission not later than 1927 and that the Indians should not be included on it. Lord Birkenhead, the Secretary of State for India, instead of appointing a mixed Commission nominated a Commission of seven members drawn solely from the British race with Sir John Simon, a Liberal, as its chairman, even though it was the future constitution of India which was to be the subject of inquiry. The ostensible reason given by Lord Birkenhead for this 'all-white' Commission only made matters worse to sensitive minds in India. He stated that there were so many mutually hostile sections that it would be quite impossible to choose Indians without offending some of them, and therefore it would be better to leave them out altogether and let British representatives decide these important matters for them. This 'rubbing-in' of Indian internal divisions was felt to be scarcely less humiliating than the racial discrimination itself.[33]

Lord Irwin admitted that the decision to exclude Indians from the Commission appeared to have been a mistake in the light of events that followed. He pointed out that one of the dangers that the Secretary of State foresaw from a mixed Commission was that, on a basis of language not precisely defined, an unreal alliance might be created between the Indian and the British Labour representatives. So long as the issue could be treated on the basis of some general and fairly vague statement, it was not unlikely that the Indians, in spite of internal differences, might find themselves able to repeat patriotic slogans together. And for political reasons of their own, the Labour representatives might not be unwilling, on the same platform of generalities, to subscribe to the case so put forward. The result might well be that proposals, which when critically analysed with knowledge would be seen to be patently ill-judged, would be presented to a not-too-well-informed public as the considered recommendations of a clear majority on the Commission.[34] The result of Lord Birkenhead's act has been to leave behind an altogether avoidable atmosphere of mistrust and resentment. It was also, if one only thinks honestly about it, a gross injustice. For it is essentially unjust to refuse to offer to eminent Indians themselves a share in drawing up a report about the future government of their own country.[35] There were also strong arguments in favour of a mixed commission on the lines of the earlier reforms enquiry committee.

Some Labour Party members advocated for a mixed Commission in the Commons. Pethick-Lawrence expressed the view that the members of the Indian races should be included in that commission. B.C. Spoor said that there should be adequate representation on that commission of every shade of opinion in India.[36] J.C. Wedgwood told the House of Commons that it would be infinitely more desirable if the initiative for that were taken by both sides, instead of being left to the sole initiative of the British Parliament.[37] Indeed the decision to appoint a 'white' commission proved to be a disastrous psychological misjudgment.

In July 1927, Lord Birkenhead and Lord Irwin began setting up the Statutory Commission. When the Secretary of State in a resolution announced to Parliament his plan for the establishment of a royal commision for India before the expiry of the ten-year period, he stressed that the commission was to be composed of members of both the houses of Parliament who were not associated with, or active in, any of the discussions or controversies concerning the Indian problem. There were seven members in the Commission, of whom two were Labourites, one (the Chairman) was a Liberal, and the rest were Conservatives. Thus the cooperation of all the political parties in Britain was secured for the work of the Commission. The Commission was to be aided in its deliberations by an Indian Commission appointed by the legislative branches of both the central and provincial governments.

Soon after the Secretary of State's plan for India was made known the Parliamentary Labour Party demanded that the Indian commissions should be equal in power and jurisdiction to the British commission. Since the Secretary of State was amenable to the suggestion, the Labour Party agreed to be represented on the Commission. In their declaration on policy, the Labour Party registered regret that the British Government had not made positive advancement to the Indian people so as to ensure their cooperation. Speaking in the House of Commons, Labour Party member, Wedgwood, said, 'May I say how strongly I support the recommendation of the Labour Party that that Commission should have equal powers with the Commission sent out from here, not merely in hearing evidence but in reporting to their own Assembly: and that that report should be on equal footing when the Joint Select Committee of the two Houses here have the other report before them.'[38] John Scurr, another Labourite while supporting the Simon Commission said that it would be a step on the road that would lead to getting the Dominion Status quickly. He advocated that the government release all the political prisoners and create an atmosphere in India which would allow the Commission to operate.[39]

These sentiments were echoed by several other Labour members. B.C. Spoor said that it was possible for the elected representatives of India to select a body of men who could work on absolutely equal terms with the British Commission and hoped that the Commission would do everything in their power to remove any suspicion or distrust that might exist in India. E. Thurtle stressed that the Indian people should have an absolute right to govern themselves in the way they thought best.[40] Lansbury summed up the views of the Labour Party: the party supported the government's proposal because it was the first step in the parliamentary process towards the establishment of a round table conference; and urged those Indians who could proceed along constitutional lines to join in doing their very best to make the proposed Commission as successful as possible.[41]

The announcement regarding the Statutory Commission evoked a chorus of condemnation from the Congress leaders in all parts of India as also from the public at large. The public had become so much accustomed to the idea of self-determination for India, that they no longer regarded the British Parliament as the arbiter of India's destiny. Moderates, Home Rulers all joined hands in denouncing the Simon Commission. The erstwhile supporters of the Montagu Reforms changed their ground and were sufficiently loud in expressing their disapprobation. There was hardly any part in India which could be found to be so poor as to do honour to the Commission. With the exception of the European Association, the Anglo-Indian Press and a small section of the Muslims headed by Sir M. Shafi in the Punjab, the whole of India stood as one man against the personnel and the proposed methods of the Commission.[42] The Congress at its session held in 1927 resolved to boycott the Commission at every stage and in every form and called upon Indians not to cooperate with it in any manner.[43]

The Indian nationalists and the Independent Labour Party criticised the decision of the Parliamentary Labour Party to participate on the Commission. It could hardly be credited that the British Labour Party, along with the Liberals, would give open sanction and support to Lord Birkenhead's policy. For this reason the news came as a shock to politically minded Indians. It led to a lack of confidence in the professions of the Labour Party.[44] With regard to the inclusion of the Labour members in the Simon Commission the Secretary of State told the House of Lords that after considerable discussion between MacDonald, the leader of the

Labour Party, and himself, the two names were put forward and were accepted.[45] The two Labour Party representatives on the Commission were Clement Attlee and Stephen Walsh but Walsh declined the nomination because of poor health and Vernon Hartshorn was appointed in his place.[46]

It should be mentioned here that on November 15, 1927, a deputation of Parliamentary Labour Party interviewed the Secretary of State for India on the question of the Statutory Commission. Before the deputation waited on Lord Birkenhead it had received instructions from the Party Executive, not to press for the inclusion of Indians on the Commission, but to press for assurance of the fullest co-operation and consultation between the Commission and the committee of the Indian Legislature. Lord Birkenhead expressed sympathy with the demand, and said that it was the intention of the government to ensure complete co-operation between the Commission and the committee, consistent with efficiency.[47] On November 24, the members of the Parliamentary Labour Party held a meeting to detemine finally the attitude of the party on the Commission. An official statement was issued by the party later :

The Labour Party regrets that the government before making its original proposals in connection with the Indian Commission, did not secure the co-operation of representatives of Indian people. In the opinion of the Labour Party the Commission appointed to proceed to India should make it its primary duty from time to time to consult, on equal terms, with the committee appointed by the Indian Legislature. The Parliamentary Labour Party is further of opinion that there should be joint meetings of the two commissions for taking evidence and that, after all the evidence has been heard and enquiries have been made, further consultations between the two commissions should be held and reports of both commissions should in due course be presented to the Joint Committee of two Houses of Parliament. The labour Party has every confidence that its representatives on the Commission will act in the spirit of this stipulation.[48]

After further discussion the Labour Party decided to cooperate with the Commission. George Lansbury while writing in the *Daily Herald* on the Simon Commission stated that whether Labour men served or not, the Commission would go out, would collect information, and would report, and there was a possibility that when the report was brought to London a Labour Government would be called upon to deal with it. That was why some representatives of the Labour Party should serve on the Commission. Lansbury mentioned that if the Indians boycotted the Commission they would make the task of their friends in England, for a time at least almost impossible.[49] In an article Lord Oliver pointed out that there was nothing in the action of Conservative Government to prejudice the cause of progress in Indian reform. There was nothing inherently insulting to India or necessarily wounding to Indian pride in the fact that the Commission was not constituted jointly of Indians and British. There was certainly in the acquiescence of Labour and Liberalism in such an arrangement no shadow of any sentiment in the slightest degree belittling to Indians. He wrote, 'It appears to friends of India wholly mistaken, it is painful to us to have it imputed, and any such mistaken and erroneous belief must weaken the position of any political body than entertain it. We do not wish the position of Indian reformers to be thus weakened, and we are therefore distressed at the feeling of grievance on this account also.'[50]

Mention may be made here that the Indian delegates at the British Commonwealth Labour Conference, held in London in July 1928, demanded that the Labour Party disavow its decision to be represented on the Statutory Commission. Chaman Lall, an Indian delegate, in his speech said that the Indians had been disappointed at the participation of the Labour Party representatives on the Commission. He told the conference that the Indians wanted two things: (1) that the Labour Party would determine to give self-government to India immediately; and (2) that the question would be considered at the round table conference of representatives of the people of India and of Great Britain.[51]

In his reply, on behalf of the British Labour Party, George Lansbury said that when a Commission was set up in the way the Simon Commission had been, whether it was set up by a Liberal, Tory or Labour Government, it was always a composite body representative of the parties in Parliament; it was a matter of procedure and had never been departed from in any single instance. He pointed out, moreover, that if the Labour Party had refused to be represented on the Commission, they would not have had the access to the information obtained and would not have been able to deal with the matter when it came up for discussion in Parliament. With regard to the statement that the Indians had been excluded from the Commission, he pointed out that from the moment the idea of setting up a Commission had been mooted, the Indians had declared their intention not to have anything to do with it, and he himself had been assured that no Indians would consent to serve on it. Therefore the Labour Party had raised no objections when Indians were not included in the personnel.[52]

Henderson, while explaining the attitude of the Labour Party to the question of India told the delegates to the conference that it was impossible for the party to alter the terms of reference of the Simon Commission, as they were part of the Act of 1919; even if there was a Labour Government it would have been absolutely impossible to alter the terms of reference of the Commission. He said that the appointment of the Commission could have remained in abeyance for another two years, but the Labour Party agreed that the matter should be expedited. Referring to the annual conferences of the party of 1925 and 1927 which declared that the Labour Party recognised the right of the Indian people to full self-government and self-determination, Henderson stated that the party were entitled to claim that when they elected Hartshorn and Attlee to act on the Commission, they did so with the intention of using every possible opportunity to give effect to the principle of self-government.[54] H. Snell of the Labour Party said that the Commission was to collect the evidence and the real round table conference was to come when that Commission reported.[54]

It will be interesting to mention that a meeting of the National Council of the Independent Labour Party was held on November 19, 1927 when the main subject of discussion was the situation created by the exclusion of Indians from the Statutory Commission. Speeches were made strongly condemning the exclusion of Indians, and deploring the association of Labour representatives with the Commission. It was pointed out that Labour was giving a legitimate cause to Indian politicians to doubt the *bona fides* of their professions regarding India. A resolution was moved by Fenner Brockway. It reads:

The Independent Labour Party strongly protests against the exclusion of Indians from the Statutory Commission appointed to report on the future Government of India. It reaffirms the right of India to self-determination, and urges that the Labour Party should ask the Labour members on the Commission to withdraw unless the Indian representatives are placed on a footing of full equality with the British representatives, or such other arrangements are made as are considered satisfactory by representative Indian opinion.[55]

As a belated concession to Indian public opinion, by September 1928, committees of the Central and Provincial Legislatures were appointed to assist the Simon Commission. These committees had, however, only an advisory status and did not soothen the wounded pride of Indian nationalism.[56] Lord Irwin hoped that the Indian committee might have been created by the Indian Legislature, and the Council of State did duly elect its proportion of members to it. But the Assembly refused all cooperation, and Lord Irwin accordingly filled the Assembly places by nomination.[57] The Governors of the provinces requested their provincial legislative councils to appoint provincial committees. All but one (Central Provinces) appointed committees from their respective legislative councils. It was Sir John Simon who after his arrival in India in February 1928 wrote to the Viceroy suggesting that the sittings of the Commission should be in the nature of a 'Joint Free Conference' consisting of the seven British members and a body of representatives of the Indian Legislatures. Sir Simon further stated that the reports submitted by the committees appointed by the legislatures would be attached to the main report to be submitted to Parliament by the Commission. In spite of the above modification proposed by Sir Simon, leaders of all parties soon after declared in a manifesto issued from Delhi that their opposition to the Simon Commission still held good.[58]

Fenner Brockway, as a delegate of the Independent Labour Party to the annual conference of the Labour Party held at Birmingham in 1928, openly attacked the action taken by the Parliamentary Labour Party and said that the commissions established in India were selected by the Indian Government, and that the Indian commissions were not given powers equal to those of the British royal commission. The accusations made by Brockway in the conference were answerd by Ramsey MacDonald. MacDonald emphasized that he had held conversation with some of the prominent Indian leaders who were in London and had suggested to them that a round table conference should be called. He disclosed that he also suggested to these men that the Indian leaders in London should consult with the Simon Commission and informally present their ideas. When the Indians undertook this course of action, the Simon Commission had refused to confer with the Indians in London.[59]

The arrival of the Simon Commission in India on February 3, 1928, was greeted with an All-India boycott-demonstration. The Commission made two visits to India. In the first visit which lasted from February 3 to March 31, 1928, its main task was to examine the papers which the Government of India had prepared on the various aspects of the system of government in India. After spending the summer months in England, it returned to India on October 11, and undertook a long tour of the country to record the evidence of those associations, individuals and officers of the provincial governments which came to urge their views or offer explanation on the points that arose out of the written memoranda.[60] Wherever the Simon Commission went, they met black flags, hostile demonstrations and shouts of 'Simon go back'. Though the boycott campaign was kept strictly within the limits of non-violence, elaborate police arrangements were made wherever the Commission went and in some places unnecessarily harsh repression was resorted to. When the Commission returned to England after their first visit in 1928 the Labour representatives on the Commission informed the executive committee of the Parliamentary Labour Party of the open hostility of large sections of the Indian population. Although the Labour Party charged the Government of India with a mishandling of the situation, the official Labour Party attitude remained that of cooperation with the Indian enquiry commission.

Nehru Report

Lord Birkenhead while moving the formation of the Statutory Commission in November 1927 said that he had twice invited the critics in India to put forward their own suggestions for a constitution and that offer remained open. The Indian leaders now decided to accept the challenge. Preliminary discussions between the Hindu and Muslim leaders for the settlement of outstanding differences between the two communities concerning the future constitution of India having been carried out in a friendly spirit, the question was taken up by the Indian National Congress in its Madras session in 1927 It passed a resolution authorising the Working Committee to confer with similar committees appointed by other organizations, political, labour, commercial and communal; to draft a Swaraj Constitution for India; and to place the same for consideration and approval before a special convention to be convened in Delhi not later than March 1928, consisting of the All-India Congress Committee and the leaders and representatives of the other organizations, and elected members of the central and provincial legislatures. In accordance with the resolution of the Congress, an All-Party Conference was summoned at Delhi in February-March, 1928, and it was agreed between the Congress and other organizations present that the question of a constitution for India should be discussed on the basis of 'full responsible government'. The second question related to communal relations and proportions. Altogether twenty-five sittings were held in those two months. [61]

The first meeting ended in a deadlock between the Hindus and the Muslims. The Hindus were willing to give the Muslims a communal electorate, but they refused to grant the Muslims control of provinces having communal electorates The Muslims under the leadership of Muhammad Ali Jinnah, insisted on the control of those provinces in which the Muslims were the largest segment of population, but they were willing to concede to the Hindus' proposal of common electorates. The Conference, in its session of May 19, 1928, attempted to reach an agreement. At this meeting a small committee under the chairmanship of Motilal Nehru was appointed to consider and determine the principles of the constitution for India. The committee submitted its report (known as Nehru Report) on August 10, 1928, and it was considered by the All-Parties' Conference held at Lucknow from August 28 to 31 1928.[62] The Muslim League was not present at that meeting.

The important recommendations were moved as separate resolutions and votes were taken on each. There was some hitch on the resolution demanding Dominion Status for India. The Congress in its Madras session (1927) had adopted independence as the goal, and the younger section, headed by Jawaharlal Nehru, son of Motilal Nehru, opposed the resolution and demanded a constitution based on full independence. They submitted a statement to this effect and abstained from voting. The resolution was passed *nem. con.* When the All-India Congress Committee met at Delhi on November 4 and 5, 1928, it decided in favour of complete independence as there could be no true freedom till the British connection was cut off. It was declared that the proposals of the Nehru Report were 'a great step towards political advance'. At its annual session held in December 1928 at Calcutta, the Congress adopted a resolution accepting the recommendations of the Nehru Report on the condition that the report was 'accepted in its entirety by the British Parliament on or before the 31st December 1929'. It was made clear by the Congress that in case its demand was not accepted before December 31, 1929, the Congress would not be bound by it and it would organise a campaign of 'non-violent non-cooperation by advising the country to refuse taxation and every aid to Government.'[63]

The main provisions of the Nehru Report: In the first place, the basis of the constitution asked for was that India should be granted a full Dominion Status forthwith. Secondly, responsible governments should be provided both at the centre as well as in the provinces. Responsibility of the cabinets was to be joint or collective. There was to be a bi-cameral legislature at the centre, but not in the provinces. The lower house of the central legislature as well as the provincial councils were to be directly elected on the basis of adult suffrage. The upper house at the centre was to be indirectly elected by the provincial councils. Thirdly, a full-fledged federation for India was considered only as a possibility. Need for autonomy to the provinces was admitted. Powers between the centre and the provinces were to be divided on a federal basis. Residuary powers were to be possessed by the centre.[64]

Two functions, defence and foreign affairs, would be left to the control of the central government. Defence would be primarily under the direction of the Governor-General, who would administer the defence department with the aid of a committee of defence. The committee of defence would include the Indian prime minister, the Indian minister of defence and the Indian minister of foreign affairs. The foreign affairs department would be administered by a minister responsible to the central legislature. The central government would have control over all affairs, national in scope and the provincial governments would have control over all local matters. Control over finance was also divided between the central and the provincial governments.[65]

The Nehru Committee made the following provisions for representation:[66]

(1) There shall be joint electorates throughout India;

(2) There shall be no reservation of seats for the central legislature except for the Muslims in provinces where they are in a

minority, and non-Muslims in the North-West Frontier Province. Such reservation will be in strict proportion to the Muslim population in every province where they are in a minority and in proportion t) the non-Muslim population in North-West Frontier Province. The Muslims or non-Muslims, where reservation is allowed to them, shall have the right to contest additional seats; (3) (a) There shall be no reservation of seats for any community in the Punjab and Bengal; (b) In provinces other than the Punjab and Bengal there will be reservation of seats for Muslim minorities on population basis with the right to contest additional seats; (c) In the North-West Frontier Province, there shall be similar reservation of seats for non-Muslims with the right to contest other seats; (4) Reservation of seats where allowed shall be for a fixed period of ten years; (5) Sind shall be separated from Bombay and constituted into a separate province; (5) The North-West Frontier Province shall be a full-fledged province.

A Supreme Court was to be established as the final Court of appeal in India. The Indian civil service would pass under the control of the Government of India.[67]

Muslim opinion was virtually unanimous in its rejection of the Nehru Report and even the old Khilafatist leaders turned against the Congress. But one of the positive contributions of the Nehru Report was the recognition of the necessity of widening the franchise and thereby accepting the introduction of adult franchise and the principle of majority rule in implementing any future scheme of constitutional reforms. This provided a great impetus to the forces interested in the introduction of a democratic political system.

Weighed in the scale of practical politics, the enormous labour that had gone into the preparation of the Nehru Report appeared to have been a waste at the close of the year. And at the annual session of the Congress, held at Lahore in December 1929, the President, Jawaharlal Nehru, declared that the Congress had fixed a year of grace for the adoption of the All-Parties scheme. That being over, the Report lapsed.[68]

Meanwhile, in May 1929 a general election took place in Britain resulting in the fall of the Conservative Government and its place was taken by a Labour Government headed by Ramsay MacDonald. By this time the Simon Commission had finished their labours in

India and had returned to England to draft their report. On October 16, 1929, Sir John Simon wrote to the Prime Minister saying:

it seems to us that what would be required would be the setting up of some sort of conference after the Reports of the Statutory Commission and the Indian Central Committee have been made, considered and published and their work has been completed, and that in this His Majesty's Government would meet both representatives of British India and representatives of the States ... for the purpose of seeking the greatest possible measure of agreement for the final proposals which it would later be the duty of H.M. Government to submit to Parliament.[69]

His proposal was welcomed by the Prime Minister, who was able to add the significant news that the leaders of other parties concurred with it.[70]

Since the report of the Statutory Commission was not published until 1930, there was very little parliamentary action taken by the new Labour Government during its first year of office. With regard to the Report, the Labour Party leader C.R. Attlee remarked that the recommendations made in the report were realistic. A great advance in self-government in the provinces was recommended but Attlee pointed out that progress at the centre was difficult because of three outstanding difficulties.

First, there was the communal tension, particularly between the two major communities, the Muslims and the Hindus. It was customary at that time to suggest that communal differences were deliberately formulated by the British on the principle of *divide et impera*. This was quite untrue, as the sequel showed, for when this problem was handed over to the Indians to settle for themselves they had to resort to partition.

Next, there was the position of the Indian States. India was an intricate mosaic of British provinces and Indian States to the rulers of which the British Government was bound by treaties. The British had no right to hand them over against their will to another power even if that power was Indian. They had the right to be maintained and the British Government had to have troops available in case of need. The report envisaged getting over this difficulty on a federal basis, but until this was done it was not possible to concede Dominion Status to British India alone.

Thirdly, there was the position of the armed forces. The armed forces of India were composed of British troops and Indian units officered for the most part by British officers, for the process of Indianising the officer cadre was still at an early stage. There were few, if any, officers who had even reached field rank. The armed forces had the double role of external defence and the maintenance of internal security. It was not possible to separate the forces for these two duties, and it would have been quite wrong and contrary to all precedent to place British troops at the disposal of a government not responsible to the House of Commons.[71]

The Parliamentary Labour Party in the report submitted to the annual conference of the Labour Party held in 1930 mentioned that the Statutory Commission Report bore evidence of a tremendous amount of work and thought, but the Commission's recommendations gave rise to some disappointment.[72] A month before the Report was published, Wedgwood Benn, the Secretary of State, referred to the functions of the Commission in the Commons and said that the Statutory Commission was authorised only to report and make recommendations. It was not a legislating body to pronounce decisions about the future government of India.[73]

Recommendations of the Statutory Commission

The Statutory Commission Report was published in two instalments.[74] The first volume contained a survey of Indian conditions. Simon himself wrote most of it. He was assisted by Attlee and Stewart. The second volume contained the recommendations. The commission considered first the ultimate constitutional framework of India and then the place of the provinces in it. That future framework, it declared, could not be of a unitary type: it had to be federal, not merely in response to the growth of provincial loyalties, but primarily because it has to embrace all India and it was only in a federation that the States could be expected in course of time to unite with British India. The Report in its major recommendation suggested that dyarchy should lapse and the whole field of provincial administration be entrusted to ministers responsible to their legislatures, since the retention of 'reserved' subjects meant the continuance of control over that part of the provincial field by the central government and the Secretary of State. The Report said, 'that in future each province should be as far as possible mistress in her own house,'[75] It recommended that provincial franchise should be extended and the legislatures enlarged. Unless there were a considerable measure of enfranchisement, there would be a danger that important elements in the population might fail to secure the voice in the affairs of the province to which they were entitled.[76] The immediate adoption of adult franchise, recommended in the Nehru Report, was declared to be impracticable. Communal representation would be retained. In all legislation and all administration—and this was now to include the control of finance and of law and order—ministers would be free from interference by the Governor or the Central Government except for such stated vital reasons as the maintenance of the safety of the province or the protection of minorities. The provincial government would be granted control of specific tax revenues, and all other taxes would be controlled by the Government of India.[77]

The Report recommended further expert examination of the question of making Sind and Orissa into separate provinces. It also said that Burma with its distinctive nationality should be separated from the Indian empire.[78] Its inclusion in India was an historical accident, and it had been included in the past for administrative convenience.

In dealing with the Centre the Report again stressed the need for preparing the way for federation. Thus the Central Legislature, it argued, which in 1919 had been established on the national or unitary principle, should be refashioned on the federal principle. The members of the 'Federal Assembly', as the lower house was to be called, should be representatives not of sections of the Indian people at large but of the provinces, and they should be elected, therefore, not by British Indian constituencies but by the provincial councils. The elections and nominations to the Council of State should be likewise on a provincial basis. For the Assembly the distribution of seats among the provinces should be roughly in accordance with their population. The functions of government of the new federated central government would remain the same as under the Act of 1919, but taxing power could be extended to the Central legislature. The Governor-General would control both defence and foreign affairs.[79]

As regards the civil services of India, the Report recommended, the Secretary of State would retain control over it and that the previously approved policy for the Indianization of the army be continued. The High Courts would be centralized. As regards the

India Office, the Governor-General in Council would remain in constitutional theory under the superintendence, direction and control of the Secretary of State. Apart from the Secretary of State's authority over the Governor-General in Council, he would exercise no control over provincial governments. The Council of India in London was to lose control over Indian finance; this function was to be transferred to the Government of India. Lastly, for the purpose of promoting closer association of the Indian States with British India in matters of common concern for India as a whole, the Report proposed that the new Act should provide that it should be lawful for the Crown to create a Council for Greater India.[80]

The Statutory Commission Report was condemned by Indians. The Indian point of view was that the recommendations of the Commission were the most unsatisfactory. There was no recommendation for a responsible government at the Centre. The report omitted any mention of Dominion Status even as the distant goal of India's political progress. The indirect election to the central legislature recommended was a retrograde step. As to the question of responsible government at the centre, the Commission made no suggestions how the process could be expedited.[81]

In British circles their immediate effect was to strengthen the widely held belief that responsible government in the provinces should be tried out before it was extended to the centre.[82] A statement issued in July 1930 by the Labour Government said : 'It [Simon Commission Report] is a document of enormous authority and intrinsic value, by far the most constructive contribution to the solution of the problem of the political situation of India that we have. But it should be noted that this Report, however authoritative and valuable, is a report only and in no sense a decision of the Government or of Parliament.'[83] The recommendation, although represented a great advance in constitutional progress, did not satisfy Labour Party opinion.[84] We shall now discuss how the Labour Government formed in 1929 dealt with the Indian problems.

The Second Labour Government

The Conservative Government which came into power on the turbid tide of the Red Letter in the late autumn of 1924, went to the country after a few months less than its legal five years' tenure of office, in the spring of 1929. On May 30 in that year there took place the British general election. The results were inconclusive for Labour and Conservatives, but a bitter disappointment to Liberals. The Liberals put up 512 candidates and secured 5.31 million votes. It was in terms of seats won that the acute disappointment lay. Labour, with 8.4 million votes, won 287 seats; the Conservatives, with 8.6 millon, won 261; the Liberals, with their 5.31, won only 59. The election had at least been a decisive vote of no-confidence in the Baldwin Government. Another remarkable—and historic—statistics about this election should be emphasised. The total registered electrorate was now nearly twenty-nine million, an increase of seven and a half million since 1918—and those figures had then included Southern Ireland. Even more remarkable was the fact that the number of women electors exceeded that of male voters by some one and a half million. The 1918 electorate had been seventy-eight per cent of all adults. By 1929 virtually the entire adult population was entitled to vote.[85] Labour was thus the strongest single party in the 1929 election. Early in June, Baldwin resigned. The King at once sent for Ramsay MacDonald, who accepted his invitation to form a government for the second time. Wedgwood Benn was appointed the new Secretary of State for India. Coming from the Liberal Party, Wedgwood Benn joined the Labour Party only in 1928. He had no contact with the nationalist leaders of India and hardly knew the problems he had to solve.

Such had been the distrust of all British political parties in India and the prejudice against the Labour Party owing to its unsympathetic Indian policy when it came into office in 1924, and also, due to the support it gave to Lord Birkenhead's scheme of the Indian Statutory Commission, that its accession to power did not give rise to any hopes or expectations among the Indian people. Lord Irwin, the Viceroy, who tried, though without success, every art to persuade Indian political leaders to lend support to the Statutory Commission and had often sought to minimize the opposition they had shown to it, seemed also to have realised that the situation called for a change of spirit and method, and that it would be impossible to work any new constitution that Parliament might ultimately enact, unless either it harmonized with

India's national demand, or succeeded in winning the general approval and support of the Indian people. Though many in England, especially the right wing Conservatives, demanded a strong policy of repression, Irwin knew that such a policy would destroy Indian confidence and goodwill. He was worried that the Statutory Commission's report would not be favourable to Indian political opinion and might lead to Indian fury. So, he felt that the moment was ripe for some gesture which could restore faith in British purpose. Irwin hoped to get support of the Labour Government and found the Secretary of State for India favourable to make a gesture of friendship. He thought of removing misunderstanding and distrust of Indians by an assurance of Dominion Status and India's right to it. Accordingly, he suggested to the Labour Government the two ideas of round table conference and formal declaration of Dominion Status as the goal of British policy for India.[86]

It should be mentioned in this connection that in the 1929 Labour Party conference, Fenner Brockway, speaking on behalf of the Independent Labour Party, wanted to know why the government had not introduced in Parliament a bill for Dominion Status for India although the Labour Party had pledged itself to a policy of self-government and self-determination for her. Brockway insisted that the Labour Party renew its pledge for Dominion self-government for India, and that the Labour Government call a round table conference so that both the British and the Indians could jointly work out the future constitution for India. He concluded by saying that as the year 1930 would be the most critical for the future constitution of India, the Labour Government should take a positive stand to attain the goodwill of the Indian people.[87] The chairman of the conference, in his speech stressed that, with the cooperation of the Indians, the Labour Government would be able to prepare the way for the satisfaction of the national aspirations of India.[88]

When Irwin came on leave to England in the summer of 1929, he held discussions with Wedgwood Benn over the proposals and the Secretary of State was disposed to concur, but wished to be satisfied that they were not going behind the backs of Simon and his Commission, who were then preparing their report. Irwin then discussed both suggestions with Simon, the Chairman of the Statu-

tory Commission. The Chairman at first saw no objection at all to
the declaration about Dominion Status, but felt difficulty about the
round table conference, on the ground that it would be likely to
affect adversely the status of the Commission's report. On the
Dominion Status declaration he argued that there was no essential
difference of kind between responsible government and Dominion
Status.[89] The Viceroy also talked to the leader of the Conservative
Party, Stanley Baldwin, and some important members of Parliament. Baldwin had no objection provided the plan was supported
by the Statutory Commission, and by all parties. When Baldwin
came to know on October 23, that the Statutory Commission
opposed it, he conferred with his colleagues and then wrote to
Philip Snowden, acting Prime Minister, and submitted the Conservative view that a new declaration 'would impair the authority of
the Simon Commission, would defeat the intention of Parliament
and compromise its liberty of action.' He, therefore, appealed to
him to avert such a disaster and at any rate postpone it until the
Prime Minister returned from abroad. The message was transmitted to Irwin, but Irwin thought that postponement would be disastrous, as he had already revealed it to some of the Indian leaders.[90]

However, with the authorization of the Labour Government,
Irwin returned to India on October 25, 1929 and on October 31,
he issued a statement in which, after pointing out that it would be
both impossible and improper to anticipate, before the report
of the Statutory Commission was published and considered, what
the final proposals of reform to be laid before Parliament would
be, and that with regard to such proposals, every British party was
bound to preserve to itself complete freedom of action, he announced the decision reached by His Majesty's Government to hold a
conference. But the most important part of the Viceregal statement was not only the announcement of the decision of His
Majesty's Government to reach, as far as possible, an agreed solution of India's constitutional problem, but the declaration with
regard to the goal of British policy in India. Irwin declared:

In view of the doubts which have been expressed both in Great Britain and
India regarding the interpretation to be placed on the intentions of the British
Government in enacting the Statute of 1919, I am authorized on behalf of His
Majesty's Government to state clearly that in their Judgment it is implicit in
the declaration of 1917 that the natural issue of India's constitutional progress,
as there contemplated, is the attainment of Dominion Status.[91]

The declaration of Dominion Status was made with the best intention aiming to restore the trust and confidence of the Indians in British policy.

In India, leaders of all shades of political opinion discussed the Viceregal announcement and issued a statement expressing their satisfaction over the declaration of the attainment of Dominion Status by India.[92] The most radical nationalists under Jawaharlal Nehru and S. C. Bose had already committed the Congress Party to the pledge that unless complete Dominion Status was granted by December 31, 1929 the Congress would campaign only for complete independence. Only with great reluctance did Jawaharlal Nehru, the president-elect of the Congress, sign a manifesto (known as Delhi manifesto) issued by Liberals, Independents and Congressmen accepting Irwin's pronuncement on certain conditions, as he had no desire to compromise on complete independence.[93] The conditions set by the Indian leaders with regard to the proposed conference were: (1) a policy of general conciliation should be definitely adopted to induce a calmer atmosphere; (2) political prisoners should be granted a general amnesty; (3) the representation of progressive political organizations should be effectively secured, and that the Indian National Congress as the largest among them should have a predominant representation.[94] The correspondent of the *Daily Telegraph*, writing from Delhi, stated; 'The effect of the Viceroy's statement may be summed up as having at a stroke removed the tension from Indian politics and reintroduced a spirit of confidence and trust between the Government and the governed . . . [95]

While the effect of Irwin's statement was excellent in India, in Great Britian the use of the sacred and ritual phrase of Dominion Status became the shibboleth that divided Churchill from Baldwin, and the diehards from the main body of the Conservative Party. Churchill himself mentioned that it was on India that his definite breach with Baldwin occurred.[96] The Liberal and Conservative Parties criticized the declaration of the goal of Dominion Status which had acquired a new meaning after the Imperial Conference of 1926. (The Dominion was defined as 'completely self-governing, it owed allegiance to the Crown; and it was freely associated with other self-governing countries, which also owed such allegiance, as a member of the British Commonwealth. The right to secede had been accepted and declared).[97] The *Daily Mail* launched a savage attack on Baldwin's leadership of his party and charged him with committing his party to the declaration without consulting his colleagues. He had joined with the Socialists to imperil the empire by promising 'full Home Rule' to the natives, the countless races, of India. The most acute political crisis of many years had arisen and the party leadership was in urgent question.[98]

In the parliamentary debate over Irwin's declaration, Lord Reading, formerly Viceroy of India (1921-26), placed a motion calling attention of the House of Lords to the statement. He objected to the use of Dominion Status because the Statutory Commission was engaged in considering its report and he thought that the declaration brought a change of policy. The Marquess of Reading further asked the Labour Government 'to state in plain terms what undoubtedly is their meaning, what undoubtedly is the true object they have in view, to make it clear...that the language used by the government in the pronouncement is only an interpretation of the ultimate goal to which India may attain when the various obstacles are surmounted.'[99]

In defence of the government, Lord Passfield (Sidney Webb), the Secretary of State for Dominion Affairs and the Colonies, stated that the announcemet was made not for the sake of using the magic phrase 'Dominion Status' and added. 'The declaration was necessary in order to proclaim the new procedure, which had actually been initiated by Sir John Simon and agreed to, of this conference—the enlargement of the scope of the Commission and the conference, which was quite a new thing, which was to come into being after the Commission had reported. That was the new policy.[100] As to the charge that Irwin's declaration undercut the Simon Commission's Report, Lord Passfield said that the Commission were not asked and authorized to express any opinion about the goal of the future in India. He added that the Commission was to consider and advise the measure, and the time that should be taken to achieve the goals set by the Act of 1919. Passfield stressed, 'They are not asked to revise and consider whether the goal should be Dominion Status.'[101]

It should be mentioned that Dominion Status was promised to India over and over again during and after the first World War. Beatrice Webb pointed out that the problem of giving one kind of uniform status to the whole of India, broken up into native states and British India, with different races, languages, castes and religions, seemed to be to put the several ruling native cliques and communities into the position of refusing instead of claiming powers from the British Government; to make those who claimed to govern India on behalf of the people of India distrust their capacity to combine in order to do it so as to delay self-government until some sort of common will had been evolved.[102] She further stated in her diaries that the cabinet was firm on Irwin's statement.[103] The Labour Government was now committed to a policy of Dominion Status for India.

The official policy was issued by the Secretary of State for India in the House of Commons on November 1, 1929. Wedgwood Benn emphasised that the Labour Party intended to fulfil the British policy statement of August 1917, and that the Governor-General was authorised to state that the declaration of 1917, so far as the Labour Party was concerned, was a pledge for Dominion Status for India. But the Labour Government, he said, would not consider questions of policy that would involve constitutional change until after the report of the Statutory Commission had been issued.[104] In reply to Lloyd George in Commons a weak later concerning the statement of Lord Irwin, Benn categorically said that the declaration was a restatement and an interpretation of the Montagu policy. 'It means', the Secretary of State for India stressed, 'what it says; no less and no more.' He further maintained that they did not shelter behind the Viceroy in their action and added that they could reject Irwin's advice regarding the statement but they did not because the advice agreed with their convictions. Continuing, Wedgwood Benn observed that it was necessary to issue a clear declaration of existing policy to demonstrate to the Indians that the British policy was not altering, that sympathy had not gone.[105] There was another reason put forward by Benn in the same speech as regards the pronouncement. He said that the Statutory Commission was going to report, and the government wanted to create a favourable atmosphere for the report. He further said that the government wanted to have an atmosphere of goodwill, and that would be better secured if the government could clear up the webs of mistrust of the Indian people.[106]

Benn's speech disappointed some friends and angered many opponents. Davidson thought it a 'lamentable parliamentary performance', Hoare, 'unworthy of a great occasion'. Although he was pressed very hard, he refused to give a clear answer to the all-important question of whether the declaration represented a change of policy. It was a party speech and it exacerbated feelings in the House. Simon who was to speak next, spoke for the Commission as a whole. He asked that the Commission be left in peace to complete the difficult task entrusted to it. Simon's speech was acclaimed as 'a perfect parliamentary performance.'[107]

The Prime Minister, Ramsay MacDonald, while speaking in the same debate stated that the declaration was necessary to establish confidence in India pending the publication of the Commission's Report. He emphatically said, 'We came to the decision that it would not be inexpedient, that it would do no harm to the Commission, that it would be beneficial from the point of view of Indian public opinion, and by that decision we stand.'[108]

The Conservative leader, Stanley Baldwin, who was much more advanced in his Indian views than were any of his colleagues, spoke about the proposed conference and the 'Dominion Status' announcement—approving the one and enquiring about the other in a mildly critical way. Speaking about the Dominion Status he said at one point that nobody knew what Dominion Status would be when India had responsible government, whether that date be near or distant, but surely no one dreamt of a self-governing India with an inferior status. 'No Indian would dream of an India,' he maintained, 'with an inferior status, nor can we wish that India should be content with an inferior status, because that would mean that we had failed in our work in India. No Tory Party with which I am concerned will fail in sympathy and endeavour to help in our time to the uttermost extent of our ability to a solution of the greatest political problem that lies before us today.'[109]

Lloyd George's speech was a very dangerous one, calculated to do considerable harm in India. But the Secretary of State was careful not to say anything to make the position worse, as were the Prime Minister, Baldwin and most of the Conservatives. On the Viceroy's declaration Lloyd George asked Benn to make it perfectly clear that the interpretation of the statement was not the right one, that they adhered by every pledge which had been given in the name of the King and the Empire and did not hold the view which had been declared in that very vital and important document that they were immediately going to set up a Dominion in India.[110] Churchill did not actually speak in the debate but cheered Lloyd George, to the concern of some of the Conservatives—thus presaging the line which he was to take later when the internal conflict in the Conservative Party on Indian affairs reached its height.[111] Birkenhead held that Irwin, 'both in his declaration and his speech, was encroaching upon a field in which he was an intruder and wanted that nothing should be done until the report of the Commission was published. According to him, there was no prospect of any government conceding Dominion Status to India in their life time.[112]

Thus we see that Lord Reading, Lloyd George of the Liberal Party and Churchill, Lord Birkenhead of the Conservative Party combined in an attack on the new policy. Their method was not that of a direct frontal onslaught, but rather to make it clear that in their opinion substantial advance in the direction of Dominion Status was so remote and unlikely as hardly to be worth discussing.[113] The shadow cabinet of the Conservative Party was summoned to discuss the matter and criticism of the statement, started by Birkenhead and supported by Austen Chamberlain. Baldwin, who had already agreed with it in principle at the time of the discussions between Irwin, Simon and MacDonald, was to sit back, listen to Birkenhead's scathing criticisms, and obtain a letter from MacDonald in which it was made clear that the Viceroy's words meant no change in British policy. Samuel Hoare also did not see anything revolutionary in the statement.[114] Lord Irwin himself mentions in his memoirs *Fulness of Days*, that 'it was surely hard to say what the progressive realisation of responsible government could mean except the ultimate achievement of status equivalent to that enjoyed by the Dominions, to which they had moved by precisely the same road as that now marked out for India.'[115]

Now that the goal was declared as Dominion Status for India the Labour Party decided that it would issue a statement of policy as to how that was to be obtained and that would be done only after consideration with the Government of India of the contents of the Statutory Commission Report, and after a conference with the Indian nationalist leaders. In October 1929, before Irwin made the statement, Sir John Simon wrote a letter to the Prime Minister, saying that their investigation into the question of constitutional development had impressed them with the necessity of fully examining the methods by which the relationship between British India and Indian States might be adjusted. He further suggested that the Indian native States should be consulted before any plan for a new constitution was drafted.[116] Later MacDonald consulted with the leader of the Conservative and Liberal Parties, and after receipt of their general consent he agreed that the Labour Government would meet the representatives of British India and the Indian States either separately or jointly. Thus the Government announced in the middle of June 1930 that a round table conference on the next steps to be taken in the advance towards Indian self-government would be constituted.

The attitude of the Labour Party, until their coming to power in 1929, did not create much enthusiasm in India. Up to that time, the party defined its Indian policy by resolutions passed at the annual conferences recommending self-government for India. Since the appointment of the Simon Commission the Labour Party had been alienated even from Indian Liberals. The Indians did not expect that the Labour Party would nominate their representatives to a Commission where Indians had no place.

The Labour Government, which remained in office until 1931, of course, gave a green light to the Viceroy of India to declare in clear terms that the natural issue of India's constitutional progress as contemplated in the August Declaration of 1917 was the attainment of Dominion Status. It was the Labour Government which took the initiative in holding a round table conference in London with the Indians to discuss the future constitution.

Notes

1. R.C. Majumdar (General Editor), op. cit., p. 439.
2. B. Shiva Rao and D. Graham Pole, *The Problem of India*, London, 1926, p. 78.
3. *The Times*, June 26, 1924.
4. 'The Indian political atmosphere' by Lord Oliver, *The Contemporary Review*, No. 740, August 1927, p. 166.
5. H.C. Deb., vol. 186, 1925, c. 748.
6. G. Milton Ochs, op. cit., pp. 122-3.
7. L.P. Report, 1925, p. 236.

8. ibid., pp. 237-8.
9. G. Milton Ochs, op. cit., p. 127.
10. H.C. Deb., vol, 186, 1925, cc. 635-640.
11. ibid., cc. 734-6.
12. ibid., c. 744.
13. H.C. Deb., vol. 188, 1925, c. 2799.
14. ibid., ce. 279 -6.
15. H.C. Deb., vol. 189, 1925, c. 386
16. Report of the first British Commonwealth Labour Conference, July 27 to August 1, 1925, pp. 13-14.
17. idid., p. 18.
18. idid., p. 19.
19. '*India to-day*' : A report on conditions in India and an outline of policy by the I.L.P. Indian Advisory Committee, 1929, pp. 21-2.
20. *The Times*, December 6, 1926.
21. G. Milton Ochs, op. cit., pp. 128-9.
22. H.C. Deb., vol. 198, 1926, cc. 1074-5.
23. ibid., cc. 1095-6.
24. ibid., c. 1130.
25. H.C. Deb., vol. 203, 1927, c. 1300.
26. ibid., c. 1314.
27. H.C. Deb., vol. 204, 1927, c. 1923.
98. H.C. Deb., vol. 207, 1927, c. 613.
29. ibid., cc. 1420-6.
30. ibid., cc. 1411-5.
31. L.P. Report, 1927, 255.
32. ibid., pp. 257-8.
33. C.F. Andrews, *India and the Simon Report*, London, 1930, pp. 31-3.
34. The Earl of Halifax (Lord Irwin), *Fulness of Days*, London, 1957, pp. 114-5.
35. C.F. Andrews, op. cit., p. 36.
36. H.C. Deb., vol. 208, 1927, c. 1679 & cc. 1708-9.
37. H,C. Deb., vol. 210, 1927, c. 1838.
38. ibid., c˙ 2239.
39. ibid., c. 2247.
40. ibid., cc. 2249-56.
41. ibid., cc. 2290-93
42. I.Q.R., 1927, vol. 2, p.60.
43. P. Sitaramayya, op. cit., p. 318.
44. C.F. Andrews, op. cit., pp. 37-8.
45. I.Q.R., 1927, vol. 2, pp. 76-7.
46. C.R. Attlee, *As it Happened*, Surrey, 1954, p. 64.
47. I.Q.R., 1927, vol. 2, pp. 95-6.
48. ibid., p. 97.
49. *The Daily Herald*, Nov. 25, 1927.

50. 'The Boycott of the Simon Commission' by Lord Olivier, *The Contemporary Review*, (monthly), May 1928.
51. Report of the Second British Commonwealth Labour Conference, July 2-6, 1928, pp. 43-4.
52. ibid., p. 44.
53. ibid., p. 45.
54 ibid., p. 48.
55. I.Q.R. 1927, vol. 2, pp. 97-8.
56. B.R. Nanda, *Mahatma Gandhi : A Biography*, New Delhi, 1968, p. 275.
57. The Earl of Halifax, op. cit., p. 116.
58. S.C. Bose, op. cit., p. 147.
59. L.P. Report, 1928, pp. 172-174.
60. Tara Chand, vol. IV, op. cit., p. 71.
61. P. Sitaramayya, op. cit., p. 322.
62. V.D. Mahajan, op. cit., p. 322.
63. ibid., p. 323.
64. R.N. Aggarwala, op. cit., pp. 151-2.
65. G. Milton Ochs, op. cit., pp. 143-4.
66. Ram Gopal, *Indian Muslims : A Polical History*, 1858-1947, Bombay, 1959, p. 201.
67. G.M Ochs, op. cit., 145.
68. Ram Gopal, p. cit., p. 221.
69. *The Times*, October 31, 1929.
70. ibid.
71. C.R. Attlee, *As it Happened*, op. cit., pp. 66-7.
72. L.P. Report, 1930, p. 84.
73. H.C. Deb., 1930, vol. 239, c. 873.
74. Report of the Indian Statutory Commission, vol. 1, Command Paper 3568, 1930.
75. Report of the Indian Statutory Commission, vol. 2, Command Paper 3569, 1930, p. 16.
76' ibid., p. 17.
†7. ibid., p. 312.
78. ibid., p. 16.
79. ibid., p. 314.
80. ibid., p. 315.
81. Article entitled 'A new constitution for India' by G.T. Garratt, *The Labour Magazine*, vol. IX, July 1930, p. 104.
82. Viscount Templewood (The Rt. Hon. Sir Samuel Hoare), *Nine Troubled Years*, London, 1954, p. 47.
83. *The Times*, July 3, 1930.
84. C.R. Attlee, op. cit., pp. 66-7.
85. R R. James, op. cit., pp. 496-7.
86. The Earl of Halifax, op. cit., p. 117.
87. L.P. Report, 1929, p. 190.
88. ibid.

89. The Earl of Halifax, op. cit., pp. 117-8.
90. K. Veerathappa, *British Conservative Party and Indian Independence*, New Delhi, 1976, pp. 18-9.
91. Quoted in *The Times*, Nov. 1, 1929.
92. *The Times*, November 1, 1929.
93. P.S. Gupta, op. cit., p. 203.
94. *The Times*, Nov. 7, 1929.
95. Article entitled 'The Outlook on the Indian refoms' by Wedgwood Benn, *The Political Quarterly*, July-September, 1935, p. 312.
96 Winston S. Churchill, *The Second World War* (The Gathering Storm), p. 33.
97. K. Veerathappa, op cit., p. 21.
98. Quoted in R.J. Moore, op. cit., pp. 80-1.
99. H.C. Deb., vol. 75, 1929, cc. 372-86.
100. ibid., c. 416.
101. ibid., c. 421.
102. *Beatrice Webb's Diaries*, 1924-1932, edited by Margaret Cole, London, 1956, p. 226.
103. ibid.
104. H.C. Deb., vol. 231, 1929, c. 473.
105. ibid., cc., 1326-30.
106. ibid.
107. R.J. Moore, op. cit., pp. 87-8.
108. H.C. Deb., vol. 231, 1929, c. 1339.
109. *Ibid*, c. 1312.
110. *Ibid.*, c. 1323.
111. Earl Winterton, op. cit., pp. 160-1.
112. *Daily Telegraph*, July 11, 1930.
113. Article entitled 'The Outlook on the Indian reforms' by Wedgwood Benn, *Political Quaterly*, July-September, 1935, p. 313.
114. Viscount Templewood, op. cit., p. 46.
115. The Earl of Halifax, op. cit., p. 46.
116. H.C. Deb., vol. 260, 1931, c. 1103.

CHAPTER 4

The Political Situation in India and the First Two Round Table Conferences, 1930-1931

In spite of the changed outlook of the Lobour Government in relation to India and its desire to help her achieve Dominion Status the way was not clear until the end of 1931. Disappointed at the handling of Indian problems by the government since their statement in the Commons in 1929, Mahatma Gandhi started the civil disobedience movement in mid-1930 and his party refused to attend the First Round Table Conference that was to be held in London before the end of that year.

The first session of the Conference was held from November 12, 1930 till January 19, 1931, in which the delegates from British India and the Indian States joined the delegates of the British parties to discuss the framing of a constitution for India. As the results of the First Round Table Conference were inconclusive, it was decided by the government to have another session of the Conference later.

But, between the first and the second session of the Conference, the Governor-General, Lord Irwin, managed to convince Gandhi of the sincerity of the Labour Government, and persuaded him to call off the civil disobedience movement. An agreement was reached between Gandhi and Irwin known as the Gandhi-Irwin Pact, as a result of which the Indian National Congress agreed to attend the Second Round Table Conference.

Before the second session of the Conference began, the government of James Ramsay MacDonald fell as a result of the financial crisis in England. A National Government was formed in August 1931. The Second Round Table Conference took place from September 7 to December 1, 1931 and it was the coalition National Government headed by MacDonald that conducted the second session. In the end, the Conference could not bring about any tangible results.

Civil Disobedience Movement

The Indian leaders offered cooperation with the Labour Government in the framing of a new constitution through a manifesto (known as Delhi Manifesto). The offer was not conditional but was accompanied by the expectation that political prisoners should be released and that the Congress should send the majority of the Indian delegates to the round table conference. The manifesto also interpreted Irwin's declaration to mean that the conference was 'to meet not to discuss when Dominion Status was to be established, but to frame a scheme of Dominion constitution for India.'[1] It was, of course, impossible for Irwin to accept the manifesto's interpretation of the purpose of the conference. That would certainly have involved the suppression of the Simon Commission, and Simon had accepted the plan for a free Conference on the assurance of MacDonald that it was to be 'a means of ascertaining views' not an 'organ for negotiating'. In view of the parliamentary debates, Gandhi was inclined to mistrust Britain's sincerity of purpose. He felt that the way of ultimate and direct action was more likely to be fruitful than the conference.

When Gandhi met Irwin on December 23, 1929 he wanted to know categorically the intentions of the government so that he could decide his course of action. Gandhi asked Irwin whether he would assure that the British Cabinet would support their demand for immediate Dominion Status, both at the Conference and in Parliament. The Viceroy indicated that it was impossible for the government to support a demand for immediate Dominion Status or to define the Conference's task as drafting a Dominion constitution. He stressed the freedom of the Conference to propose Dominion Status and to discuss the obstacles to achieving it. As the Viceroy was unable to give the assurance of immediate Dominion Status the negotiations broke down. Long afterwards Irwin continued to lament a missed opportunity and to hold his British opponents of November 1929 responsible for it. Indians felt that 'however nice the Viceroy might be a very influential chunk of the Conservative Party was against them'.[2]

Gandhi had entered into talks with the Viceroy because he did not want to miss any chance of solving a problem by means of peaceful negotions. But he knew that the government would never make any advance till it was forced to that. For the time being the door had been banged on the prospect of peaceful settlement. Gandhi and Motilal Nehru carrying the immense burden of their responsibilities proceeded to attend the Lahore session of the Congress held on December 31, 1929. As the Labour Government had refused to accept the conditions on which the Congress was prepared to forego its commitment to the goal of independence, Gandhi rejected the round table conference initiative and resolved to resort to civil disobedience for the achievement of complete independence. Gandhi moved his historic resolution at the Lahore session :

This Congress . . . . in pursuance of the resolution passed at its session at Calcutta last year, declares that the world 'Swaraj' in Article 1 of the Congress Constitution shall mean complete independence and further declares the entire scheme of the Nehru Committee's Report to have lapsed, and hopes that all Congressmen will henceforth devote their exclusive attention to the attainment of complete independence for India. . . . This Congress appeals to the Nation zealously to prosecute the constructive programme of the Congress, and authorises the All-India Committee, whenever it deems fit, to launch upon a programme of civil disobedience including non-payment of taxes, whether in selected areas or otherwise, and under such safeguards as it may consider necessary.

The resolution was put to vote and carried, and the flag of independence was unfurled on the bank of river Ravi. H. N. Brailsford while commenting on the Congress Party's demand for independence wrote that its demand was obviously tactical if one surveyed the recent history of the party. On the substance of self-government, they were resolute and united. But manifestly the main body had not yet reached the point at which it would reject the Dominion solution, if it were within its grasp. 'We should wish Mr. Wedgwood Benn', Brailsford said, 'to exhaust all the resources of leadership and negotiation, so long as a chance remains that Parliament will permit him to advance towards the definition and realisation of the Dominion Status'.[3]

As the Congress Party was steadfast in its refusal to have anything to do with the government's proposal and as it embarked upon a new passive resistance campaign, the Labour Government was left with no alternative but to continue to use special ordinances to suppress the movement. Wedgwood Benn, the Secretary of State for India, himself affirmed that the government had no other course of action left at its disposal, for it was the duty of any government to preserve public order.[4] The Congress by passing the independence resolution had, in the Viceroy's opinion, declared itself as a body which intended to puruse 'an illegitimate aim by illegal and unconstitutional means'. The Secretary of State for India acknowledged the gravity of the situation and expressed a desire to be consulted in advance if extra-ordinary powers were to be invoked, though, in an emergency, the Viceroy could act at first and inform him later.[5] In the face of firm realities of passive resistance, Irwin in April 1930 promulgated emergency ordinances and Gandhi was again arrested on April 29, because of the violation of Salt law. Faced by non-violent rebellion, the government first proceeded to make arrests. According to official figures, more than sixty thousand civil resisters were cast in prison.[6] As in the previous passive resistance campaign, the Muslims did not participate in the movement. By May 1930, the Government of India had the situation under control.

The Labour Government did not interfere with the Viceroy's tactics in dealing with the civil disobedience movement, even after Gandhi was arrested. In May 1930, while the Secretary of State placed before the House of Commons the reasons for the civil disobedience movement, J.C. Wedgwood of the Labour Party advanced the explanation that the real trouble sprang from the exclusion of Indians from the Simon Commission. He said that was a fatal step which prevented the real cooperation between English people and Indian people both desiring the same end—the earliest possible establishment of self-government in India. He cautioned against too optimistic a view on the forthcoming round table conference as an opportunity for the two groups to get together on a common plan. Wedgwood stressed that the only permanent solution to the Indian problem was for the Labour Government to come to terms with Indian political leaders.[7] In the same debate Major Graham Pole, another Labourite, maintained that they would only get cooperation if they could persuade Indians that they (Indians) could believe in them, that in the House of Commons and among the people of Great Britain there was an intense desire to do justly by India.[8]

The Secretary of State for India spoke in defence of the Labour

Government's Indian policy. He stated that he managed to have the repressive ordinances repealed on April 1, 1930 but within a few days violence had erupted in India for which they had to reintroduce the ordinances. Wedgwood Benn emphasized that the problem of internal violence in India was of Indian origin, not British; the government was only trying to maintain law and order.[9] Recapitulating the aims of British policy in relation to India the Secretary of State reminded the House of the Montagu Declaration and the statement of Irwin and stressed that that policy stood. He said that although that goal was accepted by all parties in Parliament in England, there remained great difficulties on the way to the goal. He pointed out that the problem of the future position of the minorities was more insistent. Benn stated that no settlement could be considerd satisfactory, which did not carry the consent of, and give a sense of security to, the important minority communities who would have to live under the new constitution. Concluding, he said, 'Any policy which sets before an Indian any ideal, save the Indian ideal, by which, I mean, the welfare of all those, of whatever race or colour, whose interest is in India, is foredoomed to failure.'[10]

The left wingers of the Labour Party advocated in the Commons that the real solution to the Indian problem would come true if the Indians were allowed to frame their own constitution. Fenner Brockway, an Independent Labour Party member attacked India policy of the Labour Government. He said that in order to provide a sound solution of the Indian problems, three things were essential: (1) a definite declaration of the intention of the government to accept full responsible government as its immediate policy and not as an ultimate object; (2) that the declaration should be accompanied by an amnesty to the political offenders in India; (3) that there should be called a round table conference, where representatives of Britain and of India might meet as equals and work out the necessary transition policy after the acceptance of the principle of full self-government had been laid down. Brockway said that regarding the first proposal the government did make a vague declaration of Dominion Status as its ultimate object.[11] He also contended that the forces of nationalism had captured India, and that if the Labour Government failed to recognize this fact, all their plans would come to naught. He called upon the Secretary of State for India to take immediate action which would still make a settlement by agreement possible and urged him to carry out the policy, to which his party was pledged, of full self-government for India. Furthermore, Brockway appealed to Wedwood Benn to say that the government would accept for the round table conference the principle of full self-government, and that they would allow the round table conference to work out the details of the transition period.[12]

India's problems were discussed at the third British Commonwealth Labour Conference held at Westminster Hall, London, between July 21 and 25, 1930. Speaking about the civil disobedience movement the Indian Trade Union Federation delegate N.M. Joshi pointed out at the conference that Gandhi supported the movement because the Viceroy was unable to give the assurance that the round table conference would be held to frame a constitution for the Dominion of India. He hoped that the British Labour Government would not allow itself to be used as an instrument of Tory policy. Shiva Rao, another delegate of the Federation, said that whatever might be said about Gandhi's movement Great Britian had asked for it and it was a mass movement.[13]

The Chairman of the British Parliamentary Labour Party, Harry Snell, while speaking at the conference remarked that the attainment of Dominion Status would depend largely on the possibility of marching towards it in unity of aim and method. W. Gillies Secretary of the International Department of the Labour Party and the Secretary of the Conference, said that Labour was not in power and they could not get in Great Britain all that they wanted for themselves, but they had broken with Tory traditions. He could not be so pessimistic as to believe that in India they were limited by Tory pessimistic policy. Major D.G. Pole, M.P., also spoke at the conference. He said that what the Labour Government had done was to keep themselves absolutely free to say that the round table conference could discuss anything. He said that it was not necessary that there should be absolute and unanimous agreement in the conference. Pole further maintained that if the government and Indian representatives could reach a measure of agreement for Dominion Status, the government would put it through and they would stand or fall by it. In his concluding remarks Pole said that the Secretary of State for India stood by all the pledges of the Labour Party without any reservations. He stressed if only their Indian friends could be got to believe that, then at the round table conference the outcome would be self-government for India.[14]

The Labour Government policy on India was criticised by Fenner Brockway in the 1930 annual conference of the Labour Party. In moving a resolution he said that the conference regretted that the Labour Government did not in its early stages (a) accept full responsible government as the basis of a conference with the Indian representatives, and (b) release the Indian political prisoners, thus securing an atmosphere of goodwill; and strongly condemned the severe repression with which the civil disobedience campaign had been met. The resolution called upon the government to withdraw immediately all repressive measures in India, liberate the political offenders, and open negotiations for the transfer of political power from British to Indian hands.[15] An amendment to limit Brockway's resolution was proposed by other Labour members. It congratulated the Labour Government upon its refusal to confine the round table conference with the Indian representatives to the discussion solely of the Simon Commission's Report. It hoped that the result of such a conference would be the granting of self-government to the Indian people at the earliest possible date, providing due safeguards against intensified exploitation of those who might not have political representation. Speaking at the Labour Party conference J.M. Kenworthy, and D.G. Pole, both M.P.s expressed the view that the Congress Party made a mistake by not agreeing to take part in the round table conference. Pole believed also that the Labour Party and the Labour Government were absolutely sincere in their wish to see India a free and self-governing part of the great Commonwealth of British Nations.[16]

In spite of the questionable wisdom of the Labour Government's Indian policy, it still met with some success. The repressive measures and police actions slowly restored internal peace and order. To counteract the government measures, the Working Committee of the Congress Party, which had assumed the direction of the non-co-operation civil disobedience campaign, issued an appeal to the Indian population to continue passive resistance. Because of this public appeal, the government in the first week of July 1930, under a special ordinance declared the All-India Congress Committee and the local Congress Committees unlawful. The Viceroy in his speech in the Legislative Assembly on July 9, 1930 remarked on the civil disobedience movement and said: 'In my judgement and in that of my government, it is a deliberate attempt to coerce established authority by mass action and, for this reason as also because of its natural and inevitable developments, must be regarded as unconstitutional and dangerously subversive.[17] In August, Tej Bahadur Sapru and Jayakar, the two liberal leaders, attempted some peace making between the Congress and the government, which is often described as 'Sapru-Jayakar peace parleys'. These two leaders carried on a long chain of interviews with the Viceroy on the one hand and Mahatma Gandhi and the Congress leaders on the other but they were not successful in bridging the gulf between the government and the Congress. Hence, the struggle continued for about six more months.

Conference Plan

While the movement continued the bureaucracy pursued their own plan. In June 1930, the report of the Simon Commission was published. It disappointed all shades of Indian nationalist opinion for being silent on Dominion Status. Nor did the Report propose any advance towards responsibility in the central government. It might be interesting to note at this point that Wedgwood Benn proposed some advice to the Labour Party Advisory Committee on Imperial Questions. These were : (1) The ultimate aim of an All-India federation including the States should be suspended, if its early realisation proved to involve requirements which imperiled agreement on the British Indian constitution. (2) A substantial measure of responsibility should be introduced at the centre. (3) Unless some new and better method of doing that could be devised there should be no hesitation about applying the dynamical one. (4) The control of the army should not be taken away from the Government of India, but Indianisation should be pushed forward, and an enquiry should be instituted into the feasibility of making the Indian Army self-contained and of separating it from the British Army in India, with a view to bringing the former ultimately under an Indian Minister of Defence. (5) In order to introduce elasticity into the constitution, each reservation of a subject and each ground upon which the Governor-General might exercise extraordinary powers should, so far as possible, without encroaching upon the essential reserve of authority for vital purposes, be made automatically withdrawable on the attainment of a specified stage of social or political progress. (6) the office of H.M.'s Secretary of State for India should be abolished and the residuum of his functions handed over to a Secretary of State for the Dominions.[18] The advice was of little use as the round table conference was in the offing.

Wedgwood Benn argued after the publication of the Simon Report that while the government had regarded the Report as the solution of the problem, even Indian liberal opinion was now pinning its hopes on the success of the Congress campaign. Reports from India had convinced him that the government was confronted not just with the fractious behaviour of a particular political party, but rather with a militant movement showing a great and growing sense of national and racial consciousness which found expression in opposition to foreign rule. Given its minority position in Parliament the problem that henceforth bedevilled the Labour Government was how to conciliate the Congress without giving offence to the opposition parties. There was a strong undertone in favour of an early peace in Wedgwood Benn's Cabinet papers of July 25, and August 9, 1930, but no fresh initiative was taken after the Sapru-Jayakar talks foundered on the rock of Congress determination to get a precise commitment to Indian independence from the government. The Cabinet accepted Wedgwood Benn's counsel that any parliamentary criticism for abandoning the Simon Report under the pressure of a civil disobedience movement could be met by arguing that Irwin's declaration had implied that constitution-making should respect Indian opinion. On July 8, the Cabinet managed to head off an opposition proposal to table a vote of thanks to Simon in Parliament.[19]

Meanwhile, a tentative date for the round table conference was set for the end of October 1930. Irwin, in his address to the Indian legislature, declared that the conference would be free to approach its task, greatly assisted, but with liberty unimpaired, by the Report of the Statutory Commission or by any other document which would be before it. The Labour Government's purpose for the conference was to reach a general agreement with the leading Indian political parties on a satisfactory constitution for India. Once the principles of the plan had been agreed upon by both the Indian and British leaders, it would be placed before the British Parliament. The Parliament could then discuss and recommend for its alteration. After an agreement by a joint committee of the House of Commons and the House of Lords, at which stage Indian concurrence would also be obtained, the Labour Government expected that a constitution satisfactory to both India and Britain would have been drafted.[20]

A debate on the participation of the British political parties at the round table conference was held in the Commons and it was urged that all three parties should be represented. MacDonald made no promises but he did say that he would do his best to prevent party conflict over India. *The Times* supported that a national delegation should represent at the conference in order to have a continuity of policy, dignity of the conference and security of its results. Wedgwood Benn consulted Irwin about party representation. The Viceroy was opposed to an all-party delegation. Earlier in the year Irwin had been quite prepared to accept it but now he believed that cooperative Indians would regard it as a 'breach of faith'. It was bound to be construed as a device to consolidate British opinion against India and so prejudge the outcome of the conference. Sir Samuel Hoare assured Irwin that the opposition demand was irresistible. Failure to accept it would precipitate a Parliamentary motion to secure a definite endorsement of Simon's recommendations The opposition leaders were unmoved by Irwin's protests. Indeed, they added another demand that Simon should attend the conference in an independent capacity.

The question was settled at the end of July 1930, when Ramsay MacDonald announced that each of the opposition parties would be invited to send separate deligations to the conference but that the government would retain its freedom of executive action at and after the conference. There would be not one all-party delegation but three individual delegations, the Conservatives and Liberals each having four members while the government would be represented by six to eight members of the Cabinet. Pressure for the representation of the Simon Commission was resisted effectively in both houses of Parliament partly because it was known that Baldwin would not support the demand.[22] MacDonald rejected the recommendation of the opposition that Sir John Simon attend the conference. His exclusion, MacDonald stated, would demonstrate to the Indians that the conference would not be dominated by the British members of the Statutory Commission.

While this decision was applauded in India, the Conservatives and the Liberals in England did not approve it.

In India, the general situation had grown worse during 1930. It was quite clear already that no agreement was likely to be reached by any conference between the Hindus and the Muslims on such crucial matters as communal representation, the creation of new provinces with Muslim majorities, as in the case of Sind, and the promotion of the North-West Frontier Province to the status of a full province. Of course, an attempt was made by the Congress party leaders at an All-Parties Conference to bring the Hindu and Muslim communities together but it failed. When the All-Parties Conference failed to agree on the selection of Indian representatives to the round table conference, Irwin arbitrarily chose the Indian delegation to the conference. The Congress Party rejected the Viceroy's overtures and refused to accept appointments to the conference. Nevertheless, November 12, 1930, when the Round Table Conference met for the first time to be inaugurated by King George V, was the most important date so far recorded in the history of British India, for it was an open and irrevocable declaration that henceforth the political future of India was no longer to be decided by the British Parliament alone, and that India must have a free and equal voice in its decision.[23]

The first session of the Conference

The Conference, consisting of eighty-nine delegates, fifty seven from British India, sixteen from the Indian States, and sixteen representatives of the government and the opposition in the two houses met in London. The government delegation to the First Round Table conference was eight and included the Prime Minister, Lord Chancellor Sankey, and Wedgwood Benn. The Conservative delegation comprised Earl Peel, the Marquess of Zetland, Oliver Stanley, M.P., and Sir Samuel Hoare. The Liberal delegation included the Marquess of Reading, the Marquess of Lothian, Sir Robert Hamilton, M.P., and Isaac Foot, M.P. [24] The Congress viewed the Conference as a collection of handpicked government men: their voice was not the voice of India. *The Times* remarked in its editorial :

This Conference marks a new epoch in the relations between this country and India . . . It is inconceivable that Parliament, which has the final responsibility, could disregard the unanimous conclusions of a representative body of

British and Indian leaders who had pooled their experience, their opinions, and their political courage for the general good. Even the Congress Party which is not solely composed of extremists would inevitably be influenced by such an impressive example of cooperation.[25]

For the Indian members of the Conference it must have been a useful experience. For the British members and for the public who watched the proceedings in the press and the printed reports it was an education in Indian politics. The summoning of the Round Table Conference seemed to have heralded a change in the British attitude to India. The Conference from November 12, 1930 to January 19, 1931 lasted a little over two months.

At the outset there was a marked difference in the attitude of the British and the Indian members of the Conference on the fundamental issue of Dominion Status. It was now admitted on the British side that India would obtain Dominion Status when the process of realising responsible government in India as a part of the British Empire was complete. But the British representatives, whatever their party, were not prepared to say that the process could be completed at once. Full responsible government in the provinces under temporary safeguards they were ready to concede. But most of the Indian members of the Conference wanted a concrete and immediate response to the claim for Dominion Status.[26] An important delegate representing British India, Tej Bahadur Sapru demanded a status of equality for India with other members of the Commonwealth, an equality which would make a government not merely responsive to, but responsible to the popular voice. He pleaded with the Indian Princes to move forward with the vision of an India as one whole and invited them to join an all-India federation.

The Princes of Indian States realized that an all-India federation was likely to prove the only satisfactory solution of India's problems. They played their part well, and four or five of the leading Princes showed at the very begining of the proceedings that they were as anxious as any nationalist of British India that the federation contemplated should be a self-governing unit in the British Commonwealth of Nations. The Maharaja of Patiala in his statement at the Conference said, "we can only federate with a British India which is self-governing, and not with a British India governed as it is at present." The Maharaja of Bikaner agreed at the

Conference that India must be united on a federal basis. The constitution must be federal, and, while the Princes could not be in any way coerced, they would come in to an all-India federation of their own free will, provided their rights were guaranteed.[28]

Soon after the opening discussion, both the questions—of Dominion Status (with its implication of responsible government at the centre) and of an all-India federation—now linked together were brought to a new and more practical stage by an unexpected move on the Princes' part. Since none of the British Indian representatives was contemplating a bilateral federation between a unitary British India and the States, the declaration of the Princes virtually created a common Indian front. All India federation was the dominant principle throughout the First Round Table Conference. But the Indian States would only come into the federation for certain scheduled subjects, and that they would still retain their contact with the Crown through the Viceroy in all questions of paramountcy. They would also retain their internal autonomy.

Hoare and Zetland of the Conservative Party welcomed the federal move providing an alternative constitutional road to that of parliamentary democracy. Hoare conferred with both Baldwin and his Conservative colleagues on the significance of a new development (Princes' willingness to join the federation), that had not been contemplated in the Simon Report or in the despatch of the Government of India that had commented upon it. The Shadow Cabinet of the Opposition, composed of all the principal ex-ministers, had not met since the controversy over Irwin's speech. In its stead, there were frequent meetings of a small Business Committee to which Baldwin invited Chamberlain, Churchill, Hailsham, Peel, Oliver Stanley and Hoare. It was to this committee that Hoare reported the movements of the Conference, and argued in favour of accepting the demand of an all-India federation.[29] He submitted a memorandum for the consideration of the Conservative delegation and of the Conservative Party Business Committee, in which he tried to show the advantages of federation and the kind of safeguards that were needed to ensure its security. All-India federation would provide a stable centre while the provincial experiment was being tried.

Hoare explained that Britain could yield 'a semblance of responsible government and yet retain in our hands the reality and verities of British control'. The Viceroy should have large overriding powers. The army would be reserved to British control. Finance could be tied up through a statutory currency board. Some eighty per cent of the Indian revenues could be kept out of the hands of an Indian finance minister. Furthermore, the federal executive would not be responsible or removable in the British sense, for it would depend partly on the Princes' nominations as well as on British Indian elections. Hoare also commended central 'responsibility' as expedient. The concession would create goodwill in India and its endorsement by the Conservatives would avert their becoming isolated politically. Hoare's advice to support central responsibility given certain conditions was accepted by the Party's Business Committee, with only Churchill dissenting. [30] It was soon evident that Churchill would not remain a member of a committee that accepted Hoare's view. The Conservative Party would not commit itself in general terms to responsibility in an all-India federation and it reserved judgement until the government produced a detailed proposal.

Only after the deputation from the Indian States had agreed to merge with British India was the problem of constitutional reform seriously considered. MacDonald, who realized that the scope of the task was tremendous and that very little headway was being made at the plenary meetings, divided the Conference into nine committees and assigned each committee a specific constitutional problem. Of the nine sub-committees, two were of major importance: the federal structure and the minorities committee headed respectively by Lord Sankey and Ramsay MacDonald.

Although the problems of the federal structure committee were not resolved by the termination of the Conference, there were many basic points of agreement. The federation should be provided with a bicameral federal legislature, containing representatives from both British India and the native States. The general legislative plan that was devised provided that the upper house was to be representative of the units of States of the federation, and the lower house was to be a popular body with representation therein being based on population. The members of the upper house would be elected by the provincial legislatures. The representation of British India in the upper house was to be based on the proportion of the provincial population to the total of the federation. For the lower house of the federal legislature, it was recommended that seventy-six per cent of the total representation would be from British India and twenty-four per cent from the native States. Such questions as the method of election, residual powers, control of the provinces and others were not resolved, but the committee was unanimous in demanding special representation in the federal legislature for special classes such as the depressed classes, labourers and commercial interests.[11]

The minorities sub-committee unanimously accepted the principle that the new constitution should contain provisions designed to assure communities that their interests would not be prejudiced. It was also agreed that the claims of the various communities to employment in the civil services should be adjusted by Public Service Commissions at the centre and in the provinces. The problem of representation and electorates, joint or communal, was not resolved. When the vital question of the number of representatives and the type of representation for each of the minorities was mentioned, each group insisted that it had to have its own representation and electorate and that if these were not granted, each minority threatened to oppose the entire constitution when it came into effect.[12]

Before the Conference closed the Muslim delegation made a formal statement of its position. As there was no settlement between the Hindus and the Muslims, 'We feel that the only course that is consistent alike with the position of our community...is to reiterate our claim that no advance is possible or practicable, whether in the provinces or in the central government, without adequate safeguards for the Muslims of India, and that no constitution will be acceptable to the Muslims of India without such safeguards.[13] No attempt, accordingly, was made to secure a formal acceptance of the sub-committees' reports. The failure to solve the communal problem was the most disappointing and portentous feature of the First Round Table Conference. The agreement of the leading Muslim delegates to support the federal solution momentarily papered over the communal cracks in the national front. MacDonald did allude to the need for adequate safeguards. He also undertook to deliver an award if the communities themselves failed to agree.

The reports of the other sub-committees may be briefly mentioned. The sub-committees dealing with the problems of provincial constitution was unanimous in its recommendation that dyarchy should be abolished and that all the provincial subjects should be placed under the administration of responsible ministers. Whether the legislature should be unicameral or bicameral should be decided in accordance with the wishes of each province Pending the final solution of the minority committee, the sub-committee accepted temporarily the principle of communal representation in the provincial cabinets. The powers of the governors were to be generally limited to those necessary to perform the constitutional functions of that office, but special powers were to be granted to deal with emergencies[34]. The franchise sub-committee decided by a majority that, while adult suffrage should be the goal, it could not be attained at once, and that a commission should be appointed to arrange for an extension of the existing franchise so as to include from ten to twenty-five per cent of the population, special provision being made for the adequate enfranchisement of women.[35]

The sub-committee on defence were agreed in declaring that 'the defence of India must to an increasing extent be the concern of the Indian people and not of the British Government alone', and in recommending that the pace of Indianisation in the Indian army should be substantially increased.[36] The sub-committee on civil service recommended that recruitment to the Indian Civil Service and the Indian Police Service should be on an all-India basis. As for the All-India Civil Service, the committee believed that this should come under the control of the Government of India, instead of the Secretary of State for India.[37] The remaining three sub-committees were relatively free of complexities. The Burma committee unanimously agreed that Burma should be separated from India and given its own constitution and administration.[38] The Sind sub-committee accepted the separation of Sind from Bombay in principle and recommended the appointment of a committee to examine the financial questions involved.[39] The North-West Frontier Province sub-committee recommended that the province be raised to the status of a governor's province, with a dyarchical system of government.[40]

The proceedings closed with a statement by the Prime Minister. On January 19, 1931, having accepted all the reports MacDonald summarized the accomplishments of the First Round Table conference in his concluding speech. He said that the conference had demonstrated to the Indians that the British were in sympathy with the Indian problem and had confronted the British with the complexity of the Indian problem. He observed that the view of His Majesty's Government was that responsibility for the government of India should be placed upon legislatures, central and provincial, with only such safeguards as would be necessary to guarantee, during a period of transition, the fulfilment of the Government of India's obligations. These security provisions would be required to protect the political liberties and rights of the minorities. He said that in such statutory safeguards as might be made for meeting the needs of the transitional period, it would be a primary concern of His Majesty's Govenment to see that the reserved powers were so framed and exercised as not to prejudice the advance of India through the new constitution to full responsibility for her own government.

Continuing, MacDonald stated that the government had taken note of the fact that the deliberations of the Conference had proceeded on the basis, accepted by all parties, that the central government should be a federation of all-India, embracing both the Indian States and British India in a bi-cameral legislature. The precise form and structure of the new federal government must be determined after further discussion with the Princes and representatives of British India. The Prime Minister further said that His Majesty's Government would be prepared to recognize the principle of responsibility of the executive to the legislature Under existing conditions the subjects of defence and external affairs would be reserved to the Govenor-General, and arrangements would be made to place in his hands the powers necessary for the administration of those subjects. Special powers to be given to the Governor-General would include the emergency powers to maintain the tranquillity of the state, the protection of minorities. As regards finance, the transfer of financial responsibility must necessarily be subject to such conditions as would ensure the fulfilment of the obligations incurred under the authority of the Secretary of State and the unimpaired maintenance of the financial stability and credit of India. The Indian Government would have full financial responsibility for the methods of raising revenue and for the control of expenditure on non-reserved services.

MacDonald while dealing with the Governors' provinces pointed out that these would be constituted on a basis of full responsibility. The authority of the federal government would be limited to provisions required to secure its administration of federal subjects. The Governor would have minimum of special powers that would require to preserve tranquillity and to guarantee the maintenance of rights provided by Statute for the public services and minorities. He further maintained that the government considered that the provincial legislatures should be enlarged, and that they should be based on a more liberal franchise. Finally, the Prime Minister said that it was the duty of the communities to come to an agreement among themselves on the points raised by the minorities sub-committee but not settled there. He stressed that the government would continue to render their good offices in that respect. He expressed the hope that special committees would be sent to India in order to work out solutions to the remaining problems.[41]

The Round Table in St. James's Palace was the symbol of a common purpose. Throughout the discussions the Indian delegates showed a remarkable knowledge of the almost countless questions involved in the framing of a constitution. The deliberations undoubtedly showed a large measure of agreement among the delegates in favour of a united all-India federation. The vague idea of federation, that had first floated through the ship that brought the Indian delegates to London, had been given substance and form in a series of concrete proposals.[42] *The Times* in its editorial wrote, 'MacDonald's declaration of policy was in effect a careful summary of the broad conclusions reached by the various committees, and particularly of the Federal Structure Committee whose report remains the essential document of the Conference.'[43]

The Prime Minister's statement of the government policy was a guarded and carefully worded acceptance of the proposals on which agreement had been reached. It fell short of what was demanded by the Indian nationalists, but it represented an enormous advance on anything that seemed likely to be offered by any of the British parties before the Conference began.'[44]

In a leading article on the Conference, *The Times* admitted that by common consent the government, as represented by the Prime Minister and the Lord Chancellor, had presided to the general admiration over the difficult discussions at the Round Table. It remained a matter for profound satisfaction that the Labour Party should have been in office when the occasion came, and that India should have been saved, as it could never have been saved in other circumstances, from becoming the sport of party politics in England.[45] The work of Wedgwood Benn, although greatly behind the scenes, was nonetheless vigilant and effective. Never in the foreground during the Conference, he yet smoothed the ground and oiled the wheels and made possible the success of others.[46]

Some time after the First Round Table Conference, the Prime Minister, MacDonald, in a debate in the Commons on the Conference stated that it had not been called to draw up a new constitution for India, but only to reach an agreement with the Indians on the broad general outline of the new structure.[47]

Stanley Baldwin, the leader of the Conservative Party, renewed his party's support to the Conference results, especially the idea of a federal system. He declared in the House of Commons that their duty would be to try and implement what had been done in the Conference if the Conservatives came to power.[48] Sir Samuel Hoare speaking for the Conservative members of the Conference summed up the meetings as an agreement on three main points: a federal government, provincial autonomy and safeguards. The extreme left of the Labour Party and the extreme right of the Conservatives expressed dissent. Fenner Brockway of the Labour left wing criticised the Labour Government for the imprisonment of thousands of Indians.[49] Churchill accused the Labour Government for not conforming to the regular constitutional procedure.[50] The dissident speech of Churchill was openly disowned by Baldwin. *The Times* while commenting on Churchill's speech expressed the view that if more brilliant rhetoric could destroy the work of the Conference Churchill would be the man to do that.[51] It may be mentioned that in one of his letters to Irwin, Wedgwood Benn pointed out that there was a good deal of trouble within the Conservatives over the Indian question and Wardlaw Milne told him that, 'while the mass of the party agreed that the Conference having been held the results cannot be discarded, there are some who feel that the whole plan of Indian self-government is unwise, or at any rate, that we are going ahead much too fast with it.' In the same letter Benn wrote, 'I think the issue is now decided and we may safely count upon Liberal support and a great deal, if not the majority, I should say, of Conservative support in carrying through the results of the Conference.[52]

Gandhi-Irwin Truce

The civil disobedience campaign was running its turbulent course, while the First Round Table Conference was meeting in London. The Labour Government had realized by the end of 1930 that without conciliating the Congress, no settlement was possible. Acknowledging that it was impossible to expect anything like submission, or recantation from the Congress, the Secretary of State wondered whether the Viceroy, Irwin, could help to create a 'bilateral situation' which could lead to an amnesty and to the abandonment by the Congress of civil disobedience in favour of cooperation with the Round Table Conference.[53] The Labour politicians were determined to come to a compromise with the Congress and the Viceroy was far-sighted enough to realise that if an understanding was to be arrived at, it was desirable to do so while the Mahatma was the leader of the Congress Party.

On the day the Prime Minister, Ramsay MacDonald, delivered his closing speech at the First Round Table Conference, the Viceroy made a public appeal for the cooperation of the Congress in his address before the Indian Legislative Assembly. Irwin stated that no one could fail to recognise 'the spiritual force which impels Mr. Gandhi to count no sacrifice too great in the cause, as he believes, of the India he loves'. He asked whether it was not possible for the Congress in the new circumstances created by the civil disobedience movement in India and the proceedings of the Round Table Conference in England to follow a different course.[54] Within a week of this appeal, Gandhi and the members of the working committee of the Congress were unconditionally released in order to give them an opportunity to consider MacDonald's statement at the Round Table Conference. After their arrival from London Tej Bahadur Sapru, V.S. Sastri and M.R. Jayakar met Gandhi and the Liberal leaders persuaded the Mahatma not to reject the offer of the Government without having a talk with the Viceroy who had made a generous gesture.

The Congress Party was strongly against the acceptance of any proposed round table scheme. There was, however, a minority in Congress Party that was sympathetic to the idea of entering into discussion with the British, if an amnesty from the Government of India could be obtained for the political prisoners. On February 14, 1931, following a decision of the Congress Working Committee,

Gandhi wrote to Irwin to request a heart to heart talk. The Viceroy then decided to meet Gandhi, and discussed with him patiently and simply the differences that kept them apart. The meetings taking place for three weeks were significant of the eagerness of Gandhi and the Congress Working Committee for peace that during the Gandhi-Irwin talks little difficulty was experienced with the constitutional issue. The very thought of the Viceroy closeted in Delhi with the leader of the civil disobedience campaign infuriated the diehards, whether Conservative or Liberal, and gravely disturbed many experienced Indian officials. The irritation and impatience grew with every day that the conversations continued. Indeed, so great was the prejudice against talks that the full scope of the agreement that ended them on March 5 never received due credit.[55]

The many days of discussion resulted in Gandhi's acceptance of a place at the round table when the Conference resumed its sittings, and an undertaking to call off civil disobedience, and the boycott of British goods.[56] The Viceroy, on behalf of the government agreed, *inter alia*, to release all political prisoners incarcerated in connection with the civil disobedience movement, to withdraw the emergency ordinances and to restore the Congress property.[57] In his statement to the Press on the conclusion of the settlement (Gandhi-Irwin truce) Gandhi refrained from describing it as a victory for the Congress; if anything it was a victory both for the government and the people. A few days after the signing of the agreement on March 18, Churchill in a speech at the Albert Hall, London, stated:

I am against this surrender to Gandhi. I am against these conversations and agreements between Lord Irwin and Mr. Gandhi. Gandhi stands for the expulsion of British from India.[58]

On the release of Gandhi, in order that he might become the envoy of nationalist India to the London Conference, Churchill reached the breaking-point in his relations with Baldwin. Baldwin seemed quite content with these developments, was in general accord with the Prime Minister and the Viceroy, and led the Conservative Opposition decidedly along this path.[59] But, generally speaking, the agreement was welcomed by all the British political parties and the public as opening a bright prospect of a satisfactory settlement of the Indian problem.

After the Gandhi-Irwin Pact was signed the Labour Government began to hope for a common plan for a new constitution which would have the approval of all of the political parties in India. In an interesting debate over India in the House of Commons after the agreement, Wedgwood Benn disclosed that the government would like to start the discussions initiated at the First Round Table Conference. The government had been considering a plan for sending a parliamentary delegation to India to gather specialized information on key constitutional problems. Upon their return to London another round table conference would be held.[60] Lieutenant Commander J.M. Kenworthy, a Labour M.P. while speaking in the same debate said that the declaratian of federation made the success of the Round Table Conference possible, and that was made possible by the far-sighted action of the Indian Princes. They should be consulted, he emphasized, in all future major questions of policy in India, and obviously, the strongest possible delegation must go to India to continue the conversations. He further said, 'the policy for which we have always stood in the past is right, and India should be granted her free self-government as a Dominion as soon as she is ready for it.' Kenworthy believed that they would get the cooperation of the Congress if they could show them (the Indians) that as a party the Labourites sympathised with their aspirations, and that they intended to make it possible for those aspirations to be realised.[61] Ramsay MacDonald maintained that the Labour Party cooperated with the previous government in trying to keep the problem of devising a constitution for India outside party politics. He added that they would maintain the same policy as long as they remained in office. [62]

The diehard Conservative Churchill objected to the entire round table concept and pointed out that the foundation of three-party unity on the question of India was the report of the Statutory Commission. He said that from the moment the government side-tracked the Statutory Report, the original basis of the three-party action ended. Churchill said; 'We hold that it is futile and most hampering both to constitutional changes and to administration to talk about independence and full Dominion Status at the present time.'[62] Baldwin, the leader of the Conservative Party, in his speech in the debate pointed out that if the party cooperation in England were once broken, the whole problem of the government of India would be insoluble and impossible. He appealed to the diehards to refrain from obstructing the way of those who had undertaken an almost superhuman task, on the successful fulfilment of which depended the well-being, the prosperity and the duration of the whole British Empire.[64] About the Gandhi-Irwin Pact, he said, 'it has definitely enlarged the area of goodwill and cooperation'.[65]

Baldwin's speech in the Commons was a plain-spoken and a vindication of his consistency, and a re-affirmation of the policy for which the Conservative Party, under his leadership, stood. [66] Commenting on the speech of Churchill, Colonel Wedgwood of the Labour Party said, 'Never before has a right honourable gentleman spoken to a House so hostile, and I think that is really because he does not believe in his own arguments'.[67] So hostile was his attitude on the question of India that at a meeting, in his own constituency, Churchill ventured to say that he thought it vital that the Conservative Party should without delay get itself into a strong position of resistance, and should begin to arouse public opinion throughout the country 'against those most unwise and dangerous proceedings of the Round Table Conference'. He said that the Socialists and Liberals slid and slithered down the slippery slope, and the Conservative Party must be strong and capable to resist the downward progress of the other two parties. [68]

In the House of Lords on March 18, 1931, the Duke of Marlborough brought a motion to discuss, among other things*, the effect produced by the proceedings of the First Round Table Conference and asked Lord Sankey, who chaired the Federal Structure Committee, to adumbrate the Indian policy of His Majesty's Government. Before going through the reply of Lord Sankey, the Lord Chancellor, we shall examine the speeches of Earl Peel and the Marquess of Reading, the Conservative and Liberal delegates respectively to the Round Table Conference. Earl Peel maintained that the most significant thing at the Conference was the movement initiated by the Princes and their declarations at the beginning that really diverted public attention from the old purely British-Indian problems and made everybody re-survey the problems in the light of the federal idea. He said that a great deal had been heard of the many discussions in India about Dominion Status but 'it was to some extent a success of the Conference that during those ten weeks

---

*Situation in India, Report of the Statutory Commission.

no resolution was even proposed or discussed on the general subject of Dominion Status'. Referring to Lord Sankey's earlier remarks that the conclusions they arrived at were provisional conclusions, Earl Peel maintained that he did not think that the great heads of the practical problems involved did emerge in the course of those discussions.[69]

The Marquess of Reading in his speech said that the Conference did not settle the constitution, but only agreed on some of the main principles, leaving others for further examination and reflection. With regard to the question of safeguards he stressed that these were indispensable. He said that if the responsibility was to be given at the centre, the safeguards must be accepted.

Dealing with the Gandhi-Irwin Pact, Reading said that from the moment that the conversations between Gandhi and Irwin had taken place and agreement was reached, the condition had improved in India and that if that improvement was brought about—'as it undoubtedly was'—by the Round Table Conference, that showed that the Conference did not have an adverse effect in India. He argued that Irwin did manage by those conversations to bring about a settlement. [70]

In reply to the Duke of Marlborough, Lord Sankey first gave a brief account of the reports of the sub-committees of the Round Table Conference and stated that the members of the committees were prepared to examine facts and to make suggestions. He said that in particular the object of the Federal Structure Committee was not to draft a constitution. He also said if the committee had had the time, still it would not have attempted to make final proposals. Sankey maintained that the members of the committee felt that there was an instructed body of public opinion both in England and in India whose views were not only entitled to be consulted, but whose opinions would be of real value in reaching a satisfactory solution. Continuing, he remarked that the future of India was no longer in the melting pot. He observed that the metal of its new constitution was being hammered out on the anvil of public opinion. [71]

The Labour Secretary of State for Colonies, Lord Passfield, in his reply to the criticism put forward by Lord Lloyd regarding the new policy of the government, said that the policy for which His Majesty's Government were of course responsible, was a policy which was fully concurred in by the Viceroy. He said that the Viceroy was not appointed by the Labour Government, but the government had absolute confidence in him and they were proceeding step by step without any difference between the Viceroy and the Labour Government. Lord Passfield clearly stated that it was the policy of the government to go on with the cooperation of all parties if other parties were willing, and the government would leave no stone unturned to secure that continued cooperation of the British parties, subject to its own necessary responsibility for action.[72]

Soon after the settlement with Gandhi Lord Irwin relinquished office and was succeeded by Lord Willingdon whose attitude was not favourable. The bureaucracy in India had not taken kindly to the truce. On the other side, many Congress leaders were not happy at the compromise which had come at a time when the civil disobedience was at its highest pitch. Gandhi himself was having difficulty in winning over the extremists in the Congress Party who were out to win '*Purna Swaraj*' (complete independence). When the Congress assembled at Karachi in the last week of March, 1931, Gandhi managed to secure the approval of the Pact and his own appointment as a Round Table Conference delegate, together with such others as the Congress Working Committee might nominate to serve under his leadership. However, the goal of complete independence was reaffirmed. So far as the Muslim question was concerned Gandhi did make a last-minute effort before leaving India for the Conference to arrive at a settlement. After the Karachi Congress Gandhi began to say that his going to the Round Table Conference depended on his ability to solve the Hindu-Muslim question beforehand. He also claimed that if the Muslims made a united demand on the question of representation, electorate, etc., in the new constitution he would accept the demand. The rub was that the Muslims themselves were not in agreement. The Nationalists had accepted the Nehru Report, and in particular joint electorates and a unitary polity, whereas the preponderance of non-Congress Muslims insisted upon separate electorates and strong provincial governments within a weak federation.[73] Despite his personal appeal Gandhi could not come to an agreed solution of the Hindu-Muslim problem.

On May 13, 1931, the Secretary of State for India, Wedgwood

Benn, said in the Commons that the government desired that the communal question should be settled by the communities concerned. 'We do not regard it as a matter in which we should interfere as between the Mohammedans, the Hindus and the Sikhs...The difficulty of a settlement is an inherent obstacle for the existence of which we are not responsible,' he said.[74] Unfortunately, when Mahatma Gandhi was in England, the minorities problem assumed the greatest importance. Meanwhile, in the middle of 1931, the special committees were sent to India, the principal of which were federal structure, minorities and finance. The Government of India was also compiling statistical information that would assist the next round table conference in determining specific provisions for the new constitution.

While the Labour Government was carrying out its plans for Indian constitutional reform, there arose the 1931 financial crisis that threatened the very economic life of England. Devaluation of sterling and the rising unemployment added to the budget and trade deficits created serious internal problems for the government. Consequently in August, the Labour Cabinet was replaced by a coalition government, formed on August 24, 1931, known as the National Government, with MacDonald as Premier. The coalition government sought the mandate of the country and in the elections held in October, obtained a decisive victory.

The election was, of course, a direct vote of no-confidence in Labour and left the Lloyd George Liberals in limbs. Labour, deserted and reviled by its former leaders, had gone down to catastrophic defeat, only a stunned fragment of fifty-two crawling back to House of Commons. Of the former front bench, only Lansbury, Attlee and Stafford Cripps survived. Lloyd George's party was reduced to a family quartet. Suddenly, there was no Parliamentary Opposition, and, although Labour was to win back a hundred seats in 1935 and make a modest revival, it was to remain a minority party with no real prospect of office until the events of 1940 brought its leaders into a different coalition than that which reigned in 1931.[75] As Ramsay MacDonald formed the National Government with Conservatives and Liberals, he was read out of the Labour Party. Henceforward he brooded supinely at the head of an administration which, though nominally National, was in fact overwhelmingly Conservative.[76] Sir Samuel Hoare succeeded Wedgwood

Benn at the India Office.

The Labour Party, sorely stricken at the polls, was led by George Lansbury after MacDonald was ousted from the party. Before the general election in England the Labour Party's annual conference was held in October, 1931 and in that conference the Indian problem was also discussed. The Labour Party's stand on India was reaffirmed in a resolution moved by Lansbury. It said that the Indians had a right to self-government and the resolution expressed hope that the members of the Second Round Table would co-operate in order that a new era of friendship between England and India would begin.[77] The left wingers were critical of the resolution. Fenner Brockway emphasised that the government had still not released all the political prisoners, and he called upon the Labour Party to use its influence on the government to release these prisoners.[78] Despite the criticism George Lansbury's resolution was carried.

The Labour Party's ideology which impelled it to convene the Round Table Conference and to conclude the Gandhi-Irwin Pact was abandoned by the Conservatives who became the virtual government after October 1931 election. The views of Birkenhead recovered their ascendancy. The recommendations of the Statutory Commission and not the agreement of the Round Table Conference henceforward were to guide the policy of the British Government.

The Second Session of the Conference

The Second Round Table Conference opened on September 7, 1931, and terminated on December 1 of that year. The main work of the Conference was done by two large committees on Federal Structure and Minorities. Mahatma Gandhi was a member of both committees, and it was hoped that through his mediation some compromise might be attained between the policy of the Conference—if the scheme which had emerged from the first Conference can be so described—and the policy of the Congress. Gandhi's speech in the preliminary discussion with which the Federal Structure Committee of the Round Table Conference began gave hope that the Conference would be able to see an end to the indiscriminate agitation in India. But the Conference was finally brought to an end without any agreement on the vital issue. It was a disappointing affair for everything was forced to wait on attempts to arrange a settlement of the minorities problem by agreement. In fact, not only did the Conference end without any agreement between the Indian representatives and the British Government as to the extent of the limitations to full self-government to be imposed, but it might have been allowed to end without even a cursory discussion of this issue. This is not to say, though, that much valuable and necessary work was not done in the Conference. On matters not relating to the question of responsibility at the centre, important progress was made in the Federal Structure Committee of the Conference, and its conclusions were presented to the full Conference.

The Chairman of the Federal Structure Committee, Lord Sankey, in his opening speech observed that the First Round Table Conference represented all sections of Indian opinion except one and that defect would be rectified now with the presence of Gandhi in the Conference. MacDonald assured the members that despite the change in the government 'there has been no change in public aims'.[79] Gandhi, in his speech in the meeting of the Federal Structure Committee, said that the Congress not only represented all India but was its only proper representative, since the non-Congress Indian delegates had not been chosen by the people but nominated by the government. He read out the relevant portion from the Karachi Congress resolution in which the Congress categorically stated its 'desire to make it clear that the Congress goal of *Purna Swaraj*, meaning complete independence, remains intact'. He said he had come to the Conference to treat with the British people on the basis of absolute equality between the two partners. In his speech he made it clear that the Congress would not be satisfied with anything less than a real transfer of power. He said that India's new status would not necessarily mean secession from the British Commonwealth, but only freedom to secede.[80]

In coming to their conclusions the Structure Committee had taken into account: (a) the widespread desire in India for constitutional advance; (b) the natural desire of the Indian States to conserve their integrity; (c) the indisputable claims of the minorities to fair treatments; (d) the obligations and responsibilities of His Majesty's Government; (e) the necessity of ensuring the financial credit and stability of government itself. Taking these factors into account the Report put forward a scheme for a federal legislature consisting of two houses. It recommended that the lower house should comprise three hundred members. Of this number, one hundred would be representatives of the States. The manner in which these representatives of the States would be selected was left to the judgment of the States.The report proposed that the upper house of the federal legislature should consist of two hundred members. These members would be composed of representatives of the provinces elected by the provincial legislatures, and eighty representatives of the Staes, the method of whose selection would rest with the States. While the lower house would be chosen, as far as possible, on the principle of popular election, the upper house would be chosen in the main to represent the component units of the federation as such. Since the Minorities Committee did never resolve its problems, this aspect of representation was not covered in the Federal Structure reports, but the Structure Committee recommended that there should be special representation for the landlords, the commercial interests, and the labourers.[81]

There remained the question of federal finance. This important question of the apportionment of the financial resources and obligations between the federation and the units making up the federation was not considered at length by the Federal Structure Committee. It recommended that two *ad hoc* committees should be set up by the government to investigate different aspects of this ques tion.[82]

The scheme envisaged by the Federal Structure Committee of the Conference provided for the setting up of a federal court. The report said that it was recognised by all that a federal cour was required 'both to interpret the constitution and to safeguard it'.[83]

The Committee stated that, during a period of transition, the Governor-General should be responsible for defence and he should be responsible for the external relations.[84]

As at the First Round Table Conference so at the Second the Hindu nationalists sought to unite Indian opinion before proceeding to discuss the devolution of powers. Gandhi's initial task, if he were to have any chance of extracting swaraj from Britain, was to settle the communal problem. What Gandhi found when the Conference got to work in earnest was that its attention was concentrated on the problem of the minorities, before the central issue, the transfer of power, was decided. He spent a week in a vain endeavour to reach an agreement with the Muslims and the other minorities. He took his stand on the scheme already sketched by Congress, which insisted on joint electorates, but assured by reservation of seats, a representation for the Muslim and Sikh minorities proportionate to numbers.

On October 8, 1931, Gandhi reported the failure of informal negotiations sadly to the Minorities Committee. He proposed that the new constitution should provide for a judicial tribunal to examine communal claims. Though he was opposed to separate representation for the minor minorities, and the untouchables in particular, he would accept the verdict of an arbitral body. The Muslims reiterated their demand that the communal question must be settled before the drafting of a new constitution. Together with the depressed classes they also opposed reference to arbitration and expressed willingness to accept a government decision. Like the Sikhs and the Muslims the depressed classes now insisted upon the protection of their interests as a condition precedent to constitutional advance.

What happened, after Gandhi's failure, was that all the special interests came together, under the leadership of Sir Hubert Carr, one of the delegates representing the British commercial community, and presented to the Conference an agreed document in which these groups supported each other in demanding separate electorates, not only for Muslims and Sikhs, but for Christians, Europeans, Anglo-Indians and the untouchables as well, with special representation for big landowners, Chambers of Commerce and Trade Unions.[85] The minorities' pact was presented to a meeting of the Minorities Committee on November 13, 1931. MacDonald stated in that meeting that as Prime Minister he would declare his award on the communal problem. Gandhi accepted this with the proviso that the Prime Minister's intervention should be limited only to religious communities like Hindus, Muslims and Sikhs, but he would not accept bifurcation of the Hindu community by separating the Scheduled Castes (Depressed Classes) from the mainstream of Hindu society.

In its final report, the committee only reaffirmed that the various communities in India were still far apart and that no adequate conclusions could be reached. In his concluding speech

Gandhi struck a note of warning. He felt that after so many 'weary weeks' the Conference had accomplished exactly nothing. The proposed safeguards were not in the interests of India. He did not want to break the bond between Britain and India, but he did want to transform it. 'I want to transform that slavery into complete freedom for my country.'[86]

During the Second Round Table Conference, the reports of the other seven committees that had been originally established during the first Conference were officially presented. MacDonald in his closing speech assured the representatives that the present government would adhere to the policy statement made at the end of the First Round Table Conference. He said:

The great idea of all-India federation still holds the field. The principle of a responsible federal government, subject to certain reservations and safeguards through a transition period, remains unchanged. And we are all agreed that the Governors' provinces of the future are to be responsible governed units, enjoying the greatest possible measure of freedom from outside interference and dictation in carrying out their own policies in their own sphere.

With regard to communal deadlock, MacDonald maintained, if the parties could not present a solution acceptable to all, in that case the government would be compelled to apply a provisional scheme, with a view to providing the most ample safeguards for minorities. But he emphasised that the communities should take further opportunities to meet together and present to the government with an agreement. Finally, MacDonald proposed to nominate in due course a small representative committee of that Conference which would remain in being in India, with which, through the Viceroy, the government could keep in effective touch. The committee's object would be to carrying forward the work of the Conference. He also proposed to set up further committees on the franchise, on federal and provincial finance. 'In the end', he declared, 'we shall have to meet again for a final review of the whole scheme.'[87]

The conclusions of the Conference concerning responsibility at the centre remained vague and tentative. However, the exchange of opinion which the discussion of these questions made possible, if it had no other result, led to a better appreciation on all sides of the Conference of different viewpoints on the important issues. If the actual achievements of the Conference fell short of anybody's expectations, nothing that had been said or done in the Conference precluded a settlement.[88] Jawaharlal Nehru in his autobiography remarked that it was political reaction that barred all progress and sheltered itself behind the communal issue. By careful selection of its nominees for the Conference, the British Government had collected the reactionary elements, and by controlling the procedure, they had made the communal issue the major issue, and an issue on which no agreement was possible between the irreconcilables gathered there.[89] The whole deliberation of the Second Round Table Conference came to no tangible result; rather it had a marked recession from what had been accepted in the First Round Table Conference.

For the ratification of the Prime Minister's statement of policy to the Round Table Conference, it was circulated to Parliament as a White Paper. After a brief survey of the development of responsible government in India, Ramsay MacDonald told the House of Commons that his policy was based on the fulfilment of the British promise of self-government for India. Speaking about the achievement of the Round Table Conference, he said, 'The great value of the Conference was that it enabled everyone of us who attended that body to understand (1) what is the Indian mind; (2) to try to translate that mind into a working constitution.' He reminded the House that the round table conferences were intended only to be consultative conferences. Commending the White Paper, MacDonald stated that the Princes' readiness to join the federation changed the outlook and put the question of a responsible federal government on to a new foundation. He said that the terms on which the native States would join the federation still remained to be worked out. MacDonald maintained that the National Government continued the same Indian policy as the Labour Government. But he denied that the immediate goal of the National Government was Dominion Status for India.[90]

Samuel Hoare, a Conservative M.P. and the new Secretary of State for India, explained that an all-India federation, autonomous provinces and safeguards were the objectives of the White Paper. In this speech Hoare stated that so far as India was concerned, all three parties were equally committed to accepting the fact that responsible government was the ultimate objective to which all of the parties were working. He said, 'We are prepared to make an advance to responsible government both at the centre and in the provinces.'   Hoare believed that though the Round Table Conference might have failed so far in finding agreement upon many fundamental questions and a great many details, yet it had played a useful part, and the Indian controversy would never be quite the same again.[91]

Winston Churchill, who was determined to oppose the government's India policy, moved an amendment opposing the establishment of a Dominion constitution in India as defined by the Statute of Westminster, and not to impair the ultimate responsibility of Parliament to the Government of India.   He took his stand on the Act of 1919 and the Simon Commission's Report.   He said:

The Statutory Commission ... after their profound study, deliberately excluded the expression 'Dominion Status' from their unanimous report—a tremendous fact, when you remember the atmosphere at the time ; a great august decision, which has never received the weight and attention which it deserves from Parliament.[92]

A prominent member of the Labour Party, Clement Attlee, who served in the Simon Commission as one of the two representatives from the party, and who became the leader of his party later, welcomed Prime Minister's India policy and said that the Labour Party also agreed with the idea of all-India federation.   Attlee remarked that one of the most remarkable things was the way the Indian Princes came forward and how in a short period of time the ideal of an all-India federation had forced itself to the front.   On the Statutory Commission's Report he said that it was an honest attempt to help India by an investigation of the facts and the suggestions of possible solutions.   Attlee emphasized the need for prompt action if the government was planning to continue the round table concept.[93]   Colonel Wedgwood, another Labourite, maintained that the federal solution, as long as the Indian States were governed with complete irresponsibility, was really a very reactionary step.   Regarding method of elections he said that it would be a tragedy if they took the step of starting election to legislatures by indirect election.   That would destroy the hold of the elector over his representative.[94]   Morgan Jones of the Labour Party remarked that in his judgment if they reserved completely the control of the army and control over finance, it would mean an offer to the Indians which was only the semblance of self-government.[95] G. Buchanan, a Labour left-winger, while speaking in the same debate, pointed out that the Meerut prisoners were still rotting in gaol for over two years without trial while the government released many political prisoners after the Gandhi-Irwin Pact. He accused the second Labour Government for not doing anything tangible for their trial. Buchanan expressed belief that India was ripe for full independence. He said, 'I think the Indian people are as capable of governing themselves as are the British people.'[96] George Lansbury, leader of the Labour Party, maintained in closing remarks that it was for the Indians to determine the position that India would assume in relationship to England and it was the Indians themselves who should have the final say whether or not India would remain within the Empire. Finally, he appealed to the Prime Minister to see Gandhi and to use his persuasive powers to make 'that great man understand that the differences between us are not and shall not be insurmountable.'[97]

On December 8, 1931, Indian policy of His Majesty's Government was debated in the House of Lords and in bringing the motion before the House, Marquess of Lothian, the Under-Secretary of State for India, said that the idea of India making itself responsible for its own government was no longer seditious but had been for nearly fifteen years the settled policy of Great Britain. Lothian stressed that he could see to adopt no other policy than the one set forth in the White Paper on which rested the foundation of the new constitution of India.[98]

Lord Snell, while speaking for the Labour Party, told the Lords that to take up the subject of India was like trying to grip with one hand a vast globe. Yet in his judgment the Round Table Conference came very near to achieving the miraculous. Continuing, he said that one of the great achievements of the Conference was that the conference method was to continue, and the centre of activities was to be in India itself, rather than in England. He said that His Majesty's Government was saved from the duty of imposing a decision upon the Conference, which might have turned every man in it from a cooperator to a critic. Lord Snell warned the government that if they reserved the right to impose upon

India any plan irrespective of the wishes of the Indian people then his party should feel alarmed. He expressed the view that the Labour Party reserved the right to consider future stages of the White Paper proposals upon their own merits even though they supported the policy at present. In conclusion, he sounded a note of caution and said :

Many of us in the Labour Party worked and spoke and fought in Parliament and elsewhere through many difficult and lonely years for Indian self-government, and we have earned our right to make an appeal to the Indian reformers to think twice and thrice before they bring upon India the disaster of deliberate disobedience, passive or active. It is not in that way that causes are won.

The House of Lords, after the debate, accepted the statement of policy by a handsome majority. From the debate held in both the Houses of Parliament, it became clear that irrespective of parties the policy was endorsed by Parliament and it stood by the National Government in its India policy.

The Labour Party, which was in office from 1929 till 1931, managed to bring about some changes in Indo-British politics. It was the Labour Government that arranged the Round Table Conference to discuss the future constitution of India. Although the two sessions of the Conference were consultative in nature, they could, in fact, point to no marked result. The only important thing to come to the forefront at the First Round Table Conference was willingness of the representatives of the Indian States to join in a federation with British India.

The delegates present at the Conference were not elected; but nominated by the government. It was a packed house with Britishers, Princes, landlords, communal leaders and representatives of European and Indian vested interests. There was no occasion to discuss the question of the real transfer of power. The entire discussion was side-tracked into mutual recriminations and discussions of conflicting claims. The National Government that was formed in 1931 seemed to have lost interest in the reforms, for the minds of the government delegates were pre-occupied with the internal problems of England. The hasty termination of the Second Round Table Conference was an indication of this.

On the side of the government, the expectations raised by the attendance of Gandhi at the second session of the Conference were dashed to the ground. While the government were led to believe that he would compromise on the Congress demands, Gandhi insisted upon the immediate granting of independence in accordance with the demand of the Congress. Relying on the declaration of Irwin, the Congress believed the discussions between the Indian and the British delegates would be between equal parties, implying the recognition of India as equal in status with Britain. The claims of Gandhi, however, were looked upon by the authorities as extravagant and untenable For the Labour Party, the conclusions arrived at in the second session were not as sweeping as it had hoped.

NOTES

1. *Sunday Times*, November 3, 1929.
2. R.J. Moore, op cit., pp. 99-100.
3. *The New Leader*, January 3, 1930.
4. H.C. Deb., vol. 254, 1931, c. 2315.
5. B.R. Nanda, *Mahatma Gandhi: A Biography*, op. cit·, p. 289.
6. S.C. Bose, op. cit., pp. 181-4.
7. H.C. Deb., vol. 239, 1930, cc. 841-2.
8. ibid., cc. 903-4.
9. ibid., cc. 869-870.
10. ibid., cc. 871-873
11. ibid., cc. 905-6
12. ibid., cc. 906-914.
13. Report of the third British Commonwealth Labour Conference, pp. 26, 28.
14. ibid. pp. 26-9.
15. L.P. Report, 1930, p. 216.
16. ibid., pp. 217-220.
17. Quoted in Indian Annual Register, 1930, vol. 2, p. 154.
18. Wedgwood Benn Papers, ST/223/37-39, July, 1930.
19. P.S. Gupta, op. cit., pp. 207-8.
20. H.C. Deb., vol. 242, 1930, c. 4.
21. *The Times*, July 10, 1930.
22. R.J. Moore, op. cit., p. 144.
23. John Coatman, op. cit,, pp. 101-103.
24. Indian Round Table Conference, 12 November, 1930—19 January, 1931, *Proceedings*, Command Paper 3778.
25. *The Times*, November 12, 1930.
26. R. Coupland, op. cit , p. 114.
27. Article entitled "The Indian Round Table Conference" by D. Graham Pole, M.P., *The Labour Magazine*, vol. 9, Feb., 1931, pp. 435-438.

28. Command Paper 3778, 1930-1931, pp. 36-7.
29. Viscount Templewood (Sir Samuel Hoare), op. cit., p. 48.
30. R.J. Moore, op. cit., pp. 155-6.
31. Command Paper 3778, 1930-1931, p. 21 *et seq.*
32. ibid., p. 46 *et seq.*
33. ibid., p. 246. The delegates of the Hindus were in favour of joint electorates but were prepared to concede reservation of seats for the minorities.
34. ibid., p. 42 *et seq.*
35. ibid., p. 57 *et seq.*
36. ibid., p. 61 *et seq,*
37. ibid., p. 65 *et seq.*
38. ibid., p. 50.
39. ibid., p. 70.
40. ibid., p. 53.
41, Command Paper 3778, 1930-31, pp. 498-509.
42. Viscount Templewood, op. cit., pp. 52-3.
43. *The Times*, January 20, 1931.
44. *The New Leader,* (Weekly), January 23, 1931.
45. Cited in *The Labour Magazine*, vol. 9, Feb. 1931, pp. 435-8.
46. ibid.
47. H.C. Deb., vol. 247, 1931, c. 643.
48. ibid., cc. 744-8.
49. ibid., c. 717.
50. ibid., c. 691.
51. *The Times*, January 27, 1931.
52. Wedgwood Benn to Irwin, February, 9, 1931, I.O.L., MSS. Eur. c. 152/6, pp. 357-8.
53. B.R. Nanda, op. cit., pp. 301-2.
54. I.A.R., vol. 1, 1931, p. 127.
55. Viscount Templewood, op. cit., p. 55.
56. ibid.
57. S.C. Bose, op. cit., p. 202.
58. *Sir Winston Churchill : A Self-Portrait*, constructed from his own sayings and writings and framed with an introduction by Colin R. Coote with the collaboration of P.D. Bunyan, London, 1954, pp. 242.
59. Winston S. Churchill, *The Second World War*: *The Gathering Storm*, Boston, 1948, p. 33.
60. H.C. Deb., vol. 249, 1931, c. 1437.
61. ibid., cc. 1518-1519.
62. ibid., c. 1538.
63. ibid., cc. 1456-1465.
64. ibid., cc. 1424-1426.
65. ibid , cc. 1422-1423.
66. *The Daily Telegraph*, March 13, 1931.
67. H.C. Deb., vol. 249, 1931, cc. 1467,

68. *The Times*, February 24, 1931.
69. H.L. Deb., vol. 80, 1931, cc. 397-8.
70. ibid., cc. 414, 420, 424-5.
71. ibid., cc. 389-394.
72. ibid., cc. 438-439.
73. R.J. Moore, op. cit., p. 189.
74. H.C. Deb., vol. 252, 1931, c. 1325.
75. R.R. James, op. cit., pp. 520-522.
76. Winston Churchill, *The Gathering Storm*, op. cit., p. 66.
77. L.P. Report, 1931, p. 215.
78. ibid., p. 170.
79. A.C. Guha, Part 1, op. cit., p. 256.
80. R. Coupland, op. cit., p. 125.
81. The Indian Round Table Conference; second session, September 7, 1931 to December 1, 1931, Command Paper 3997, p. 16 *et seq.*
82. ibid., p. 24 *et seq.*
83. ibid., p. 27 *et seq.*
84. ibid., p. 51 *et seq.*
85. H.S.L. Polak, H.N. Brailsford, and Lord Pethick-Lawrence, *Mahatma Gandhi*, London, 1949, p. 192.
86. ibid., p. 194.
87. Command Paper 3997, 1931, pp. 414-421.
88. "The Second Round Table Conference" by D.G. Pole, *The Labour Magazine*, vol. 10, 1931, p, 455.
89. Jawaharlal Nehru, *An Autobiography*; London, 1936, p. 294.
90. H.C. Deb., vol. 260, 1931, c. 1101 *et seq.*
91. ibid., cc. 1210-1211.
92. ibid., c. 1292.
93. ibid., cc. 1119-1123.
94. ibid., cc. 1148-1149.
95. ibid., c. 1334.
96. ibid., cc. 1358-1359.
97. ibid., cc. 1392-1396.
98. H.L. Deb., vol. 83, 1931, c. 307.
99. ibid., cc. 346-350.

CHAPTER 5

From the Third Round Table Conference to the Passing of the Act of 1935

The political situation in India became tense after the Second Round Table Conference. The Indian Government tried to suppress the Congress movement f r independence and when Gandhi reached home after attending the Conference in London he was arrested. In England, the Parliamentary Labour Party began to criticise the repressive policy of the National Government and to advocate Dominion Status for India. Although the National Government maintained the Indian policy of the Labour Government, the spirit was changed. MacDonald's coalition government stressed that they would not negotiate with the Congress until the party abandoned its attempt to disrupt the Indian Government machine.

Meanwhile, in November 1932, the Third Round Table Conference began. The most striking feature of this Conference was that it was not attended either by the Labour Party or by the Indian Congress Party because of the repressive policy pursued by the National Government. The Conference cleared the way for the preparation of a White Paper with proposals for a new constitution.

A joint committee of both the House of Commons and Lords was then formed in 1933 to examine the feasibility of the Indian scheme and to report back to Parliament. The committee sat almost continuously from April 1933, till November 1934. The Labour Party sent four members to this committee, but they could not change the provisions during the discussions. The report did not substantially differ from the proposals in the White Paper. Finally, it was presented to Parliament as the Government of India Bill. The Bill was debated in Parliament where the Labour Party proposed some amendments, which were all rejected. The Bill was carried by an overwhelming majority in both the House of Commons and the Lords and it received royal assent in August 1935.

National Government's India Policy

Towards the close of the second session of the Round Table Conference, even before Mahatma Gandhi and other Indian leaders left the English shores, it was believed that forces were already at work to sabotage the Conference, make a clean sweep of the whole Indian muddle of the previous Labour Government, and go back to the 'buried' Simon Commission. It was feared that federal responsibility might be shelved, and only provincial autonomy such as contemplated by the Simon Report would be granted. An influential section of the Indian team of the Conference had to formally protest against such a plan. The result was that the whole question of responsible government in India was shelved for the time being. In a letter to George Lansbury, leader of the Labour Party, Indian Liberal leader Tej Bahadur Sapru wrote :

We take our stand on the definite pledges given by the Prime Minister in his speech at the last Round Table Conference and in his speech in the House of Commons in December 1931, when the White Paper relating to Indian policy came up for debate in Commons. We see absolutely no reason for abandoning that procedure and . . . I regret to observe that the policy of Lord Irwin and Mr Wedgwood Benn which was endorsed by His Majesty's Government at that time is no longer the favoured policy. We do not believe in and have no faith in the Conservative point of view in regard to India.[1]

At the conclusion of the second session, and when returning from England, Gandhi had made it perfectly clear that the Congress would not only not bring down its demand for immediate effective control over the army, finance and so forth which any British government, Labour or Conservative, was not prepared to grant, but that the Congress would revive the civil disobedience movement, in case the negotiations ultimately broke down.[2]

During Gandhi's absence from India, the Government of India under Willingdon adopted repressive measures and broke the spirit of the Gandhi-Irwin agreement. At the end of the second session of the Round Table Conference, Gandhi had intimated that he and the Prime Minister had probably 'come to the parting of the ways'; and indeed, before he returned to India, the truce had broken down. The civil disobedience movement was started again. Willingdon

considered the restoration of law and order as the paramount pre-
requisite to any negotiations with the nationalists. On January
4, 1932, Gandhi and the Congress President, Vallabhbhai Patel, were
arrested and confined without trial as State prisoners. Gandhi's
arrest was accompanied by the battery of repressive ordinances.
These actions of the Viceroy were supported by Sir Samuel Hoare,
the Secretary of State for India and he assured Willingdon that no
bargain could be struck with the Congress in order to obtain its
cooperation.[3] The failure of the Congress to call off the civil
disobedience movement convinced the Viceroy that the party was
revolutionary, and he thereupon declared it illegal.

In England, during the year 1932, the Labour Party, whose unity
had been disrupted when Ramsay MacDonald formed the National
Government, continued its fight for Dominion Status for India. The
small Parliamentary Labour Party condemned the Indian policy of
the National Government in a debate in the Commons on February
29, 1932. MacDonald was accused of breaking faith with the
Indians when he deliberately ended the second session of the
Round Table Conference. The Parliamentary Labour Party pointed
out the changed attitude of the government towards India, especially in its treatment of Gandhi. The Labour members criticised the
government for the sudden and swift decision of imprisoning Gandhi
immediately after he reached India. The Labour members argued
that as Gandhi represented a solid body of opinion his imprisonment had contributed in some degree to the destruction of the
remaining faith that the Indians had in the British Government.
They were critical of the repressive ordinances put into effect in
India by Lord Willingdon. The Labourites maintained that the only
way of winning over the Indians was, 'not by the method of force,
but by the arbitrament of reason.'[4]

It may be mentioned here that Colonel Wedgwood, an outspoken
member of the Parliamentary Labour Party, remarked in Commons
that what Gandhi did in conjunction with Lord Irwin was probably
the best thing that had happened to the relations between England
and India. But they failed, and the possibilities of cooperation had
come to nothing. He said that they had come to naught because
Congress and the Congress leaders were determined that these
negotiations should come to nothing. Wedgwood told the House
that Congress asked for trouble and they got that, and he did not

think that they could complain of the action that the present government took. With regard to the Round Table Conference he said, 'nothing could come out of the Conference'. He was all along against the federal plan, an 'alliance with the Princes and the rich of India'. He believed that the entire round table concept and all the British committees that were trying to lay the basis for an Indian constitution would fail in their purpose.[5]

Immediately after Wedgwood's speech, Sir Reginald Craddock, a diehard Conservative, attacked the Labour Party for its support of the Congress Party which, he claimed, consisted of only a few of the intelligentsia and the Labourites were persistently deceived by the Congress. He doubted that the Labour Party did not realise what they were doing when they spoke for the Congress and the interests at the back of the Congress. He said that he was not accusing the Labourites of anything but being readily persuaded by people 'whose veracity or judgment they cannot readily discern'. He pointed out that the Labour Party by its policy during the last two or three years, had brought about the situation in which the present government had had to act firmly, and to resort to ordinances of various kinds.[6]

Clement Attlee of the Labour Party in reply said that if someone thought of repressing the Congress movement by force, would make a profound mistake. He stressed that they should recognise the nationalist movement in India and endeavour to work with all that was best in the Congress movement. Referring to the situation in India, Attlee expressed the view that the experiment of trying to crush Congress was likely to fail. 'I believe that so far from it succeeding you will get only class after class joining in the movement until eventually you find yourselves, despite yourselves, creating a united India, united by a common hostility to the British connection: and that is the last thing I should wish to happen', he concluded.[7]

The leader of the Labour Party, George Lansbury, maintained that he knew to his own knowledge that Gandhi went from England full of the belief that after he landed he would be able to discuss with the Viceroy what the ordinances were expected to accomplish, but he was not allowed to meet Willingdon. Lansbury observed that had Gandhi been allowed to discuss with the Viceroy they would have found a way out.[8]

On March 24, 1932, India was again discussed in the Commons and in that debate Morgan Jones and David Grenfell of the Labour Party brought two charges against the government. First, they pointed out that the government had introduced a chapter of extreme repression in India by putting into effect the ordinances and secondly, the government had broken up the atmosphere of the Round Table Conference. Besides, Morgan Jones invited the Secretary of State for India, Sir Samuel Hoare, to make an explicit declaration that the position of the government remained precisely as it was at the end of the Round Table Conference.[9] David Grenfell in his speech called attention of the Secretary of State and suggested to him to extend an invitation to further conferences between the leaders of Indian nationalism and the British Government, and to withdraw at the earliest date the 'oppressive and un-British' ordinances.[10]

While responding to the Labourites, the Secretary of State for India admitted that the ordinances that they approved were very drastic and severe. He said that they covered almost every activity of Indian life. Hoare made it a point that the ordinances would be kept in force in India just so long as the emergency continued. He told the House that the government had been proceeding with the policy of the Round Table Conference and informed that the committees formed to investigate on the spot certain important details connected with the all-India federation had made substantial progress in their efforts. On the communal issue Hoare categorically said that in any new Indian constitution there must be adequate safeguards for the minorities. He further pointed out that if the communities did not agree among themselves and His Majesty's Government stood out of the controversy altogether, there could be no constitutional advance of any kind, either at the centre or in the provinces. The Secretary of State in the course of his speech made it clear that the British Government were intensely interested in the success of an all-India federation.[11]

On April 29, Sir Samuel Hoare while maintaining that the government was pursuing exactly the policy approved by 'an overwhelming majority of this House last December' challenged the members to produce a better policy than the one adumbrated in the White Paper issued after the termination of the Second Round Table Conference. The leader of the Labour Party, George Lansbury, again criti-

cised the government and expressed the view that the Indians themselves had to be given the right of self-determination. He said that
no peace and security in India would be possible unless the people
there had the right to settle their own problems. Replying to the
charge that during the second Labour Government double the number of persons were imprisoned, Lansbury said that from the very
beginning of that administration, and before they came into office,
Irwin did his best in the midst of great trouble and difficulty in
India to maintain the principle of conciliation. He pointed out that
the Labourites were not able to go through without imprisoning
people; but no one could deny that the Viceroy never lost any
opportunity of upholding the full right of the Indian people to self-
government. He further stated that a very difficult situation had been
created before the Labour Party came into office by the appointment of the all-white Simon Commission. Lansbury maintained
that the Tory Government had to face all the difficulties which
arose, but when Irwin and Wedgwood Benn were together in office,
they tried to overcome those difficulties by bringing about the
Round Table Conference in place of a Statutory Commission. He
then castigated the government for imprisoning Gandhi. Lansbury
emphasized that it had destroyed all the goodwill that the Labour
Government had been able to build.[12]

The National Government defended its action by declaring that
the policy conformed with the policy of the Labour Government.
While it is true that the National Government maintained the form
of the Labour Government's policy, the spirit was greatly altered.
The Labour Government was sincerely interested in winning the
cooperation of all Indian political parties, while the National
Government was willing to deal only with the moderate Indian
political parties.

On June 27, 1932, Sir Samuel Hoare presented to the Commons
a review of the situation in India and informed that the actions
that had been taken by the Government of India were 'completely
successful in keeping the civil disobedience movement in check'.
He said that although the powers were drastic they were justified
by the necessity of proving that civil disobedience could not
succeed against the organised resources of the State. He intimated
that the campaign against the government had been held
in check, but it had not been called off. With regard to the

constitutional question Hoare pointed out that the Government would proceed by the introduction of a single bill covering the whole constitutional problem, rather than approach it in two stages with a provincial autonomy first and a federal bill subsequently. He further made it known to the India Committee of the House of Commons that the government had already started conversations with representative Princes and that these talks would be continued in India with a view to ascertaining the extent to which it could proceed with the all-India federal scheme. Hoare said that the government would take the next immediate step towards the removal of communal obstacles that retarded constitutional progress. He declared that it would invite both houses of Parliament to set up a joint select committee to examine the proposals for constitutional reform and to give the committee power to confer with representatives of Indian opinion in that respect.[13]

The Labour Party in their protest against the Government plan of action vehemently criticised the sweeping use of the ordinances in the suppression of opposition to the Government of India. This action tended to dishearten even moderate opinion in India which was anxious to cooperate with the government. The Labour member, Morgan Jones, told the House of Commons that he was in doubt whether the Secretary of State would find it easy to bridge the gulf yawning between the government and the moderate forces in India. He observed that the legislation which was to be presented later to the House of Commons must depend ultimately for its success upon the cordial cooperation of the average Indian in India. He remarked that he found no trace of desire in the speech of the Secretary of State to effect some policy of reconciliation between the government and that vast section of opinion represented by the Congress Party [14]

The Labour opposition continued to claim that the bitterness between the Hindus and the Muslims and between the Indians and the British Government was increasing everyday. Colonel Wedgwood, another Labourite, while criticising the safeguards said:

If they are safeguards for the common people of India I shall be all for them, but we know what these safeguards will be. They will be for our investments, for the vested interests; they will be safeguards for the landlords, and safeguards for the Mohammedans or the depressed classes or Anglo-Indians.[15]

J. McGovern, an I.L.P. member, in his speech charged the Labour Party by saying that when the party was out of office they spoke with the voice of the Congress of India, and when in office they spoke with the voice of the British imperialist, the British ruling class.[16]

The Labour leader, George Lansbury, observed that under the Labour Government and before that, as well as under the present government, there was a long period of coercive measures, and the necessity for those had arisen solely because the Indian people did not believe that the Britishers intended to carry out their pledges and promises.[19] It should be noted that the National Government of Ramsay MacDonald made it clear that until the Congress Party, as the Secretary of State put it, 'definitely abandon the attempt to smash the machine of government and to set themselves up as a rival organisation to the accredited Government of India, there can be no question of negotiations of any kind'.[18]

A meeting of the Labour Party Advisory Committee on Imperial Questions was held on June 1, 1932, in which a draft statement on the situation in India and the party policy was considered. The draft statement mentioned that the National Government, by a general resort to rule by ordinance, appeared to have imperilled the whole principle of constitution-making by the Conference method, which had been the basis of Labour Party policy. The draft stated that Round Table Conference was broken up with unnecessary haste before any opportunity was given for proper reports to be drawn up on such subjects as the proposed safeguards. It said that the return of the delegates to India coincided with a policy of wholesale internments and imprisonments of those associated with the national movement. The Committee considered the revival of the Conference method and resummoning of the Round Table conference in London. The draft urged the government to convince Indians by declaring that it would continue the work of constitution-making on a basis of equality. It believed that the best method of ending the existing deadlock was to make such changes in the administration as would ensure the future cooperation of those who had already shown their willingness to work with the government.[19]

Meanwhile, the civil disobedience movement did not prevent the continuance of preparations for the final stage of the Round Table

Conference. The Franchise Committee under Lord Lothian, the Federal Finance Committee under Lord Eustace Percy, and the States' Inquiry Committee under J.C.C. Davidson went out to India and drafted their reports. In August 1932, since further discussions had proved fruitless, the Prime Minister announced the government's provisional scheme of minority representation, commonly called the Communal Award. Separate electorates were retained for the minority communities and also for the Muslims in Bengal and the Punjab despite their numerical majority. Weightage was also conceded to the Muslims in provinces in which they were in a minority and to the Sikhs and Hindus in the Punjab. Ramsay MacDonald while declaring the award stated that the government would be glad if, 'at any stage before the proposed bill becomes law, the communities can reach an agreement amongst themselves'. He said that the government would be ready and willing to substitute for their scheme any scheme whether in respect of any one or more of Governors' Provinces or in respect of the whole of British India that was generally agreed and accepted by all the parties affected.[20]

When the details were announced, the inevitable criticism in India was concentrated upon two points. First, the Sikhs, a martial community, resented Muslim predominance in the Punjab, and Congress, personified in Gandhi, refused to accept the segregation of the Depressed Classes from the main Hindu community. Whilst nothing could be done to mollify the Sikhs, a Hindu crisis was averted by the 'Poona Pact' between Gandhi and Ambedkar (leader of the Depressed Classes), by which the Depressed Classes, under the threat of Gandhi's 'fast unto death', abandoned their separate electorates in exchange for double the number of seats in joint electorates.[21] The Prime Minister accepted the Poona agreement.

In Great Britain the annual Labour Party Conference was held in October 1932, in which the British Government's Indian policy was reviewed. The Labour parliamentarians reported to the conference that as the National Government undertook a policy of coercion and imprisonment of 'large masses of the Indian people', and outlawed the Congress Party, the Parliamentary Labour Party refused to associate themselves with the policy of the government. They informed the conference that during a debate in the Commons last June Parliamentary Labour Party made it clear to the House that the Labour Party supported to its fullest extent the right of the Indian people to self-government and self-determination.[22]

George Lansbury moved a resolution in that conference which reaffirmed the right of the Indian people to choose the form of government which they considered to be in harmony with their national aspirations. The resolution considered that the government should take steps to convince Indians that the British Government had not departed, and did not intend to depart from its avowed policy of establishing a responsible federal government, with such provincial assemblies as might be decided upon, and that it was the government's intention to continue the work of constitution-making on a basis of equality. It urged the government for an amnesty of all persons not guilty of crimes of violence in India, and the renewal of an effective round table conference for the consideration of the proposals of the government and the discussion of all outstanding questions[23].

After moving the resolution, Lansbury said that the Indians had the sympathy of the British Labour Party and they would have the help of the party in their struggle. He condemned the actions in India of the National Government which he termed as a Tory Government. After giving support to Lansbury's resolution, Wedgwood Benn told the conference that he regretted the fact that the National Government had abandoned the Indian policy pursued by the Labour Government and stressed that if they could get the various sections in India together, and if they were willing to give them what they asked, then there would be peace. The resolution was carried.[24]

The Third Session of the Conference

A few weeks before the Labour Party annual conference was held, the British Government announced that soon there would be another round table conference in London. The Conference assembled on November 17, 1932, for its third and last session and continued till December 24. This Conference was smaller than the earlier conferences. Only forty-six delegates attended it, as against some 112 at the previous session. The British delegation consisted of twelve members. The Labour Party did not participate in the Conference. The party at its annual conference the month before resolved to abstain, reserving its comment until the joint committee stage.

It was attended by eight members of India Committee of the Cabinet, except that R.A. Butler, Hoare's under-secretary, replaced Runciman, and by four party representatives, Reading and Lothian, Peel and Winterton. The Indian delegation consisted only of Indian moderates, who had worked with the British committees in India. It comprised twelve representatives from the Indian States, and twenty-two from British India.[25] The only serious gap, at this session as at the first, was the gap left by the Congress.

The main business of this last session was a further consideration of the central organisation in the light of the reports of the Lothian, Percy and Davidson committees. As to the franchise, it was agreed that adult suffrage was impracticable at present, that the existing franchise should be extended and the principle of direct voting retained, and that provision should be made for the enfranchisement of a substantial proportion of women. It was also agreed that the elections to the federal upper chamber should be made by the provincial legislatures. As to the lower house, the balance of opinion, after some discussion favoured direct rather than indirect election. On the question of the distribution of powers between the centre and the provinces, the divergence between Hindu and Muslim opinion concerning the character of the federation was reflected in their disagreement about 'residuary powers', that is, the control of any subjects not expressly allocated to the centre or the provinces or to the concurrent jurisdiction of both. The Hindus wanted them to go to the centre, the Muslims to the provinces. To overcome this deadlock it was suggested, though no without dissent, that the Governor-General might be empowered to decide such cases as arose.[26]

As for reserve powers, the government insisted upon defence and external relations remaining with officials appointed by the Governor-General, who was ultimately responsible to the home government. Hoare noted privately that external relations could not be transferred 'within any measurable time'. Sapru and Jayakar pressed in vain for the defence minister to be an Indian.

With regard to finance, reservation was favoured by Hoare and the India Committee of Cabinet but it was contested successfully, arguing that unless finance were transferred there could be no effective responsibility in any department of state. However, it was accepted that a reserve bank should be established to control India's currency and exchange; and that the Governor-General, with a financial adviser, should have a special responsibility for the financial stability and credit of India. It was insisted only that delay in setting up the reserve bank should not be allowed to retard federation. The other special responsibilities assigned to the Governor-General (and the Governors) were for peace and tranquillity, the protection of the minorities and the rights of the states and services, and the prevention of commercial discrimination. The Governor-General was to intervene in only the law and order field of provincial administration, and then only to counter menaces to India's internal security.[27]

During the general discussion Sapru pleaded for the inclusion of an accession deadline into the bill for the Princes, because he was alarmed at the possibility of the states' failure to accede delaying federation indefinitely. In case a sufficient number of Princes did not join within one year a British Indian federation should be set up. Hoare argued that the nomination of a deadline might delay the early creation of a federation. On the question of safeguards, Hoare remarked, 'They are not intended to obstruct a real transfer of responsible power. They are rather ultimate controls that we hope will never need to be exercised for the greater reassurance of the world outside both in India itself and in Great Britain.'[28] Remarking on federation Winterton said that in his judgment in all recent political events in England and political policy there had never been a bigger conception or a greater ideal than that of all-India federation.[29]

The Conference ended without any high hopes. However, it put the aspirations of Indian nationalism to the test of practical politics and all the problems were dealt with exhaustively. Since the National Government was dominated by the Conservatives, the attitude was hardened under pressure from the extremist group. The majority of the Indian delegates disbelieved in the necessity of the safeguards but in spite of their dislike for them accepted them as *quid pro quo* which they were to concede as the price of responsible government.[30] The Conference cleared the way for the measured series of stages necessary to parliamentary legislation. The government would prepare a White Paper embodying its proposals. The paper would be presented to Parliament. A joint committee of both houses would, after hearing witnesses, report back to Parliament on the proposed legislation. Finally, a bill would be prepared and presented for Parliament's approval.

The Joint Select Committee Report

In March, 1933, the British Government came out with the White Paper containing the proposals of the government indicating the line on which the new constitution of India was to take shape. It was drafted in the light of the conclusions of the Round Table Conferences and the Statutory Commission Report. It provided for an all-India federation, provincial autonomy, responsibility and safeguards. It invited Parliament to appoint a Joint Select Committee with power to call into consultation representatives of Indian States and provinces to examine the proposals.

On a motion by the Secretary of State for India to appoint a Joint Select Committee to consider the White Paper proposals, the British Parliament debated for three days and expressed their views before they consented to the formation of a committee. Moving the resolution in the House of Commons Sir Samuel Hoare urged the members to take the Indian question out of party politics to safeguard both Indian and British interests.[31]

After the resolution was moved, the Labour Party attacked the government scheme. Attlee, while speaking on behalf of the Labourites, complained that the idea of Dominion Status had disappeared even as the ultimate goal, and that there was no provision for progressive advance to full responsible government. He said that the Labour Party believed that the new constitution should contain the principle laid down in the Gandhi-Irwin Pact, that such safeguards as were necessary should be in the interests of India, and 'we think they should be agreed on in co-operation with the leaders of Indian opinion'. Attlee stated that the new constitution should adopt the principle put forward by the Labour Government at the First Round Table Conference and repeated as their policy by the National Government at the Second Round Table Conference, that the reserved powers should not be such as to prejudice the advance of India through the new constitution to full responsibility for her own government. He said that the Labour Party had conviction that no settlement could be reached without the cooperation of all sections in India.

About the Joint Select Committee, Attlee maintained that his party would nominate representatives to serve on the committee and they would do their utmost to get their views discussed and incorporated in the committee's report. He accused Ramsay Mac-Donald of violating the spirit of cooperation that was the keynote of the Labour Government's Indian policy. Regarding the Third Round Table Conference, he complained that it contained a small number of unrepresentative Indian delegates lacking support of the Indian people. Attlee accused the Prime Minister of being a captive of the Conservative Party. He expressed doubt of getting full cooperation in India. He said that in the draft constitution it was proposed to start a limited amount of responsible government and it was hedged about by safeguards.[32]

Attlee further maintained that there was no suggestion that the powers of the Governor-General would be relaxed at any time. The Labour leader complained that there was no indication when the Indian Army would be Indianised and the financial safeguards would be relaxed. Adoption of dyarchical system at the central government level was also criticised and Attlee said that the system of dyarchy was the most unfortunate one. Other criticisms of the Labourite centred around the vagueness of the requirements imposed on States for joining the federation; the granting of equal powers to both houses of the federal legislature; the limited franchise given to women; and the over-representation given to special economic groups. Although some proposals of the White Paper were criticised by the Labour leader, he acknowledged that there were also things of value in it; such as, the conception of federation, the freedom of the provinces from the centre.[33]

Baldwin, the leader of the Conservative Party, pointed out in the debates that improvement in Indian situation and a cessation of civil disobedience were largely due to the firm policy of the government and progress made in constitutional reforms. He admitted that there were difficulties in the course, but he was convinced that there were infinitely greater difficulties if they did not take that step. Hence he supported the proposals.[34] After considering the different viewpoints, the House of Commons adopted the government's resolution by a vote of 449 against 43. A similar motion passed by the House of Lords, and a 32-member Joint Select Committee, composed of sixteen members from each House, was created. The Labour Party had only four appointments to the Committee, the Liberals three, and the remaining were government supporters. The Labour members were C.R. Attlee, Lord Snell, Morgan Jones and F. Seymour Cocks.[35]

The Joint Select Committee held 159 meetings and 120 witnesses were examined during the course of its eighteen months' session. The Committee reported to Parliament on November 22, 1934. In the Joint Committee, the report had been carried by nineteen votes to nine, the minority being made up of five diehards who thought it went too far, and four Labour members who did not think that it went far enough.[36]

The Joint Select Committee Report, in general, approved the White Paper proposals. The main recommendations of the Committee were : an all-India federation of eleven self-governing provinces linked with the States (which would enter the federation voluntarily). Burma to be separated from India. Defence and external affairs would remain the responsibility of the Governor-General. In other matters, both at the federal centre and in the provinces, ministers would be responsible to the legislatures. The powers of the provincial governments would include law and order. The Governor-General and the provincial Governors would be guided by the advice of their ministers, so long as this did not conflict with certain special responsibilities. These responsibilities would include 'the prevention of grave menace to peace and tranquillity', the safeguarding of minorities, and (in the case of the Governor-General) the safeguarding of 'financial stability and credit'.[37]

A draft report known as 'Attlee Draft', was also prepared for the Joint Select Committee by the Labour Party members. The conclusions made in the report put forward the same arguments made by the Labour Party members in the debates in Commons when the Secretary of State for India proposed for the establishment of the Joint Select Committee. The Attlee Draft emphatically stated that real responsibility should be conceded at the centre. It said that it was the desire of the Labourites that Indian nationalism should find its full expression within the constitution, and they thought that it was only possible if real responsibility was given at the centre as well as in the provinces. The Draft stressed that the new constitution should state beyond all cavil that it was the intention of England to grant full Dominion Status to India within a measurable period of years.[35]

The Labourites, in the Draft, advocated for a single chamber. They said that their objections to second chamber in the provinces applied also to the centre. It was suggested in the White Paper that there should be two chambers of equal power and of very similar composition, and that in the event of differences between the two houses, the device of a joint session should be employed. The Labourites argued that, in effect, it made the central legislature a single chamber, meeting for certain purposes in two sections, and made an unnecessary duplication of representation which resulted in an unwieldy body of legislatures. They opposed the limited franchise and desired provisions to be written into the plan so that ultimately universal suffrage would be attained.

The Draft said that the Labourites found no reason why India should not have as full a control over her external affairs as any other Dominion. It further said that they did not think it necessary that the Governor-General should have a special responsibility for safeguarding the financial stability and credit of the federation. The Labour members pointed out that it was useless to give power and responsibility with one hand and take that away with the other. 'If Indian representatives are not capable of conducting on sound lines the finances of the federation, they are not capable of self-government,' the Draft said. Regarding defence the Draft agreed that it must for some years be a reserved department and accepted the proposal that the Governor-General should exercise his functions through a counsellor. The Labourites considered that there should be a definite programme of Indianization with a time-limit of thirty years.

The Draft, in principle, agreed to the communal representation as a temporary measure. Further, it said that there was a necessity that special representation should be given to those classes of the community whose poverty rendered them most vulnerable to exploitation. The Labourites approved of the reservation of seats for the depressed classes which might have to be continued for many years. They believed that the power of intervention of the Governors and the Governer-General should be essentially for use in emergency and in future they would tend to rely more on their powers of persuasion and advice than on the putting into force of an actual exercise of their will. The Draft accepted the principle of federation and preferred to see the federation fully representative of all-India from the start, but the entry of the States should not be made a condition of the establishment of responsible government at the centre. All proposals put forward by the Labour Party members were voted down in the Joint Select Committee.[39]

While the Joint Select Committee Report did not substantially differ from the proposals in the White Paper, it contained one important change. For direct election upon a limited franchise for the central assembly, it substituted indirect election by the provincial chambers. On December 12, 1934, a motion that a bill should be submitted to Parliament on the lines of the Committee's report was carried in the Commons by 491 votes to 49 and in the Lords by 239 votes to 62 and on December 19 the bill (known as Government of India Bill) was introduced. The debates on it lasted for forty-three days in the House of Commons and for thirteen days in the House of Lords. The second and third readings were carried in Commons by 404 votes to 133 and 386 to 122, and in Lords by 236 votes to 55 and without a division. On August 2, 1935, the Bill received the royal assent.[40]

Parliamentary Debates on the Government of India Bill, 1934

The Labour Party's amendments, like the amendments which the party proposed to the 1919 constitution, were all rejected. However, the Labour Party made a better parliamentary showing because the Churchillians, at times, were allied with the Labourites in protest against the provisions of the Government of India Bill. It should be mentioned, however, that the alliance was temporary and for diametrically opposite reasons. The right wing of the Conservative Party wanted more restrictions, and the left wing Labourites desired liberalization of the government's proposals.[41]

The amendments of the Labour Party, mainly, centred on three major historic principles of Dominion Status for India, of the protection of the interests of the common man, and of the development of a constitution by the Indians. The Labour Party's criticism of the India bill began at the second reading. Attlee moved an amendment in the name of the leader of the opposition Labour Party which said :

No legislation for the better government of India will be satisfactory which does not secure the good-will and cooperation of the Indian people by recognising explicitly India's right to Dominion Status by providing within it the means of its attainment, and which does not by its provisions as to franchise and representation secure to the workers and peasants of India the possibility of achieving by constitutional means their social and economic emancipation.[42]

In his speech, after the amendment was moved, Attlee said that it was not merely a matter of saying in a Preamble that Dominion Status was the goal. He said that Dominion Status meant the recognition of the right of India to that status and an admission that the Indians had the right to deal with their own constitutional affairs. He pointed out that there was nowhere any recognition of the right of the Indian people to self-government and stressed the fact that no constitution could possibly be worked which was not accepted by Indians.[43]

The Labourites stated that the keynote of the Government of India Bill was mistrust. They lamented that India would not have control of her foreign affairs and of her finances; the legislature was to be overloaded with Conservative interests, landlords, commerce, and second chambers were to be set up with the wealthy and the privileged. Besides, the Labourites deplored that the Princes had the right to refuse to accept the federal system, but the Indian representatives had no option. The Labour party suggested that there should be a time limit with regard to Indianization. They urged that the weakest members of the community, the workers, the women, the depressed classes should be given political power.[44]

Gordon MacDonald while speaking in the Commons warned that the Indian masses were not a set of people to be used as pawns in the political game and said one of the reasons for his party's objection to the Bill was that the provisions of the franchise and representation did not enable the worker to secure his own emancipation.[45] David Grenfell maintained that India could not establish constitutions for self-government unless she knew that in the constitution she was permitted to stand on terms of equality and to work for the attainment of equality of status. He emphasised that a considered declaration on the question of status would enable the government to overcome the suspicion of India. Continuing, he said that the Indians had declared against the Bill in its present form and insisted that the British Government should consult with them, and endeavour to make the Bill acceptable. He said that one of the grave defects of the machinery of government in that Bill was that it was not sufficiently representative. Finally, Grenfell expressed the view that it was not likely that the Indians would tolerate a franchise where only an insignificant percentage of the people vote for the federal legislature, and only a minority for the provincial legislatures.[46]

Colonel Wedgwood objected to the Bill arguing that it put the Indian people under the control of non-representative Princes of India. He did attach great importance to the question of the finality of the scheme. 'If this Bill becomes an Act any words about Dominion Status in the Preamble would be meaningless, for we have to realize that this Bill, when we pass it, is the Act,' he said. Wedgwood was against the system of communal representation in India.[47] He deplored the fact that the British Government was imposing the constitution on Indians and by imposing that scheme they could continue to rule India behind the shelter of the people who stood to benefit by the scheme.[48]

The Labourites maintained that foreign affairs should be under the control of a responsible minister rather than under the Governor-General and they also objected to the clause about the Governor-General's control of the military or defence. While the Labour Party agreed, in principle, that defence had to remain under the control of the Governor-General, it demanded a definite date set for the transfer of all control over the military to the Indians.[49] About the second chamber Attlee said that the Labour Party stood for its abolition. He maintained that the arrangements at the centre were such as to make it certain that the live political movement in India would never get effective representation at the centre and argued that whether it was direct or indirect election did not affect the matter, because in every case they were to be kept in check all the time by the second chamber—a second chamber with equal power, and which was to meet the first chamber in joint meeting in the event of any dispute.[50] Wedgwood in his argument about the abolition of the second chamber observed that the work to be done would be so small that the composition of the lower and the upper chamber would be very largely decorative and nothing else.[51]

On the third reading of the Government of India Bill in Commons Morgan Jones of the Labour Party said that instead of permitting the Princes to join the federation without prejudicing the future progress of British India, the government proceeded to safeguard the Princes—to make British India join the federation without prejudicing the Princes. He deplored that the Princes would come into the federation on their own terms, and the terms were to be stated through the medium of an instrument called the Instrument of Accession. It was impossible, and it would be impossible for any future government, to permit any constitutional change to take place in India except with the assent of the Princes thereto, because, Jones pointed out that the moment any change of a constitutional kind took place, every Prince would be entitled to say, 'I never entered the federation on those terms, and I am absolved, therefore, from the Instrument under which I came in.' The second point of Jones' indictment was the under-representation of the workers of India. He told the Commons that even in their country, the workers were not able to protect themselves adequately until they had political power, and they would not in India either, until they had a larger measure of representation in the instruments of constitutional authority in the land. Thirdly, he maintained that the Labour Party deplored the inadequate share of control of the Indian people over the problem of finance. He said that the safeguards in the hands of the Governor-General and of the Governor were a little too sweeping. He criticised the powers of the Governor-General and said that he had the power to stop a bill from being introduced, the power to stop it in its passage, and the power to withhold his consent when it was passed.[52]

During the debates on the third reading of the Bill, the Labour Party leader C.R. Attlee objected to it by saying that the Government of India Bill was deliberately framed to exclude as far as possible the Congress Party from effective powers in the new constitution. He explained that it was done at the centre by giving an undue weight to the Princes, and he pointed to the fact that they were represented as a conservative element to keep left wing elements in check. 'It has been done by the creation of a reactionary and unrepresentative Council of State at the centre and by the creation of reactionary second chambers in the provinces, and also in the formation of the British side of the assembly by the methods which set a premium on communalism,' he complained. Another accusation made by Attlee was that the government had yielded time after time to the States and also to minority communities, but had always stood strongly against any yielding to Congress or the nationalists. The Labour leader stressed the need for making a stronger provision in the Bill for the transference of the reserved subjects, and particularly of defence. He observed that in all federations there was a possibility of separatist tendencies and in a great continent like India it was a great danger, and where the centre was ineffective, where it did not really provide a field for the national forces to work, there might be a gradual breaking up. He stated that the other great danger was communalism. Attlee said that the special representation given to vested interests and the creation of second chambers meant that the economic life would be ineffective and the tendency would be right the way through to get divisions on mere communal lines. Finally, the Labour leader remarked that instead of the Bill being received with joy in India it would be received grudgingly and worked in that spirit.[53]

In closing the Labour Party's attack on the Bill the leader of the Party, George Lansbury, said that the policy of the party, since the first Labour Government, had been that the Indians themselves should determine the type of constitution that they wanted. He said:

We do not believe that you can settle the Indian question by imposing on Indians a constitution without consultation with them and without their consent. We understand self-determination to mean that whatever constitution they live under is one which they accept.[54]

In the House of Lords, the Labour Party Peers raised similar objections but they failed to alter the government's proposals. The Bill passed through the House of Lords without the adoption of any of the Labour Party's amendments. In a broadcast Lansbury commented on the Bill by saying: 'Autocracy veiled by a facade of make-believe democracy is the best description of this scheme.'[55]

The Act of 1935

The Government of India Bill received the royal assent in August 1935, after the second and third readings were carried in both Houses of Parliament. It became known as the Government of India Act, 1935. Provincial elections were held in India in 1936, and the provincial clauses of the Act of 1935 were put into effect the following year. Since the rulers of the States never gave their consent, the federation envisaged by the Act of 1935 never came into being. The main provisions of the Government of India Act of 1935 were as follows:

Two new provinces—Sindh and Orissa—were created, and together with the North-West Frontier Province, they were placed on an equal footing with the older provinces. The number of povinces in India now became eleven; Burma ceased to be a part of India. In the provinces dyarchy was abolished and they gained virtually complete autonomy. They acquired a separate legal personality and were now substantially liberated from the superintendence, direction and control of the Government of India and the Secretary of State in London.

The executive authority of a province was vested in the Governor as the representative of the Crown. He was provided with a council of ministers to aid and advise him in the discharge of the functions conferred on him by the Act. These functions included almost the entire sphere of provincial government, except in matters like law and order for which he had a special responsibility and for which he could act at his own discretion. All departments of provincial administration were now to be controlled by ministers responsible to their legislatures. The Governors were to accept their ministers' advice in all matters except those in which they had 'special responsibilities', for example, the prevention of any grave menace to the peace and tranquility of the province and the safeguarding of the legitimate interests of the minorities. In case it became impossible to carry on the government of a province in accordance with the provisions of the Act, the Governor could assume control of the whole administration of the province at his discretion for a specified period. The Governor was also invested with some extraordinary powers. The special powers of the Governor were regarded as serious limitations on real responsible government in India.

Provincial legislatures consisted of one or two chambers.*

*Madras, Bombay, Bengal, the United Provinces, Bihar, and Assam had each two chambers, known as the legislative council and the legislative assembly. Punjab, the Central Provinces, the North-West Frontier Province, Sindh and Orissa had only one chamber, known as the legislative assembly. The strength of the legislative assembly or the lower chamber varied from 50 to 250 members, almost all of whom were elected.

Representation in the legislatures was arranged in accordance with the 'communal award' as modified by the Poona Pact. Special electorates were retained and certain seats were reserved for the scheduled castes. About ten per cent of the population of India— roughly thirty million—was enfranchised.

The federal proposals of the Government of India Act, 1935, may be summarized as follows:

The federation of India could only come into operation when an address to the Crown by Parliament would ask for a proclamation to that effect, and the proclamation could not be issued until a sufficient number of States (1) to occupy 52 of the 104 seats allotted to the States in the upper house of the federal legislature and (2) to make up half the total population of all the States had acceded to the federation.

The federal legislature was to be bicameral. The Council of State, or the federal upper house, was to consist of 156 representatives of British India and not more than 104 of the States. It was not to be subject to dissolution. The States' representatives were to be appointed by their rulers, the smaller States being grouped together as units for electoral purposes. Six of the British Indian representatives were to be nominated by the Governor-General. Of the remaining 150 seats all but ten were distributed among the provinces mainly on a population basis. The other ten seats were given to the Anglo-Indian, European and Indian Christian communities in British India as a whole. In the second place, the seats were allocated, as in the provincial legislatures, to separate communal electorates. The General, Muslim and Sikh seats were to be filled by direct election by members of those communities in territorial constituencies. The representatives of the Depressed Classes, Indian Christians, Anglo-Indians and Europeans were to be elected by the members of those communities who were members of the provincial legislative councils or assemblies. The provincial legislature as a whole was to elect to the seats reserved for women in any province.

The federal assembly which was to be elected every five years, if not dissolved earlier, was to consist of 250 representatives of British India and not more than 125 of the States. The distribution of seats allotted to the States was based mainly on population. Comparatively few of the States were to be represented individually.

In most cases there was to be one representative for a group of States. The British Indian seats were allocated on the same principles as those in the upper house, but in the federal assembly the General, Muslim and Sikh seats, numbering together 193, were to be filled by indirect election, namely, by the members of those communities who were members of the provincial legislative assemblies on the principle of proportional representation with the single transferable vote. The Indian Christian, Anglo-Indian and European representatives and the women were to be elected by members of those classes in the provincial assemblies. The representatives of the Scheduled Castes were to be elected by the holders of the General seats in the assemblies from candidates previously elected by Scheduled Caste voters only.

The Governor-General was to have a council of ministers of not more than ten. He was charged with special responsibilities. The Governor-General was required to act in his discretion, not only like the Governors in such matters as the appointment of ministers and the summoning of the legislature, but also as regards defence, external affairs, and ecclesiastical affairs. He was empowered to appoint a financial adviser who was to be responsible to him and was to assist him in the discharge of the special responsibility for safeguarding the financial stability and credit of the federal government. Finance in general was, however, to be entrusted to a finance minister, responsible to the legislature.

As to the civil service, the Secretary of State was to recruit, control and secure the rights of the Indian Civil Service.

The Act of 1935 was to re-establish the high courts in the provinces, and create a new federal court.

Lastly, the Secretary of State's Council in London was to be abolished and he was to be provided in its place with a body of advisers, not less than three and not more than six. The India Office remained, but its cost was to be charged to the British revenues.

In India, the Congress found the whole scheme objectionable as a denial both of India's right to immediate independence and of the principles of democracy. It was opposed to the proposed federal scheme because (according to the Congress) vital functions of the government were excluded from the sphere of responsibility. With defence and external affairs as reserved subjects, added to the special responsibilities and the veto power of the Governor-General, there remained no responsibility at the centre. The Congress found nothing to choose between the centre and the provinces. In the federal structure, there was a juxtaposition of the nominees of the autocratic Princes of the Indian States and the democratically elected representatives of the people of British India. The Congress declared that 'no constitution which curtails the sovereignty of the people of India and does not recognise their right to shape and control fully their political and economic future can be accepted.'[56] The Congress also pointed out that a constitution acceptable to it must be 'based on the independence of India as a nation and it can only be framed by a constituent assembly elected on adult franchise.'[57]

Although the unity of the Labour Party was disrupted when Ramsay MacDonald formed the National Government in August 1931, the party continued its fight for Dominion Status for India. After the Second Round Table Conference, the National Government, which was indeed a Conservative-dominated government, embarked upon a policy of repression in India. The Labour Party severely criticised this in Parliament. The Party did not even participate in the Third Round Table Conference, which was also boycotted by the Indian National Congress. The non-participation of the Labour Party in the Third Conference was a clear demonstration of their sympathy with the Congress movement.

The Labour Party did nominate four members to the Joint Select Committee and also prepared Draft proposals stressing that real responsibility should be conceded to the centre. Their Draft also emphasised that the new constitution should state clearly that it was the intention of Britain to grant full Dominion Status to India within a 'measurable period of years'. All the proposals of the Labour Party members that were put before the Committee were voted down. Although their proposals were made in answer to the Indian demands, the Labour Party representatives did not mention that India should be granted Dominion Status immediately; instead they said that she should attain Dominion Status within a 'measurable period of years'. This implied that India was not yet fit for Dominion Status. Indian nationalists certainly did not expect such an opinion from a Labour Party sympathetic to the Indian causes.

The Joint Committee Report was later discussed in Parliament, where the Labour Party tried to amend some provisions of the Government of India Bill without success, because the Party was a minority in Parliament. The Bill was ultimately passed with a large majority and became known as the Act of 1935.

NOTES

1. W. Gillies Papers, WG/INC/ 1931, Letter from Sapru to Lansbury, Labour Party Archive.
2. I.A.R,, vol. 2, 1932, p. 25.
3. T. Chand, vol. 4, op. cit., p. 179.
4. H.C. Deb., vol. 262, 1932, cc. 809-823.
5. ibid,, cc. 830-834.
6. ibid,, cc. 835-837.
7. ibid., cc. 840-845.
8. ibid., c. 901.
9. H.C. Deb., vol. 263, 1932, c. 1220.
10. ibid., cc. 1212-3.
11. ibid., c. 1226-1236.
12. H.C. Deb., vol. 265, 1932, cc. 716-727.
13. H.C. Deb., vol. 267, 1932, cc. 1488-1498.
14. ibid., cc. 1499-1502.
15. ibid., c. 1515.
16. ibid.
17. ibid. cc. 1589-1590.
18. ibid., c. 1604.
19. W. Gillies Papers, L.P. No. 103A. June, 1932, Labour Party Archive.
20. M. Gwyer and A. Appadorai, vol. 1, op. cit., p. 260.
21. Templewood, op. cit., pp. 61-2.
22. L.P. Report, 1932, p. 95.
23. ibid., p. 178.
24. ibid., pp. 180-1.
25. Indian Round Table Conference, Third Session, 17 November—24 December, 1932, Command Paper 4238.
26. R. Coupland, op. cit., p. 129.
27. R.J. Moore, op. cit., pp. 287-8.
28. Command Paper, 4238, 1932, p. 142.
29. ibid., p. 109.
30. *The Times*, January 17, 1933.
31. H.C. Deb., vol. 276, 1933, c. 695 *et seq.*
32. H.C. Deb., vol. 276, 1933, cc. 719-722.
33. ibid., c. 732.
34. ibid., c. 1131 *et seq.*
35. G. Milton Ochs, op. cit., pp. 208-9.

36. Viscount Templewood, op. cit., p. 99.
37. Report of the Joint Select Committee, House of Commons Sessional Papers, 1933-1934, VIII (5). *passim.*
38. Joint Committee on Indian Constitutional Reform, vol. 1, Part 2, 1934, pp. 255-61.
39. ibid., pp. 258-9, 262-274.
40. R. Coupland, op. cit., p. 133.
41. G Milton Ochs, op. cit., p. 215.
42. H.C. Deb., vol. 297, 1935, c. 1167.
43. ibid., cc. 1168-9.
44. ibid., cc. 1169-1173.
45. ibid., c. 1220.
46. ibid., cc. 1326-1328.
47. ibid., cc. 1675-1683.
48. H.C. Deb., vol. 298, 1935, c. 289.
49. ibid., c. 1417.
50. ibid., cc. 1965-1966.
51. ibid., cc. 1969-1970.
52. ibid., cc. 1723-1732.
53. ibid., cc. 1823-1828.
54. ibid., cc. 1996-7.
55. George Lansbury Collection, Broadcast by Lansbury, February, 1 1935, vol. 24, III K, folio K 694, London School of Economics and Political Science Library.
56. Congress Resolution, 12 April 1936, cited in R.S. Gautam, op. cit., p. 92.
57. ibid p. 93.

CHAPTER 6

India before the Second World War, 1935-39

During the years 1935-1939, the Labour Party was unable to advance the cause of Indian constitutional reform in Parliament. This lack of success should be attributed to Labour's weakened position and to the complex international problems that increasingly disturbed England. Even if the Labour Party was inclined to give India responsible self-rule, its strength with only 154 seats in parliament could not challenge the National Government, which was in reality a Conservative Government.

In the 1935 British elections India was not a prominent political issue, even though the Labour Party had pledged itself to further constitutional reform in its annual conference held in October 1935. The Labour Party passed a policy resolution in that conference which committed the party to continue its fight for self-determination and self-government for India.

In India, after the passage of the Act of 1935, elections for provincial legislatures were held in 1937 and the Congress Party won a notable victory. Later, with regard to the acceptance of office by the Congress, there arose a constitutional deadlock. The All-India Congress Committee, despite the determined opposition of its small left wing, permitted their members to form ministries provided that the leader of the Congress Party in the legislature was able to state publicly that the Governor would not use his special powers of interference or over-rule the advice of ministers in the course of their constitutional activities. In June 1937, the Governor-General, Lord Linlithgow, made a public statement which was regarded by the Congress as satisfactory on this point. They then formed the ministries in six provinces. Later, in 1937-38 Congress was able to form ministries in two other provinces.

When the Indian constitutional deadlock came up for discussion in Parliament, the Labour Party suggested that the Governor-

General reassure the Indians by making a general statement along the lines suggested by Gandhi. The Labour Party expressed the hope that the Indians would work the 1935 constitution.

The Act of 1935 was bitterly opposed by all sections of Indian opinion. The operation of the part of the Act concerned with the central government depended on the fulfilment of the pre-condition that a sufficient number of Indian States would accede to the federation. Federation as such was not opposed and it was generally recognized that a federal structure was desirable for India, but the proposed federation petrified British rule and vested interests in India. The apparent enthusiasm which some of the Indian princely States had shown for the idea of a federation in the early stages of the Round Table Conference had cooled off by the time the Act of 1935 came to be enacted. The Government of India, under the viceroyalties of Willingdon and Linlithgow, showed neither urgency nor firmness in dealing with the States. The negotiations dragged on leisurely for years until the Second World War broke out in September 1939 and the federation was shelved.

Working of the 1935 Act
Indian nationalists had consistently agitated for a constituent assembly to frame their own constitution. Hoping to satisfy some of the demands of Indian nationalists, British Government passed the Act of 1935, but they were not satisfied with the pace of advance. While the Congress 'rejected' the Act and resolved not to submit to the constitution or to cooperate with, but to combat it, both inside and outside the legislature, so as to end it, there was an influential section within the Congress which felt that the provincial portion of the Act should be permitted to function. Both the right and the left in the Congress were agreed on the desirability of contesting the elections for the provincial legislatures, but they were divided on the question of acceptance of office. The Congress, at its Faizpur session in December 1936, accordingly, decided to contest the elections to the provincial legislatures due early in 1937, but postponed decision on the controversial issue of 'acceptance of office' till after the elections.[1] In his presidential address to the Congress in that session, Jawaharlal Nehru mentioned that the Congress clarified its position in the election manifesto and declared that 'we are not going to the legislatures to cooperate in any way

with the Act but to combat it. That limits the field of our decision in regard to offices, and those who incline to acceptance of them must demonstrate that this is the way to non-cooperate with the Act, and to end it.'[2] The Congress decided to pursue simultaneously a dual policy: to carry on the struggle for independence and at the same time to carrry through the legislatures constructive measures of reform.[3]

In England, in the general elections of November 1935, the National Government and its supporters won 427 seats and the Labour party got 154 seats. The Liberal Party was reduced to a mere seventeen seats.[4] Although the government was designated as 'national' it was essentially a Conservative Government headed by Stanley Baldwin. A month before the election, the Labour Party in its annual conference in Brighton vowed to further Indian constitutional reform. The party in its resolution deplored the Indian policy of the National Government, both legislative and administrative, and maintained that it was neither a solution of the Indian problem nor it made any contribution in that direction. The Labour Party further resolved:

To stand by the policy of self-determination and self-government, and, whether in power or in opposition, to demand that the freely elected representatives of the Indian people shall formulate a settlement of the problems of India, in the interests of the Indian masses.[5]

After the resolution was moved by Betty Fraser of the London University Labour Party, she criticised the Attlee Draft which advocated the same principle of veto and remarked that it was inconsistent with the Labour Party policy. She stressed that a constituent assembly should be set up in India to give to the people the machinery by which they could have an immediate election, and after that it would be their job to rule their country in their own way. Later, speaking in the conference, Attlee said that Parliamentary Labour Party fought the Government of India Bill fought their methods and advocated the party's policy. 'When it came to the point of considering specific proposals,' Attlee intimated, then we had to take out part in them and we did, both in Committee and on the floor of the House of Commons.' He claimed that they objected to the government's policy and to their proposals, but in

Commons the Labour Party had also to consider other proposals as well and to try to modify those with which they did not agree.[6]

Even if the Labour Party was inclined to give India responsible self-rule, its strength in Parliament was not sufficient to challenge the government. What is significant is that the 1935 election was the last held in the United Kingdom until the termination of the War in Europe in May 1945, and that for the next decade the Labour Party remained a weak minority. During the period 1935-1939, before the outbreak of the Second World War, there was very little parliamentary debate on India. It is not clear whether this was due to members' preoccupation with more urgent problems like the abdication crisis and the events leading to the War, or to the feeling of self-satisfaction that having introduced a new constitution, they hoped that Indians would make the most of it.

After 1935 the British public had become absorbed in the pressing international problems and they were relatively unconcerned with India. Sir Samuel Hoare whose management of Indian affairs had raised him in public estimation was entrusted with the more important portfolio of Foreign Secretary and Marquess of Zetland (Lord Ronaldshay) took his place at the India Office, in June 1935. Soon after, Willingdon retired, and Linlithgow was installed as Viceroy of India on April 18, 1936.[7] The new Viceroy was instructed by the Home Government to take the initiative in effecting the constitutional changes under the Act of 1935. The Government of India started negotiations with the Princes for their acceptance of the federal scheme, which alone would have made it possible for the inauguration of the federation. In spite of the various sorts of special considerations given to the States for persuading them to enter the federation, they failed in the end to accept the conditions of union.

In the elections for provincial legislatures held early in 1937 under the Act of 1935, the Congress Party had an absolute majority in five provinces—Orissa, Bihar, Madras, Central Provinces and United Provinces; it was the largest single party in Bengal, Bombay, North-West Frontier Province.[8] Such an overwhelming election success was unprecedented in the history of the Congress. The election immediately raised the problem of acceptance of office. The Congress leadership was divided on the issue. Jawaharlal

Nehru was against the acceptance of office, but he was in a minority both among the members of the Congress Working Committee and the All-India Congress Committee who regarded acceptance of office as the inevitable corollary of participation in the elections. The consequence was that the All-India Congress Committee which met at Delhi on March 17 and 18, 1937, permitted the acceptance of office in provinces where the Congress commanded a majority in the legislatures, 'provided...the leader of the Congress Party in the legislature is satisfied and is able to state publicly that the Governor will not use his special power of inter-ference and set aside the advice of ministers in regard to constitutional activities.'[9] The demand created a deadlock, for it raised the question whether it could be met without amendment of the law of the constitution. The Governors regretted that 'it was impossible for the Governors to give any assurances as regards the use of the powers vested in them under the Act.'[10]

Constitutional Deadlock

The question of Indian constitutional impasse, created by the Congress Party's decision not to join the provincial cabinets, came up for discussion in British Parliament after the provincial autonomy came into force on April 1, 1937. The Marquess of Zetland, Conservative Secretary of State for India, made a formal statement in the House of Lords on April 8, 1937, in which he said : '. . . it seems to be desirable that I should make it clear beyond all possibility of doubt that the demand made to the Governors was one which, without an amendment of the constitution, they could not possibly have accepted.' He further maintained that the reserve powers were an integral part of the constitution, that they could not be abrogated except by Parliament itself, and that the Governors therefore could not treat the Congress as a privileged body which was exempt from the provisions of the constitution by which all other parties were bound. The Secretary of State, in conclusion, stated that the constitution would be administered in a spirit of cordial cooperation and sympathetic understanding of the position of ministers.[11]

Lord Snell, speaking on behalf of the Labour Party, maintained that he agreed that the Governors could not swear away their responsibilities under the constitution and he could not feel that such a constitution be inaugurated by a process of political manoeuvre. But, whilst he believed that even a Governor must be treated fairly, he also wanted to treat fairly the Indian people and to recognise the difficulties that they had. He stressed that those difficulties must be surmounted in some way. "Merely to say to the Indian people 'Here is the constitution ; take it or leave it' will not help us to bridge the gulf that has arisen," he opined. Lord Snell further pointed out that the Indians were confessedly disappointed with the Act while they hoped that it would give them so much more than it actually did give them. He always believed that if the government had been bold enough to say frankly and openly that at the end of all that at some time it would mean full Dominion Status, the Indian people would have taken that and been satisfied. He deplored that the government did very little to reassure them, and the present attitude of the Indian people towards that constitution was the measure of their distrust. Lord Snell suggested that the Viceroy could allay some of the fears of the Indian people and remove their misapprehension by giving a kind of general assurance. By general assurance he meant the following viewpoints mentioned in the Minority Report of the Labour Party :

The success of the provincial governments will be shown just insofar as such a power does not have to be exercised, and we consider that powers given to the Governor must be adequate, but in our view they should essentially be emergency powers to be used only where a breakdown threatens, and not to be part of the ordinary operation of government.

Lord Snell maintained that an assurance of that kind, if it were conveyed to the Indian people, would be helpful at the present time. Finally, he urged the Indians to work the 'constitution for what it is worth.'[12]

It should be mentioned here that Mahatma Gandhi issued a Press statement on March 30, 1937, in which he categorically said that it would be distinctly discourteous if the Governors interfered with their ministers in matters over which the law gave the latter full control and with which Governors were under no legal obligation to interfere.[13] R.A. Butler, the Under-Secretary of State for India, in his reply in the House of Commons to the question asked by Attlee about the position in India, referred to Gandhi's Press statement and said that it had been the cause of much confusion both in England and India. The Under-Secretary expressed the hope that the representatives of the Congress Party would reconsider their refusal to assume the responsibilities which their constituents had imposed upon them. Butler reiterated that the Congress representatives could depend upon the most cordial co-operation and support from the Governors.[14]

Months passed as the controversy continued. On May 6, 1937, Lord Snell, again speaking for the Labour Party in the House of Lords, suggested that the most immediate need was to give to the Indian people an assurance that their wishes and their work would not be continuously thwarted either by the Government of India or in the India Office. In the same breath he also appealed to the leaders of the Indian people to try out that great experiment and not to lead the Indians into a mere wilderness of barren negation.[15]

The Secretary of State for India, Marquess of Zetland, in his remarks in the same debate, stated that the essence of the new constitution was that the initiative and the responsibility for the whole of the government of a province, though in form certainly vesting in the Governor, pass to the ministry the moment the ministry took office. He said that it would be the Governor's duty to help his ministers in every way by his political knowledge and his administrative experience. He further expressed that the reserved powers, of which the Congress made so much, would not normally be in operation at all. Zetland said that they could only come into the picture if the Governor considered that the carefully limited special responsibilities laid upon him by the Instrument of Instructions which Parliament approved, became involved.[16]

Though it was generally admitted that Lord Zetland clarified the constitutional aspects of the situation, the main criticism of his speech was that it went too far in upholding the constitutional position but did not go far enough in suggesting how this particular constitutional controversy was to be solved. Gandhi suggested that a tribunal should be created to decide the competence of the Governors to give the assurance for the use of their special powers. He took exception to Zetland's remark that the Congress could not be treated as a privileged body and said that he would prefer an honourable deadlock to dishonourable daily scenes between the Congress and the Governors.[17]   Lord Lothian, who was directly concerned with the framing of the Act of 1935, said in two articles published in *The Times* as well as in a speech in the House of Lords, that the Governor could not give the pledge asked for by the Congress, and suggested that safeguards would in practice be controlled by public opinion. He further added that if a Governor's decision differed from his ministers', that depended upon whether they could command the support of the electorate. If they could, the Governor would not precipitate a constitutional crisis of which there would be no solution save the suspension of the normal functioning of the constitution.   Lothian thought that the real key to a solution lay in the recognition that under the system of a responsible government the ultimate decision against abuse of power came to rest with the electorate.[18]

Some of the Congress leaders including Jawaharlal Nehru, accepted the interpretation of Lothian and the Congress modified its demand to the effect that if a Governor differed, he must ask the ministers to resign or dismiss them.   Zetland in another debate in the House of Lords expressed that he did not think it would be either wise or in accordance with the intentions of Parliament to lay down that in these circumstances the Governor must necessarily call for the resignation of his ministers. He observed if that had been the intention of Parliament, it would have said so in the Act itself.   Zetland referred in this respect to the last section of the Act of 1935 which defined the Governor's position insofar as his special responsibilities were concerned.   It said : 'If and insofar as any special responsibility of the Governor is involved, he shall, in the exercise of his functions, exercise his individual judgment as to the action to be taken.'[19]   Zetland maintained that the Governor could always dismiss his ministers and, equally, the ministers could always resign ; but it would be better to leave it both to the Governor to decide whether he desired to dismiss his ministers and to the ministers to decide whether they desired to resign, until the case arose.[20]

On June 14, 1937, George Lansbury of the Labour Party lent his support in the House of Commons to the stand taken by Gandhi who, according to Lansbury, had given a definite lead to clarify the position. He quoted Gandhi and said that the Congress was eager to accept office but 'only if the government show their willingness to conciliate'. He expressed his surprise that the small difference of resignation by the minister or dismissal by the Governor could not be removed and formation of majority ministries might not be facilitated. He urged that the Viceroy should be advised to call the leaders of the majority party into consultation in order to bridge the gulf between them. The Labour leader argued that the Congress did not give way because there was a tremendous feeling of distrust among Indian politicians. Finally, Lansbury said that he had always hoped that the Act would work, even though he thoroughly disagreed with and voted against it. 'I hope that the government will help men like Mr Gandhi and others who want the Act tried out, and will take the necessary means for helping them to carry the rest of the Congress Party,' he concluded.[21]

When it was stated in Parliament that the Governors could not give the assurance without amending the Act, the Congress Working Committee between April 26 and 29, considered this matter and passed a resolution that the Congress had not contemplated any amendment of the Act nor was such an amendment necessary for giving the assurance demanded. The resolution further said that the pronouncements of the policy of the British Government made by Lord Zetland and Butler were utterly inadequate to meet the requirements of the Congress.[22]

A ray of hope appeared when Lord Linlithgow, the Viceroy, said on June 21, 1937, that the three months' experience of the operation of the constitution had conclusively shown that assurances from the Governors were not essential to the smooth and harmonious working of the constitution. Besides, he stressed that there was no foundation for any suggestion that a Governor was free, or was entitled, or would have the power to interfere with the day-to-day administration of a province outside the limited range of the responsibilities specially confined to him. Finally, he said :'...whatever emerges you may count upon me, in face even of bitter disappointment, to strive unstirringly towards the full and final establishment in India of the principles of parliamentary government.'[23]

It should be mentioned here that when the Governors found after the elections that Congress was hesitating to form the ministry, they sent for the parties which had the second largest support in the legislature, even though they did not command a majority. These interim ministries were formed by non-Congress and, in some cases, anti-Congress elements.[24] The Congress leaders were convinced that in spite of their failure to secure the assurance they had sought, they had at least achieved something in having the purposes of the Act explained to them. After the Viceroy's clarification, some members of the Congress Working Committee changed their opinion in favour of acceptance of office. The Committee meeting in the first week of July at Wardha permitted Congressmen to accept office where they were invited. At the same time, it directed them to utilize the office for carrying out the election manifesto in combating the new Act on the one hand and of prosecuting the constructive programme on the other.[25] The Congress leaders in six provinces where they had a majority, were invited by the respective Governors to form new ministries. The British Government without losing any constitutional ground succeeded in securing at least temporary Congress support. The Congress perhaps lost its argument but not its objective. Thus the constitutional deadlock was solved for the time being.

Meanwhile, the British authorities tried to expedite the inauguration of federation under the Act of 1935. But the Act had unfortunately placed the fate of federation in the hands of the Princes. Though the Princes regarded federation as inevitable, none was enthusiastic about it and very few had as yet grasped the importance of getting the federal scheme underway early. During his leave of absence the Viceroy had consultations with the Secretary of State for India, the Prime Minister, and other members of the Cabinet and as a result it was understood that the programme for bringing federation into being was begun to take definite shape. On his return to India, he planned the steps to be taken to enable the rulers to determine their attitude towards federation. It was the strong desire of the government to start the work for federation by the middle of 1939. Viceroy Linlithgow declared that British policy towards Indian constitutional advance and the establishment of federation were unchanged in spite of the emphasis on totalitarian tendencies in the world.[26]

The Congress Party approved of the federal principle but

disagreed with Britain over its method of implementing federation as embodied in the Act of 1935. The Congress wanted to include the States people in its fight for freedom. In a resolution passed by the Tripuri session of the Congress on March 12, 1939, it said that the Congress desired to reiterate that its objective, complete independence, was for the whole of India inclusive of the States which could not be separated and which must have the same measure of political, social, economic and religious freedom as a part of India.[27] The Congress thought that the Princes should be represented in the federal government by elected members and not by their own nominees. It was the belief of the Congress that nominated representatives were bound to form a reactionary group and act as a brake upon the expression of the democratic theory. The Congress also doubted whether the Princes would ever surrender sufficient sovereignty, especially in fiscal matters, to give reality to the federation. Its inauguration was also made impossible because the government had given pledges to the Muslim League that no constitutional advance would be undertaken which was not approved by it. So that even if the Princes agreed and the Liberals supported, the government would not have ignored the opposition of the League.

Both Zetland and Linlithgow from time to time enunciated the determination of His Majesty's Government to secure the inauguration of the federation. Indian nationalists were unanimous that federation was the ultimate goal, but they urged a federation on the findings of a constituent assembly. Before the slow moving machinery of the Government of India could deal with this situation the Great War supervened, and on September 5, 1939, the Viceroy informed the Legislative Assembly that the scheme of federal union forming part of the 1935 Act had lapsed for the duration of the War.

The two years, 1937-1939, of responsible government in all eleven of the Governors' provinces supply evidence that the new constitution would have had a good chance of succeeding, had not war upset the peace-time developments. When Great Britain declared war upon Germany in September 1939, the Governor-General, without the support of the central legislatures, declared war on Germany. Since the Governor-General controlled the foreign affairs as a reserved subject, the constitutionality of the

Act could not be questioned. But this action of the Government of India was deeply resented by the Indians, and, therefore, the Congress Working Committee called for the immediate resignation of all Congress ministries. And it was done accordingly. The Congress leaders then sought an immediate constitutional advance, towards independent, responsible government, and moved towards open resistance to the central government.

The Labour Party during this period did advocate for granting Dominion Status to India. When the Indian constitutional impasse was debated in Parliament the Labour leaders supported the stand taken by Mahatma Gandhi and also urged the Indians to make use of the 1935 constitution.

NOTES

1. S.R. Mehrotra, op. cit., p. 182.
2. M. Gwyer and A. Appadorai, vol. 1, op. cit., p. 388.
3. Jawaharlal Nehru, *The Discovery of India*, Bombay, 1961, p. 390.
4. *The Times*, Nov. 18, 1935.
5. L.P. Report, 1935, p. 240.
6. ibid., pp. 241-2.
7. T. Chand, vol. IV, op. cit., p. 216.
8. A.C. Guha, Part 1, op. cit., p. 369.
9. I.A.R., 1937, vol. 1, p. 178.
10. ibid., p. 243.
11. H.L. Deb., vol. 104, 1937, cc. 879-885.
12. ibid., cc. 885-889.
13. M. Gwyer and A. Appadorai, vol. 1, op. cit., p. 393.
14. H.C. Deb., vol. 322, 1937, cc. 361-363.
15. H.L. Deb., vol. 105, 1937, c. 183.
16. ibid., c. 193.
17. *The Times*, April 12, 1937,
18. *The Times*, April 6, 13, 1937; H.L. Deb.. vol. 104, 1937, cc. 867-875.
19. H.L. Deb., vol. 105, 1937, cc. 415-416.
20. ibid., c. 416.
21. H.C. Deb.. vol. 325, 1937, cc. 165-167.
22. M. Gwyer and Appadorai, vol 1, op. cit., p, 394.
23. I.A.R., vol. 1, 1937, p. 265.
24. A.K. Azad, *India Wins Freedom*, Bombay, 1959, p. 14.
25. P. Sitaramayya, vol. 2, op. cit., p. 51.
26. *The Times*, December 20, 1938.
27. I.A.R., vol. 1, 1939, p. 337.

CHAPTER 7

Conclusion

The Labour Party formulated no Indian policy until the beginning of the First World War. In the years before the War, the party merely attacked the Government's India policy. It was in 1918 that the Labour Party adopted a programme of socialism at home and of Home Rule for India. The Labour Party's annual conference in that year endorsed the policy of 'Home Rule for India' and expressed the hope that the Labour members in the House of Commons would do everything possible so that the Indian people would have their just rights, including the right to self-government.

From the inception of the Labour Party down to its adoption of the socialist programme in 1918, two prominent leaders of the Labour Party, James Keir Hardie and James Ramsay MacDonald, pressed for a liberal treatment of India by the British Government. The Labour Party's interest in India grew through its contact with the London branch of the Congress Party. The office became the centre of operations for the Congress Party's propaganda in England.

After the partition of Bengal in 1905, the Congress Party began agitating against the government for its annulment. The unrest in India was countered by repressive measures by the Government of India. It was not till the partition of Bengal had been annulled in 1911 that the agitation subsided. Meanwhile, the Morley-Minto reforms became law as the Indian Councils Act of 1909. The aim of the reforms of 1909, according to Morley, the Secretary of State for India, and Minto, the Viceroy, was greater association of Indians with the government. The Labour Party had little influence, in the passage of the 1909 Act during the Asquith government but did oppose the communal clause and condemned the limited scope of the self-government granted to India.

The reforms did not come upto the expectation of the Indians. Between 1909 and 1917, India was burdened with many political upheavals. When the World War started in 1914, the first reaction to this tremendous event in India was a spontaneous rally to England's cause. India's war effort surprised the British people and the British statesmen. India's reaction to the war brought the nationalists to the forefront of Indian politics. Annie Besant, a former Fabian, and B.G. Tilak, a nationalist leader, started the Home Rule Movement in India. The Home Rulers demanded self-government for India while retaining the British connection. For the first time, in 1916-17, the agitation spread on a nation-wide scale and a network of political committees covered much of India.

While the movement was going on, the British Government made an historic announcement of future Indian policy in August 1917. The Secretary of State   declared in the House of Commons: 'The policy of His Majesty's Government. . . .is the gradual deve-lopment of self-governing institutions, with a view to the progres-sive realisation of responsible government in India as an integral part of the British Empire.' The declaration, which became the preamble of   the reforms Act of 1919, was the response to the insistent demand of patriotic Indians for a goal and a policy. Although the Lloyd George coalition and the subsequent Conser-vative Party governments denied that the 1917 Declaration bound Britain to the granting of responsible government and Dominion Status to India in the near future, the Labour Party was convinced that the Declaration did pledge these very things, and acted accordingly. The Labour Party was greatly influenced in its inter-pretation of the 1917 Declaration by the London branch of the Congress Party, on which it relied primarily for its information on India.

About three months after the August Declaration, Montagu, the Secretary of State, visited India. While touring various parts of the country in the company of Chelmsford, the Governor-General, Montagu met many national leaders, received many deputations and considered various proposals for constitutional advance. The Montagu-Chelmsford Report containing proposals for constitu-tional reform was published in 1918, with the joint signatures of Montagu and Chelmsford. It recommended, *inter alia*, that a system of dyarchy should be introduced in the provinces. The report proposed a legislature of two houses. It disapproved of communal representation. Later, the Government of India Bill of 1919 based on the Montford Report, was introduced in Parliament.

During the debates on the bill, all attempts of the Labour Party to liberalize it failed. The main reasons for the failure were the paucity of Labour Party members in the House of Commons and the lack of experienced parliamentary leaders. Even though Labour had improved its numerical position in Parliament in the 1918 election, it still could count only fifty-seven members. The Labour Party attracted radicals of the Liberal Party to its banner and one convert, Colonel Wedgwood, led the Labour Party attack on the Government of India Bill of 1919. The Labourites attacked the Bill because of its limited liberal concessions, William Adamson, Chairman of the Parliamentary Labour Party, maintained that although the Bill was a definite move in the right direction it did not go far enough. The criticisms of the Labour Party were justified because the new constitution gave the Indians only limited self-government at the provincial level and none at the centre. All the essential powers remained in the hands of the British officials in the Government of India.

If we look at the criticisms made by the Labour Party members in Parliament of the Government of India Bill we see that the party tried to liberalize the Bill thereby advancing the cause of self-government for India. But the Parliamentary Labour Party fell short of advocating Dominion Status for India. The party maintained that self-government should be granted to India by 'stages'. It means that the Indians were not fit for full self-government at that time and which is why the Labourites wanted that she should have self-government step by step. Besides, the Labour Party favoured the extension of the right of self-determination to the Indian peoples within the framework of the Empire which meant that the Indians would not be able to secede if she so desired. This conditional approach of the party was certainly undesirable. The Labour Party, of course, at a later stage withdrew this condition.

Political reforms in India were accompanied by coercion. The repressive Rowlatt Acts and the Jallianwala Bagh massacre poisoned the Indian political atmosphere. Mahatma Gandhi, leader of the Congress Party, then started the non-cooperation movement. After the tragedy of Chauri-Chaura in 1922 in which twenty-two Indian policemen were burnt to death by an angry mob, Gandhi suspended the movement. Although the Labour Party condemned the Rowlatt Acts and the Jallianwala Bagh massacre, it did not support the non-cooperation movement. The Labourites while denouncing the non-cooperation movement of Gandhi held the view that the Indians should confine their agitation for liberty within the constitutional limits. It is surprising that the Labour Party which claimed to be the torch-bearer of anti-imperialism condemned the principle of non-cooperation to obtain self-rule by legitimate means. But the radicals of Labour Party supported the non-cooperation movement. While sending greetings to the non-cooperators the Independent Labour Party observed that the Indian people had the absolute right to decide the extent and nature of their freedom. The Independent Labour Party believed that the non-cooperation movement had reawakened the people of India to a true sense of their national responsibility in the way that no other means could have achieved. The Independent Labour Party was very active in support of the Indian freedom movement. Indeed, their discourse was almost identical to that of the Congress Party. In England, the government of Baldwin was turned out of office in January 1924, and James Ramsay MacDonald, the leader of the Labour Party, formed the first Labour Government. The Labour Party came to office with Liberal support and it remained as a minority government for a period of only nine months. The keynote of the Labour Government's policy was to achieve Indian cooperation.

Following the termination of the non-cooperation movement a branch of the Congress Party formed the Swaraj Party. The aim of the party was to resort to a policy of a uniform and consistent obstruction in the Assembly and make government impossible until the right of the Indian people to control the machinery and system of government was conceded. Assuming that the Indians would cooperate with the Labour Government, MacDonald appealed to the nationalists for cooperation in finding a solution to the constitutional problem. When the Congress Party did not respond favourably, the Government was at a loss. Both houses of the British Parliament severely criticised the Labour Government for its indecision in formulating an Indian policy. The only advance made by the Labour Government was to direct the Government of India to examine the working of the 1919 Act, for making recommendations for amendments. Since the Labour Party was out of office when the reports were completed, the recommendations were ignored by the Conservative Government.

It should be pointed out that during the Labour administration Gandhi was released from jail after a serious illness, having served two years of a six-years sentence. But, the government of MacDonald gave a blow to Indians by sanctioning the infamous Bengal Ordinance. MacDonald's liberal professions, particularly of the doctrine of self-determination, won for him admirers among the Indian nationalist leaders. They looked up to MacDonald's advent to office as the beginning of the era when the principle of self-determination would be put into practice in India. But the MacDonald Government did nothing to prove their sincerity of purpose. The nationalists asked the Labour Government for a round table conference to discuss their position which was denied to them. Besides, the Indian indignation was aroused by the introduction of Bengal Ordinance, which cut clean across the most elementary right of citizenship. The introduction of this sort of repressive ordinance was unexpected from a socialist government as the Labour Party always stood against the repressive measures in India. So, we see here the gulf clearly between the prophecy and practice of the Labour Party.

It is true that faith of Indian nationalists was misplaced in Ramsay MacDonald. He wrote much about India; but he never ardently advocated self-determination for India. The message that MacDonald sent to India upon his accession to office is well known. In the course of his message to India, the Labour Prime Minister said that no party in Great Britain would be cowed by threats of force or by politics designed to bring Government to a standstill. Any other Prime Minister might have attached his name to such a communication. It was wondered, why he sent such an excessively discouraging message. There was ample reason; it was to counteract the effects of some of the statements on India made by Colonel Wedgwood, an outspoken member of the Labour Party, and, who was sympathetic to the Indian cause. A few days before the Labour Party came into office Wedgwood maintained in a speech before the University Labour Federation that India would prove the test of a Labour Government. He said that the Labour Party hoped to overcome the difficulties by accelerating the conversion of India into a self-governing dominion.

This was too much for the British bourgeoisie. They could not permit a party with such ideas to be at the helm of the country. When MacDonald looked hungrily at the votes of the Liberal minority, he was reminded of those indiscreet pronouncements of his colleague. MacDonald had to inform his Indian admirers that self-determination was all right when it did not concern the Empire too closely, but when the safety of the British Empire was involved he would not tolerate any monkey tricks.

Between 1924 and 1930, the Labour Party began to take more interest in Indian constitutional problems. Early in 1924, the moderate Indian leaders drafted the Commonwealth of India Bill. The Bill would have granted India responsible self-government. Before it was presented to the Labour Party, the Labour Government was out of office. The Commonwealth of India Bill appealed to the Labour left and became the basis for the principle of policy that all future constitutional changes for India had to have the concurrence of the Indians. It received a cool reception in the House of Commons although the Labour Party made an unsuccessful appeal for a second reading.

The appointment of the Indian Statutory Commision in 1927 by the Conservative Government according to the provisions of the Act of 1919, whose purpose was to inquire into the working of the system of government and to make recommendations for the development of responsible government in India, was resented by the Indians because they were not included in the Commission. The Indians were all the more shocked because the Labour Party nominated two members in that all-white Commission. The radical Labourites, however, advocated a mixed commission in Parliament. India's faith in Labour had been shattered by its action in connection with the Simon Commission. Here again, we see a wide gulf between Labour Party's word and its deed. At the annual conference at Blackpool in 1927, in anticipation of the appointment of a royal commission to consider the future constitution of India, the party declared unanimously that the royal commission to be appointed 'should be so constituted, and the method of doing its work so arranged, that it will enjoy the confidence and cooperation of the Indian people.' If this resolution meant anything at all it meant that the Labour Party regarded the confidence and cooperation of the Indian people as indispensable to the success of any commission. Yet what happened ? Within a few months of the passing of the foregoing resolution it was announced that an Indian parliamentary commission had been appointed, on which there were two Labour Party representatives, which meant that the commission had the approval and support of the party. This commission did not enjoy the confidence of the Indian people. On the contrary, it was greeted with fierce hostility by every section of Indian nationalist opinion, from the most moderate to the most extreme.

It may be conceded that when Labour agreed to support and identify itself with the Simon Commission it was unaware that this body would not enjoy the cooperation and confidence of the Indians, and that its action was a mistake due to ignorance of this fact, rather than a deliberate flouting of the decision of the Blackpool conference. Even on this point, however, the party cannot be acquitted of grave negligence. Having declared Indian confidence and cooperation necessary, it was surely under an obligation to ascertain whether or not these would be forthcoming before identifying itself with the Commission. Yet the fact is that, in spite of the conference resolution, the Parliamentary Labour Party proceeded to nominate representatives to the Commission, with complete indifference to the attitude which Indian opinion would adopt towards the latter body.

In 1928, the Indian political leaders at an All-Party Conference formed a committee headed by Motilal Nehru to consider and determine the principles of constitution for India. The Committee prepared a report (known as Nehru Report) in which it was stated that the basic aim of the constitution was that India should be granted full Dominion Status forthwith. One of the positive contributions of the Report was the recognition of the necessity of widening the franchise, thereby accepting universal suffrage and the principle of majority rule in the implementation of any future scheme of constitutional reforms. The contents of the Nehru plan were well-known to the Labourites, but the Labour Party that came into office for the second time in 1929 could not proclaim a policy for India until the Indian Statutory Commission Report had been published.

The Report of the Statutory Commission was published in mid-1930. In its major recommendations, the report suggested that dyarchy should be discontinued and the whole field of provincial administration be entrusted to ministers responsible to their respective legislatures. The Labour Government issued a statement in July 1930 in which it wrote that 'the report, however authoritative and valuable, is a report only and in no sense a decision of the government or of Parliament.' The recommendations did not satisfy the Labour opinion. On the question of responsible government at the centre, the Commission made no suggestions how the process could be expedited.

The second Labour Government remained in office till August 1931. During its tenure of office the Viceroy, Irwin, with the authorization of the Labour Government, made his famous statement of October 1929, promising India responsible government and Dominion Status. Whilst the effect of the statement was excellent in India, in England the use of the ritual phrase "Dominion Status" became the shibboleth that divided Churchill from Baldwin, and the diehards from the main body of the Conservative Party. Prime Minister Ramsay MacDonald stated in the House of Commons that Irwin's declaration was necessary to establish confidence in India pending the publication of the Statutory Commission Report. Now that the goal was declared to be Dominion Status for India, the Labour Party decided that it would issue a statement of policy as to how that should be obtained. Later, the Labour Government announced that a Round Table Conference would be held between the Indians and the British to discuss the future constitution of India.

The years 1930-1931 were eventful, as during this time the civil disobedience movement was started in India and in England the first two sessions of the Round Table Conference were held. The Indian political leaders issued the Delhi Manifesto after the announcement by the government that the Round Table Conference would be held. In the Manifesto, Irwin's declaration was interpreted to mean that the conference would discuss the framing of a Dominion constitution for India. As the Labour Government had refused to accept the conditions on which the Congress Party wanted to attend the conference, Gandhi began the civil disobedience movement for the achievement of complete independence. Repressive ordinances were introduced to check the movement and the government defended its policy by saying that they were trying to maintain law and order in India.

The First and the Second sessions of the Round Table Conference were held in London before the end of 1930 and 1931 respectively. While the Congress Party boycotted the First Round Table Conference, they did attend the Second as a result of the Gandhi-Irwin Pact. The First Round Table Conference could bring no tangible results, except for the willingness shown by the Princes to join in an all-India federation, but that idea was abandoned by them after the passage of the Act of 1935. While the Labour Government was carrying out its plans for Indian constitutional reform, there arose the 1931 financial crisis in England, and in August the Labour Government was replaced by a coalition government, known as the National Government and headed by Ramsay MacDonald. As MacDonald formed the National Government with the Conservatives and Liberals, he was expelled from the Labour Party.

Gandhi, on behalf of Congress could not offer his cooperation to the First Round Table Conference because the Congress had already voted for independence, and, therefore it was not possible to persuade the party to agree to any proposal which in its preamble did not concede without question that the substance of independence was forthwith to be granted to India. The Congress expressed the view that the Conference must proceed to hammer the substance of independence into definite shape; to show, for instance, what adjustments must be brought about during the transition period of transference of power from British hands into Indians. This the Labour Government could not guarantee. There would have been little practical difficulty about the Congress view if Labour could command courage to stick to its principles and professions. But it was not prepared to risk its life on the Indian issue. It was perhaps more anxious to carry the British Liberals and Tories with them than the Indian nationalists. The Congress rightly felt that such a promiscuous conference could hardly be expected to yield any results even remotely foreshadowing the fruition of Indian aspirations.

The plea of official Labour was that it was sincere in its solicitude for Indian emancipation, but that its actual   course of action was determined by conditions of political reality which required a cautious slow movement along the line of least resistance. It is to be noted that the Labour handling of the Indian situation was in two respects a departure from the Tory treatment of it. First, it admitted the fundamental blunder of the Simon Commission plan and substituted for it the round table method. Secondly, it had the courage to act and open negotiations with the Congress while the latter was carrying on the civil disobedience movement. The Gandhi-Irwin agreement was in no sense an agreement between the victor and the vanquished—a circumstance which made it so galling and bitter to the Indian bureaucratic throat that was to swallow it. The Congress participated in the Second Round Table Conference on the distinct understanding that all reservations and safeguards in the transition period would be demonstrably in the interest of India.

The second Labour government had made two initial mistakes which it would not or could not rectify. It had made a pact with the Tories and Liberals, and the collaboration with these parties in the Round Table Conference and in the Parliament necessarily meant that the measure of responsibility to be conceded in the Indian constitution would be the least possible, and that of the reservations and safeguards largest possible.   By that pact official Labour consented to move with a perpetual Tory halter round its neck. The second mistake was due to its failure to make the Indian representation in the Conference, truly representative in character. The Congress, which was practically the sole factor in the field of Indian political struggle, was sought to be cornered in the St. James' Palace. The Labour Government which was still in power persisted in refusing 'to disclose its own Indian plans. Its mind seemed to be undecided. The inconclusive session of the Conference broke up in an atmosphere of vagueness and mutual distrust. There had been nothing left for the great constitutional question itself but to wait for the reports of committees.

The Labour Government called the Round Table Conference which was a deliberative body only, and not a constituent assembly empowered to frame a constitution for India. It was said that the

British Government would draw up its final proposals on the basis of an agreement reached in the Conference, and present them in the shape of a bill to the British Parliament. This might not be tantamount to a denial of the right of self-determination to India. If the Labour Government had acceded to the Congress request to call the Conference for the purpose of framing forthwith a Dominion constitution for India, that is to say, for deciding by negotiation the necessary adjustments for the speedy transference of authority from British hands to Indian hands, then, in the hypothesis of immediate Dominion Status for India being accepted by England as a settled question not further to be reopened, the passing of a necessary bill by the British Parliament might be regarded as more or less a formal affair not meaning anything like dictation by one party in relation to the other.

The overwhelming Conservative Party victory in October 1931 doomed the Second, and most important, Round Table Conference to failure. That was the Conference that had to succeed, for Gandhi was present as the sole representative of the Congress Party. The Secretary of State for India, Sir Samuel Hoare, who had promised to continue the Labour Government's policy, inspired hopes that an amicable solution could be negotiated. But the emptiness of Hoare's promise, together with the mutual distrust between Gandhi and the Conservatives, rendered a meeting of minds impossible. Gandhi was as uncompromising on the communal problem as were the minorities that claimed communal rights, and the British Conservatives usually supported the minorities against the Hindus, if for no other reason than to preserve the Empire against the threat of Indian nationalism.

The Labour Party criticised the Indian policy of the National Government both in and outside Parliament. It condemned the repression in India introduced by the Government and the jailing of Gandhi immediately after his return to India from the Round Table Conference. The Party urged the National Government to cooperate with the Congress Party to reach a settlement of the Indian problem. It may be pointed out that while the 1929-31 Labour Government was interested in winning the cooperation of all Indian political parties, the National Government was willing only to deal with the moderate political parties.

After the third session of the Round Table Conference, which was not attended by both the British Labour Party and the Indian Congress Party, the National Government drafted a White Paper in the light of the conclusions of the round table conferences and the Statutory Commission Report. It provided for an all-India federation, provincial autonomy, responsibility and safeguards. In the debates in the House of Commons on the appointment of the Joint Select Committee, the Labour Party complained that the idea of Dominion Status had disappeared even as the ultimate goal, and that there was no provision in the White Paper for the progressive advancement to full responsible government. Although the Labour Party criticised the White Paper proposals, it did nominate its representatives to the Joint Select Committee. The Committee, in general, approved the White Paper proposals. It may be noted that a draft report was also prepared for the Committee by the Labour Party representative (known as Attlee Draft). The conclusions made in the Draft put forward the same arguments as those made by the Labour Party members in Commons debates at the time of the proposal for the establishment of the Joint Select Committee. But the Draft proposals were voted down in the Committee. It was expected that Attlee Draft would come into line with the Labour Party policy. Instead, the Draft advocated the same principle of veto as mentioned by the majority report of the Joint Select Committee. It did not criticise the principle of veto, and the only real improvement that it did make upon the majority report was to try to set up provision for adult suffrage in India. Later, when the Committee's Report came up for discussion in Parliament as the Government of India Bill, in December 1934, the Labour Party brought forward some amendments to liberalize the Bill, without success. The reason for their failure to liberalize the Bill was that the party was a minority in Parliament. In their criticisms they maintained that the Bill did not contain the means for the realisation of Dominion Status and imposed undue restrictions on the exercise of self-government. While closing the Labour Party's attack on the Bill, the leader of the party, George Lansbury, advocated that the Indians themselves should determine the type of constitution that they wanted. The Bill when passed in August 1935, became known as the Act of 1935.

After the passage of the Act, the elections for provincial legisla- tures were held in early 1937, and the Congress Party had a notable victory in five of the eleven provinces. But after the elections there appeared a constitutional impasse on the question of the acceptance of office by the Congress. The Congress wanted an assurance from the Governors that they would not interfere with the activities of the ministers. The matter was later settled and the Congress formed the ministries. The Act of 1935 was not promulgated at the federal level. Before the Second World War, not a single State had joined or even expressed the desire to join the federation. In 1939, when Britain declared war upon Germany, the Viceroy, without support of the legislatures, also declared war. The Congress ministries then resigned as a protest against the Viceroy's unilateral decision.

Although the idea of Dominion Status was first proclaimed as a Labour Party objective in the 1918 annual conference and in subsequent conferences, and the Party declared that it recognized the right of the Indian people to full self-government and self-determination, there was little the Party could do for India during the first and the second Labour Governments. The accomplishments of the first Labour Government were unimpressive; its tenure of office was only nine months, and it had to rely upon the support of the Liberals to get any of its programmes fulfilled. The Prime Minister MacDonald after the fall of the first Labour Government expressed that the chief reason he and his government were unable to take any effective action to grant additional liberty to India was because of the recalcitrance of Indian nationalist leaders at the very time the Labour Party took control of the British Government. This is not completely true. The Prime Minister, indeed, aimed at winning confidence in England, and to this end he postponed any attempt to apply Labour's own principles to India.

India in all probability would have received Dominion Status under the aegis of the second Labour Government had not the financial crisis supervened to overthrow that government, to wreck the Labour Party for the next fifteen years, and to throw the question of Indian constitutional reform into the hands of reactionary Conservatives. Had the Labour Government been able to reach an agreement with the Indian delegation to the First Round Table Conference and to present a bill to Parliament before the August 1931 crisis, there was a chance for India to have become a Dominion at the time. Statistically, the 1929 election gave the Labour Party

287 seats, 260 for the Conservatives; the Liberals had fifty-nine and the independents nine. A bare government majority of 308 would have secured the passage of the bill in Commons. Consequently, the Labour Government would have needed only twenty-one votes to secure a majority. This was not a formidable obstacle, since even Stanley Baldwin, on the strength of his pledge to MacDonald, considered himself personally bound to support MacDonald's India bill, and the vehement attacks of some of the Liberals on the repressive government measures in India indicated that considerable Liberal support would have been forthcoming.

The Labour Party in the 1930s advocated the granting of Dominion Status to India under an Indian-drafted constitution. The party did not alter its basic position until the partition of India into the two independent States of India and Pakistan in August 1947.

Bibliography

Primary sources

British Commonwealth Labour Conference Reports, 1925, 1928, 1930. Published by the T U.C. and The Labour Party, London.

Gillies Papers. Labour Party Archive, London.

Independent Labour Party Annual Report, 1911.

India To-day. A report on conditions in India and an outline of policy by the I.L.P. Indian Advisory Committee. I.L.P., London, 1926

Indian Statutory Commission Report, Vol. I. I1 and III. Printed and published by His Majesty's Stationery Office. London, 1930,

Indian Round Table Conference, Second Session, *Proceedings*, Command Paper 3778. November 12, 1930—January 19, 1931.

Indian Round Table Conference, Second Session, *Proceedings*, Command Paper 3997. September 7, 1931—Dec. 1, 1931.

Indian Round Table Conference, Third Session, *Proceedings*, Command Paper 4238. November 17, 1932—Dec. 1, 1932.

Joint Select Committee Report, 1933-1934. House of Commons Sessional Papers.

Labour Party Annual Reports, 1918-1939.

Labour Representation Committee Annual Report, 1903.

Lansbury Collections. British Library of Economics and Political Science, London.

Middleton Papers. Labour Party Archive, London.

Parliamentary Debates. House of Commons. 1906-1937.

Parliamentary Debates. House of Lords. 1920-1939.

William Wedgwood Benn Papers. House of Lords Record Office, London.

Secondary sources

Aggarwala, Rama Nand: *National Movement and Constitutional Development*. Metropolitan Book Co., New Delhi, 1962.

Andrews, C.F. : *India and the Simon Report.* George Allen & Unwin, London, 1930.

Attlee, C.R. : *As it Happened,* The Windmill Press, Surrey, 1954.

————: *Empire into Commonwealth.* Oxford University Press, London, 1961.

————: *The Labour Party in Perspective and Twelve Years Later.* Victor Gollancz, London, 1949.

Azad, Abul Kalam : *India Wins Freedom.* Orient Longmans, Bombay, 1959.

Baillie, Adrian : *India from a Back Bench.* Methuen & Co., London, 1934.

Beauchamp, Joan : *British Imperialism in India.* Martin Lawrence, London, 1934.

Bellamy M. Joyce & Saville John : *Dictionary of Labour Biography* (Vol. 1). The Macmillan Press, London, 1972.

Besant, Annie : *India: Bond or Free.* G.P. Putnam's Sons, London, 1926.

Bhatia, O.P. Singh: *History of India, 1857-1916.* S. Amardeep Publishers, New Delhi, 1968.

Bose, Subhas Chandra : *The Indian Struggle, 1920-1942.* Asia Publishing House, Bombay, 1964.

Brailford, Henry Noel : *Subject India.* Victor Gollancz, London, 1943.

Brand, Carl F. : *The British Labour Party.* Stanford University Press, California, 1964.

Bulmer-Thomas, Ivor : *The Growth of the British Party System,* Vol. I. 1640-1923. Pall Mall, London, 1967.

Chand, Tara. : *History of the Freedom Movement in India.* Vol. I—IV. Publications Division, Ministry of Information and Broadcasting, Government of India, New Delhi, 1972.

Chandra, Bipan; Tripathi, Amalesh De, Barun : *Freedom Struggle.* National Book Trust, New Delhi, 1972.

Churchill, Winston : *A Self-Portrait;* Constructed from his own sayings and writings and framed with an introduction by Colin R. Coote with the collaboration of P. D. Bunyan, Eyre & Spottiswoode, London, 1954.

————: *The Second World War — The Gathering Storm.* Houghton Mifflin Co. Boston, 1948.

Coates, David. : *The Labour Party and the Struggle for Socialism.* Cambridge University Press, London, 1975.

Coatman John : *India*: *The Road to Self-Government*. George Allen & Unwin, London, 1941.

Cole, G.D.H. : *British Working Class Politics, 1832-1914*. George Routledge and Sons, London, 1941.

————: *History of the Labour Party from 1914*. Routledge & Kegan Paul, London, 1948.

———: *A History of Socialist Thought*. Macmillan & Co. London, 1956.

Cole, Margaret (Editor) : *Beatrice Webb's Diaries 1924-1932*. Longmans, Green & Co , London, 1956.

Collins, Larry and Lapierre, Dominique : *Freedom at Midnight*. Vikas Publishing House, New Delhi, 1976.

Cooke, Colin : *The Life of Richard Stafford Cripps*. Hodder and Stoughton, London, 1957.

Coupland, R. : *The Indian Problems, 1833-1935*. Oxford University Press, London, 1942.

Das, M. N. : *India under Morley and Minto—Politics behind Revolution, Repression and Reforms*. George Allen & Unwin, London, 1964.

Dutt, R. Palme : *India To-day*. Manisha Granthalaya, Calcutta, 1947 (Revised and enlarged edition).

Edwardes, Michael : *A History of India*. Thames and Hudson, London, 1961.

Emerson, Rupert : *From Empire to Nation*. Cambridge University Press, Cambridge, 1967.

Fischer, Georges : *Le Parti travailliste et la decolonisation de l'inde*. francois maspero, Paris, 1966.

Forester, Tom : *The Labour Party and the Working Class*, Heinemann, London, 1976.

Gandhi, M. K. : *Young India*. S. Ganesan Publisher, Triplicane, Madras, 1922.

————: *Communal Unity* (Compilation of Gandhi's writings). Navajivan Publishing House, Ahmedabad, 1949.

Gautam, Ram Sakha : *Indian National Congress and Constitutional Changes in India, 1885-1979*. Chetna Publications, New Delhi, 1981.

Ghose, S. : *Indian National Congress*, Pauls Press. New Delhi, 1975.

Gopal, Ram : *Indian Muslims—A Political History, 1858-1947*. Asia Publishing House, Bombay, 1959,

Gopal, Ram : *Lokmanya Tilak—A Biography.* Asia Publishing House, Bombay, 1956.

Gupta, Partha Sarathi : *Imperialism and the British Labour Movement, 1914-1964.* Macmillan, London, 1975.

Gwyer, Maurice and Appadorai, A. : *Speeches and Documents on the Indian Constitution, 1921-1947.* Vol. I and II, Oxford University Press, London, 1957.

Halifax, (The Earl of) : *Fulness of Days.* Collins, London, 1957.

Hamid, Abdul : *Muslim Separatism in India, 1858-1947.* Oxford University Press, Lahore, 1967.

Hardie, J. Keir : *India—Impressions and Suggestions.* I.L.P., London, 1909.

Hinden, Rita : *Empire and After—A Study of British Imperial Attitudes.* Essential Books, London, 1949.

Hinton, James : *Labour and Socialism—A History of the British Labour Movement 1867-1974.* Wheatsheaf Books, Sussex. 1983.

Howe, Irving (Editor) : *A Handbook of Socialist Thought.* Victor Gollancz, London, 1972.

Indian Annual Register : Published by Annual Register Office, Calcutta.

Indian Quarterly Register : Published by Annual Register Office, Calcutta.

James, Robert Rhodes : *The British Revolution—British Politics, 1880-1939.* Vol. I and II Hamish Hamilton, London, 1977.

Jennings, Ivor : *Party Politics.* Vol. I & III. Cambridge University Press, Cambridge, 1962.

Jones, Morgan : *Whither India.* Published by Labour Party, London, 1935.

Judd, Denis : *Balfour and the British Empire, A Study in imperial Evolution, 1874-1932.* Macmillan, London, 1968.

Keith, Arthur Berriedale : *A Constitutional History of India, 1600-1935.* Methuen & Co., London, 1936.

———: (Editor) : *Speeches and Documents on Indian Policy 1750-1921.* Vol. I and II, Oxford University Press, London, 1922.

Kennedy, J. : *Asian Nationalism in the Twentieth Century.* Macmillan, London, 1968.

Kenworthy, J.M. (The Rt. Hon.) : *India : A Warning.* Elkin Mathews & Marrot, London, 1931.

Khan, Aga (The) : *India in Transition, A Study in Political Evolution*. Medici Society, London, 1918.

Knaplund, Paul : *Britain, Commonwealth and Empire, 1901-1955*. Hamish Hamilton, London, 1956.

Kulkarni, V.B. : *British Dominion in India and After*. Bharatiya Vidya Bhavan, Bombay, 1964.

Laidler, Harry W. : *History of Socialism*. Thomas Y. Crowell Co. New York, 1968.

Lal, Chaman : *The Vanishing Empire*. Sagar Publications, New Delhi, 1969.

Lawrence, Henry : *The Indian White Paper*. B.H. Blackwell, Oxford, 1934.

Lewis, Martin D. (Editor) : *Problems in European Civilization—The British in India—Imperialism or Trusteeship* ? D.C. Heath & Co., Boston, 1962.

Lyman, Richard W. : *The First Labour Government, 1924*. Chapman & Hall, London, 1957.

MacDonald, James Ramsay : *The Awakening of India*. Hodderand Stoughton, London, 1910.

———: *The Government of India*. The Swarthmore Press, London, 1919.

Mahajan, Vidya Dhar : *The Nationalist Movement in India*. Sterling Publishers, New Delhi, 1976.

Majumdar, R C. : *History of the Freedom Movement in India*. vol. I-III. Firma K.L. Mukhopadhyay, Calcutta, 1963.

Majumdar, R.C. (General Editor) : *The History and Culture of the Indian People, Struggle for Freedom*. Bharatiya Vidya Bhavan, Bombay, 1969.

Mansergh, Nicolas : *Survey of British Commonwealth Affairs, Problems of External Policy, 1931-1939*. Oxford University Press, London, 1952.

Marquand, David : *Ramsay MacDonald*. Jonathan Cape, London, 1977.

Masani, R.P. : *Britain in India*. Oxford University Press, London, 1960.

McBriar, A.M. : *Fabian Socialism and English Politics*, 1884-1918. Cambridge University Press, London, 1962.

MacKibbin, Ross : *The Evolution of the Labour Party*. Oxford University Press, London, 1974.

Mehrotra, S.R. : *Towards India's Freedom and Partition.* Vikas Publishing House, New Delhi, 1979.

Menon, V.P. : *The Transfer of Power in India.* Orient Longmans, Calcutta, 1957.

Mishra, Shreegovind : *Constitutional Development and National Movement in India 1919-47.* Janaki Prakashan, Patna, 1978.

Montagu, Edwin S. : *An Indian Diary.* Edited by Venetia Montagu. William Heinemann, London, 1930.

Moore, R.J. : *The Crisis of Indian Unity.* Clarendon Press, Oxford, 1974.

Nanda, B.R. : *The Indian Moderates and the British Raj.* Oxford University Press, New Delhi, 1977.

———: *Mahatma Gandhi—A Biography.* Allied Publishers, New Delhi, 1968.

Nehru, Jawaharlal: *The Discovery of India.* Asia Publishing House, Bombay, 1961.

———: *An Autobiography.* The Bodley Head, London, 1958. First published in 1936.

———: *A Bunch of Old Letters—Written Mostly to Jawaharlal Nehru and Some Written by Him.* Asia Publishing House, Bombay, 1958.

Nethercot, A.H. : *The Last Four Lives of Annie Besant.* Rupert Hart-Davis, London, 1963

Ochs, George Milton : *The Labour Party and Constitutional Reform for India.* University of Illinois, 1960.

Osburn, Arthur : *Must England Lose India.* Alfred A. Knopf, London, 1930.

Pandey, B.N. : *The Indian Nationalist Movement, 1885-1947.* Macmillan, London, 1979.

Pelling, Henry : *Origins of the Labour Party, 1880-1900.* Oxford University Press, Oxford, 1977.

Pethick-Lawrence F.W. : *Fate has been Kind.* Hutchinson & Co., London, 1943.

Philips, C.H. (editor) : *Politics and Society in India.* George Allen & Unwin, London, 1963.

Pimlott, Benn : *Labour and the Left in the 1930s.* Cambridge University Press, Cambridge, 1977.

Polak, H.S.L , Brailsford H. N., & Pethic-Lawrence, Lord : *Mahatma Gandhi.* Odhams Press Ltd., London, 1949.

Postgate, Raymond : *The Life of George Lansbury.* Longmans, Green & Co., London, 1951.

Powell-Price, J.C. : *A History of India.* Thomas Nelson and Sons, London, 1955.

Pradhan, R.G. : *India's Struggle for Swaraj.* G.A. Natesan & Co., Madras, 1930.

Prasad, Bisheshwar : *Bondage and Freedom—A History of Modern India, 1858-1947.* Vol- I-II. Rajesh Publications. New Delhi, 1979.

Pravate, T.V. : *Gopal Krishna Gokhale* (*A Narrative and Interpretative Review of his Life, Career and Contemporary Events*) Navajivan Press, Ahmedabad, 1959.

Rao, B. Shiva and Pole, D. Graham : *The Problem of India.* The Labour Publishing Co., London, 1926.

Rao, B. Shiva : *India's Freedom Movement—Some Notable Figures.* Orient Longman, New Delhi, 1972.

Rao, P. Kodanda : *Foreign Friends of India's Freedom.* The P.T.I. Book Co., Bangalore, 1973.

Ridley, George : *India.* Published by Labour Party, London, 1942.

Roberts, P.E. : *History of British India.* Oxford University Press, London, 1952.

Rutherford, V.H. : *India and the Labour Party.* The Labour Publishing Co., London, 1928.

———— : *Modern India—Its Problems and Their Solution.* The Labour Publishing Co., London, 1927.

Sanderson, Gorham D. : *India and British Imperialism.* Bookman Associates, New York, 1951.

Simmons, Jack : *From Empire to Commonwealth* (*Principles of British Imperial Government*) Odhams Press, Long Acre, London, 1949.

Singh, Khazan : *Indian Freedom Movement.* Published by Manjeet Singh, New Delhi, 1974.

Sitaramayya, Pattabhi : *The History of the Indian National Congress, 1885-1935.* Padma Publications, Bombay, 1935.

Suda, Jyoti Prasad : *The Indian National Movement.* Jai Prakash Nath & Co., Meerut City, 1969.

Symonds, Richard : *The Making of Pakistan.* Faber & Faber, London, 1949.

Templewood, Viscount (The Rt. Hon. Sir Samuel Hoare) : *Nine Troubled Years*. Collins, London, 1954.

Thompson E. & Garratt G.T. : *Rise and Fulfilment of British Rule in India*. A.M.S. Press, New York, 1934.

Tsiang, Tingfu F. : *Labour and Empire*. Longmans, Green & Co., New York, 1923.

Veerathappa K. : *British Conservative Party and Indian Independence*. Ashish Publishing House, New Delhi, 1976.

Wedgwood, Josiah C. : *Memoirs of a Fighting Life*. Hutchinson & Co., London, 1940.

————: *Essays : and Adventures of a Labour M.P.* George Allen & Unwin, London, 1924.

Williams, Rushbrook L.F. : *India in 1923-24. A Statement Prepared for Presentation to Parliament*. Government of India Central Publication Brands; 1924.

Winterton, Earl : *Orders of the Day*. Cassell & Co., London, 1953.

Wolpert, Stanley. : *A New History of India* . Oxford University Press, New York, 1977.

Periodicals and Newspapers
—*Contemporary Review* (*The*)
—*Herald* (*The*)
—*International Affairs*
—*Journal of Asian Studies* (*The*)
—*Labour Magazine* (*The*)
—*Labour Monthly* (*The*)
—*New Leader* (*The*)
—*Nineteenth Century and After* (*The*)
—*Parliamentary Affairs*
—*Political Quarterly* (*The*)
—*Political Studies*
—*Socialist Review* (*The*)
—*Telegraph* (*The*)
—*Times* (*The*)
—*Tribune* (*The*)

INDEX